Autism and Personality

D1562971

Taking a psychoanalytic and developmental approach, *Autism and Personality* outlines in considerable detail the new developments in therapeutic techniques used by the Tavistock Autism Team and Workshop to treat autistic children. It also underlines the importance of support for parents and siblings, who are all too often under considerable stress.

The book presents fresh ideas about the importance of personality for the developmental course of the condition, and the implications for psychotherapeutic technique. Using case vignettes to illustrate the theoretical ideas emerging from the Workshop, coupled with case studies which highlight the patient's changing contact with the therapist, it gives a fascinating picture of the individuality of each child and of the sensitivity and skill required for each treatment.

Accessible to professionals and also to parents, *Autism and Personality* is a valuable insight into the nature and course of this condition and its treatment.

Anne Alvarez is a Consultant Child and Adolescent Psychotherapist and Co-convenor of the Tavistock Clinic Autism Service and Workshop. She is the author of *Live Company: Psychoanalytic Psychotherapy with Autistic, Borderline, Deprived and Abused Children* (1992).

Susan Reid is a Consultant Child and Adolescent Psychotherapist in the Child and Family Department of the Tavistock Clinic, involved in the training of child psychotherapists. She founded the Autism Research Workshop in 1986 and is Co-convenor of the Workshop and of the Tavistock Autism Service. She is the editor of *Developments in Infant Observation: the Tavistock approach* (1997).

Contributors: Pamela Bartram; Janet Bungener; Judith Edwards; Carol Hanson; Trudy Klauber; Branka Pecotic; Michele Pundick; Maria Rhode; Biddy Youell.

Autism and Personality
Findings from the Tavistock Autism Workshop

Edited by
Anne Alvarez and Susan Reid

With the assistance of
Judith Edwards and Biddy Youell

Routledge
Taylor & Francis Group

LONDON AND NEW YORK

First published 1999
by Routledge
27 Church Road, Hove, East Sussex, BN3 2FA

Simultaneously published in the USA and Canada
by Routledge
270 Madison Ave, New York NY 10016

Transferred to Digital Printing 2008

Routledge is an imprint of the Taylor & Francis Group, an informa business

Typeset in Galliard by Routledge

British Library Cataloguing in Publication Data
A catalogue record for this book is available from the British Library

Library of Congress Cataloging in Publication Data
Autism and Personality/edited by Anne Alvarez and Susan Reid
p. cm.
Includes bibliographical references and index.
1. Autistic children. I. Alvarez, Anne, 1936– . II. Reid, Susan, 1946– .
RJ506.A9A896 1999
618.92'8982–dc21   98–43904
CIP

ISBN 978-0-415-14602-9 (pbk)

Contents

Notes on contributors

Anne Alvarez is a consultant child and adolescent psychotherapist and Co-convener of the Tavistock Clinic Autism Service and Workshop. She trained originally as a Clinical Psychologist in Canada and the USA. She is the author of *Live Company: Psychoanalytic Psychotherapy with Autistic, Borderline, Deprived and Abused Children* and of many other publications related to the treatment of severely disturbed children. She is director of an individual case study research project on autism at the Tavistock, and consultant to a research project on parent-infant psychotherapy with toddlers with Pervasive Development Disorder at the University of Pisa. She has lectured widely in the UK and around the world.

Pamela Bartram is a child psychotherapist working in the West Hertfordshire Health Trust and in private practice. She originally trained as a music therapist, specialising in work with autistic and multiply handicapped children. She retains a particular interest in the non-verbal aspects of therapeutic communication.

Janet Bungener qualified initially as a primary school teacher then went on to train as a child psychotherapist at the Tavistock Clinic. She has worked in various settings in the National Health Service as well as privately as a clinician and supervisor. She has a special interest in psychodynamic work with children and families with learning and physical disabilities as well as autism. She is a visiting teacher at the Tavistock Clinic for various courses on learning disability.

Judith Edwards is a child and adolescent psychotherapist currently working in a family consultation centre. She also teaches Child Development at the Tavistock Clinic, and is joint editor of the *Journal of Child Psychotherapy*. Other published work includes a chapter in a book on *School Refusal*, a chapter on Latency in a forthcoming book on *Personality Development*, and a chapter on Autism in the *Handbook of Child and Adolescent Psychoanalytic Psychotherapy*.

Carol Hanson trained as a child and adolescent psychotherapist at the Tavistock Clinic. She is Senior Child and Adolescent Psychotherapist at the

South Brent Child and Family Clinic, London, and a visiting teacher at the Tavistock. She has a special interest in autism and was a member of the Autism Workshop for several years.

Trudy Klauber is a consultant child and adolescent psychotherapist in the Child and Family Department at the Tavistock Clinic, and was formerly Director of the Donald Winnicott Centre in East London. She was a member of the Tavistock Autism Workshop from 1987 to 1997 and worked extensively in assessment and long-term work with parents. She is assistant organising tutor of the M.A. in Psychoanalytic Observational Studies at the Tavistock Clinic, and teaches and supervises on the clinical training in child psychotherapy. She also teaches and lectures in the UK and in Italy.

Branka Pecotic is a senior child and adolescent psychotherapist working in Brent Child and Adolescent Mental Health Team and in Enfield. She originally trained as a clinical psychologist. She was a member of the Autism Workshop for several years and is a member of the research team observing infants in families where there is a child with autism. She teaches infant and young child observation at the Tavistock Clinic.

Michele Pundick has a background in developmental psychology. She is a child psychotherapist at a child and family consultation service. She teaches Infant Observation and Child Development at the Tavistock and for the North of England Training in Psychoanalytic Psychotherapy. She has a special interest in autism and learning disability. She is a member of the research team, observing infants in families where there is a child with autism, and was a member of the Autism Workshop for several years.

Susan Reid is a consultant child and adolescent psychotherapist in the Child and Family Department of the Tavistock Clinic, involved in the training of child psychotherapists. She founded the Autism Research Workshop in 1986 and is Co-convenor of the Workshop and of the Tavistock Autism Service. She is director of four research projects in the field – an individual case study and an outcome study of psychotherapy with children with autism, both with Dr Anthony Lee; an observational study of infants in families where there is an autistic child; and an outcome study of group psychotherapy for the siblings of children with autism. She is editor of *Developments in Infant Observation: The Tavistock Model*, and has lectured widely in the UK, Europe and the USA.

Maria Rhode is consultant child and adolescent psychotherapist in the Department of Children and Families at the Tavistock Clinic where she is Co-organising Tutor of the training in adult psychotherapy for child psychotherapists. She is co-editor (with Margaret Rustin and Alex and Hélène Dubinsky) of *Psychotic States in Children* (Tavistock Clinic Book Series) and guest editor of an issue of the *Journal of Infant Observation and its Applications*. She has contributed journal articles and book chapters on autism, psychosis and infant observation, and has a particular interest in language development in children with autism.

Biddy Youell works as a child and adolescent psychotherapist in Buckinghamshire and North London. She is an academic tutor at the Tavistock Clinic and teaches on a number of postgraduate courses. Her interest in autism began during the Child Psychotherapy training and she was a member of the Tavistock Autism Workshop for three years.

Preface

Both the Tavistock Autism Team and its Workshop are based in the Child and Family Department at the Tavistock Clinic. The members of the Team are privileged to work in a National Health Service setting to which a wide range of patients with autism is referred – from the mild, high-functioning Asperger's children and young people, to those who are severely handicapped by their condition. We treat not only those who are sufficiently young and responsive to be helped back onto the path of normal development, but also those at the other end of the spectrum, in terms both of the severity of their autism and of its chronicity. In the latter cases it may be impossible to effect a major reversal of the process, but it is possible to have a significant impact on the quality of the autistic person's life and that of the family. Chronicity brings problems in its own right, and this has important implications for early detection and treatment. Indeed, our work with the very handicapped children informs and illuminates the work with the less damaged children. The study of the more chronic conditions throws much light on the course of the autism, and so, by definition, on its nature.

Some of the cases described in the book have been treated by members of the Tavistock Team: the rest have been treated by other members of the Workshop, who work elsewhere in the UK in a variety of National Health Service settings. The Workshop was founded by Sue Reid in 1986 in order to give clinical support to child psychotherapists working with these puzzling children. The Workshop is now a multidisciplinary forum with several research projects in progress. Anne Alvarez joined as Co-convener in 1990, after several colleagues drew our attention to the similarities in our views regarding the urgent need to rethink and revise psychoanalytic technique with these mysterious children. This volume is the fruit of our collaboration. It presents our ideas about the importance of personality for the developmental course of the illness, and the implications for psychotherapeutic technique. (Anne Alvarez's book, *Live Company* [1992], published by Routledge, discussed some of the problems of chronicity, and also the need to revise psychotherapeutic technique and theory in the light of developmental thinking.)

Our clinical work over the years has made it impossible to ignore the existence of sub-groups in the autistic spectrum. This has had far-reaching implications for considering which technique is the best for any particular child. It has also led to more effective consultation with parents and professionals, and continues to inform our ideas about the treatability of each child or young person. We try to identify where the autism arises from deficit, where from defence against trauma, where from disorder, and where from deviance. We are concerned with the manner in which any of the first three, if left untreated, may lead to the fourth.

Part I of this volume introduces some of the theoretical ideas emerging from the workshop: these are illustrated by clinical vignettes. Each chapter in Part II is written as the story of the patient's changing contact with the therapist and with the outside world. Each of the patients presents different problems, and the variety, we think, will give a clear picture of the unique personality of each child and of the way this interacts with the autism to exacerbate or reduce it. We hope that the narrative style will make the book accessible to fellow professionals, to those from other disciplines, and, importantly, to parents of autistic children and other interested lay people. We think that our findings have implications far beyond the consulting room.

Our approach is both psychoanalytic and developmental. It is psychoanalytic in its emphasis on the close observation of events in their interpersonal context. This tradition of naturalistic observation and an open-minded attempt to find a way through to the patient – instead of making the patient fit the theory – is in the best psychoanalytic tradition. We try to see the world through the child's eyes, not through the lens of some beloved theory or methodology. A major and ongoing preoccupation of the Workshop is the development of an increasingly effective treatment methodology which takes account of these patients' particular levels of developmental delay – to know when to be attune to these levels, and when to be alert to the moments when the child is ready for a more demanding and imperfectly attuned world. The struggle to reach the more severely autistic patients has caused us to question and reflect upon every aspect of our psychotherapeutic method, and often upon the very nature of human relatedness.

The suffering of children with autism is often underestimated, as is the stress on their families and the tragic limitations on normal life. The debate continues as to whether autism is an emotional, cognitive or, as we suggest, an emotional/cognitive disorder. What is clear, however, is that an impairment in the capacity for social communication, whatever its cause, can be enormously distressing emotionally, both for impaired people and for those who live with them. It can have devastating effects on morale. Despite all the cutbacks within the National Health Service, it is essential, therefore, to continue to offer intensive psychotherapy to those who need it, as well as support to their families. We regularly work with colleagues who use different approaches, and usually we find these to be complementary to our own. Some older children referred to us with a diagnosis of mild Asperger's Syndrome have apparently been severely autistic when young. Sometimes the improvements seem to have come about through parental determination, sometimes through interventions in special schools. The important issue is whether and how the condition can be modified, not who does the modifying.

Fundamental to our approach is the degree of work pursued with the children's parents, other family members, and the wider network of schools, nurseries, paediatricians, language and arts therapists. This approach is central to all the work in the Child and Family Department at the Tavistock, but autism is a communication disorder, and there is extra potential for non-communication and miscommunication both within the family and between the family and other helping agencies, or between the agencies themselves. The provision of support for parents and siblings carries no aetiological implication: it may, however, help parents to find their child easier to understand and to live with. We wish to help the parents to find the non-autistic child behind the autism, and to help the child to find a strengthened parent behind the often traumatised and sometimes nearly despairing carer. Our Tavistock view is that both sides of the work are essential if benign circles are to be set in motion.

The reader will find many observations of the conditions under which the autistic symptomatology waxes and wanes, and the conditions under which the normal, non-autistic part of the personality of the child emerges. It is our view that our close and intense observation of these children – and of our own responses to them – may provide important information likely to be missed in purely behavioural analyses of symptoms. We study not only what the patient just did or seems about to do, but, importantly, the differing states of mind *in ourselves* which may have preceded or accompanied these changes. Our current research projects with Dr Anthony Lee, using video, process recordings and independent psychological evaluations, should throw further light on these important issues. This book presents our clinical findings.

Anne Alvarez and **Sue Reid**

Acknowledgements

The largest debt of gratitude goes to our patients, from whom we have learned so much. We have been overwhelmed by their parents' enthusiasm for this project, and they have generously given us permission to write about their children in the hope that it might help other children with autism and their parents.

This book could also not have been written without the invaluable secretarial support of Debi Schifreen, whose tolerance and forbearance we have greatly appreciated. Many other secretaries have also been generous in their assistance – Pamela Gair, Anne Joyce, Tracy Lakin, Jane Rayner and Jane Stockwell. We have been grateful for the friendly interest in our patients' progress provided by Jenny Allen, Allen Kirby and Juliet Tash in reception.

We are indebted to the staff of the Tavistock library; Margaret Walker, Angela Haselton and Helen Oliver have generously given us their time and expertise.

Our research projects are heavily dependent upon the technical support of David Wisker, Paul Watson, Andrew Mewitt and Suzanne Pike. A particular vote of thanks must go to our colleague, Dr Anthony Lee, who has put his time, advice and research and editing experience at our disposal. Dr Mary Sue Moore brought another dimension to our thinking in presenting relevant neurobiological research to the Autism Workshop, and she has given us much helpful advice in our research. Collaboration with colleagues in education and in other professions has been central to helping these children and their families. There are many with whom we have only recently begun to work, but we would particularly like to thank Johanna Ruggeri, Teresa Wasilewska, Enid Colmer and Jenny Gridley, with whom we have enjoyed a long association. We also need to mention our long association with Dr Sally Hodges and Dr David Simpson, both of whom have, to our delight, recently joined the Autism Team and Workshop at the Tavistock Clinic.

Our research and clinical activities have been supported by grants from the Winnicott Trust, the Tavistock Foundation, the Handicapped Children's Aid Committee, the Variety Club Children's Charity and the Goldsmith's Company, and we are very grateful to them.

An earlier version of Chapter 2 was presented to the annual conference of the Association of Child Psychotherapists in 1992, and some of the material appeared in *Clinical Child Psychology and Psychiatry*, 1998. Some of the material from Chapter 3 appeared in the *Journal of Child Psychotherapy*, 1998. An earlier version of Chapter 4 appeared in *Clinical Child Psychology and Psychiatry* in 1996. Earlier versions of Chapters 5, 8 and 13 were read at the Tavistock Autism Conference in July 1995. An earlier version of Chapter 16 was published in the *Journal of Child Psychotherapy* in 1994. We would like to thank the above journals for permission to reproduce copyright material.

Finally we must thank Al Alvarez, Albert Reid and Ben Reid for reading earlier drafts of our chapters and for their invaluable comments, support and assistance, and our families for allowing us time to work together in preparing this book.

1 Introduction

Autism, personality and the family

Anne Alvarez and Susan Reid

This is not just a book about autism. It is a book about children and young people with autism and the ways in which their individual and unique personalities may interact with autistic symptomatology. The *Oxford English Dictionary* (1971) defines personality as 'the quality, character or fact of being a person as distinct from a thing', or 'that quality or principle which makes a being personal'. It also defines it as 'that quality or assemblage of qualities which makes a person what he is, as distinct from other persons'. There is something so striking, so mysterious and disturbing about the condition of autism, especially the reduction of personhood in the sufferer, that it seems inevitable that researchers and clinicians tended to concentrate in the early decades on the features which autistic people had in common, rather than on those which distinguished them. Here we emphasise that every person with autism is different, and that there is a close and dense interweaving between the symptoms and the personal motivation of the children, adolescents and young adults described in these pages. We also intend to illustrate the way in which each patient described has, interwoven with their autism, an intact, non-autistic part of their personality. This non-autistic part may use, misuse and exploit the autistic symptoms, or it may oppose them and make efforts to reduce their influence. As patients begin to notice and to enjoy the feeling of coming out of the 'deep freeze' of autism, they may begin to value states of greater emotional depth and even to struggle to preserve and maintain them.

The autistic condition

Autism is a severe disorder which affects young children massively in their mental and emotional development. Children with autism do not engage in normal emotional relationships with people. They do not seek communication with people in the ordinary way. They do not play normally, and frequently carry out strange repetitive rituals and behaviours (Kanner 1943). These features are often accompanied by severe developmental delay in all areas of the child's functioning. They seem to lack a sense of a world in which there are people with minds who could be both interesting and interested in them. This is now known to be essential for the development of a human mind, where thoughts may occur, experiences be remembered, links made and imaginative life develop (Stern 1985). The majority of us have a capacity to judge mental states and some intuition about the feelings and motivation of others – in an ordinary sense to be 'mind-readers'. Normally developing children naturally acquire a set of increasingly sophisticated social and communication skills. They can imagine, pretend, interpret and recognise the feelings of others and detect intentions that are not communicated by speech alone. They come to know, and be interested in, when another person says one thing but means something else. They come to understand humour and irony. Their acts acquire intentionality. They know that if they do A, then B is likely to follow: experiences, experiments, repeated over time form a vast storehouse, a repository to be drawn on. From this bank of experiences ordinary children recognise what is similar and what is different about whatever situation they are in – they become emotionally literate.

Children with autism, in contrast, do not have rich inner worlds in which experiences and phantasies can be stored ready for some lively interaction with others and where new thoughts can be stimulated by new experiences. An inner world implies a three-dimensional space, including perspective, vertices, and differentiated contents. This is what the person with autism lacks for *most* of the time. However, close observation shows that, although it is not fully available or accessible, an inner world is rarely entirely absent. It is as if the three-dimensional space were fragile and unstable: a small breeze might cause it to collapse in on itself like a pack of cards.

There is much controversy about how best to describe autism, about where to locate the core damage, and about the nature of the core impairment. Some authors prefer a cognitive explanation, i.e. that people with autism are born without the capacity eventually to form an adequate 'theory of mind' (Leslie 1987; Frith 1989). Because of our study of very early infantile development and its stress on the social/emotional foundations of cognition – that is, on *the precursors of* 'the precursors of theory of mind' (Baron-Cohen 1992) – we tend to concur with writers like Hobson (1993) and Trevarthen *et al.* (1996) who view autism as a disorder of intersubjectivity, as a lack of a sense of other persons. We formulate it as an impairment of the normal *sense of emotionally based curiosity about, and desire for, interpersonal relationships.*

It is important to remember that autism is a condition which arises in early childhood: however fixed and limited its symptomatology may seem, it is exposed to developmental forces which compound the picture and complicate the course of the illness in myriad ways. In recent years many children have been referred to our service with a current diagnosis of mild Asperger's Syndrome: we learn that some of these children were diagnosed as severely autistic at the age of 2 or 3. Sometimes the parents tell us of their own heroic efforts to draw the child back into contact; in other cases we hear of improvements after the child went to a particular language unit or nursery school. Our own clinical findings of improved outcome after treatment lead us to be unsurprised by these changes and partial recoveries, but to be nonetheless even more interested in learning about the conditions for amelioration or deterioration. The child and adolescent psychotherapist's long and intensive contact with these patients may have much to offer to the subject of autism, not only for purposes of intervention and treatment, but also because such contact provides a rich source of data for the study of the nature of the condition itself.

In Chapter 2 on assessment, and in Chapter 5 on disorder and deviance, we consider the factors in the persistence of the condition of autism, but our focus everywhere in the book is equally on its mutability and its responsivity. Although people with autism have much in common, we are particularly interested in the differences between them as people, and in the fact that the autistic state of mind fluctuates from moment to moment within any individual with autism. This factor makes it extremely confusing for parents and professionals in their attempts to make contact.

The impact of autism on the family

For parents, sisters and brothers, the burden of living with an apparently uninterested and unreachable child may produce a state of permanent hurt, shock and grief: outside the home, the families of these normal-looking but severely handicapped and strangely behaved children are often exposed to public and humiliating embarrassments. Their lives may become severely limited, with consequent stress on the parents' marriage and effects on the mental health of everyone.

Unfortunately for people with autism and their distressed families, there has been great controversy about the cause of their mysterious condition. In the past, some professionals took extreme points of view, leading them to split into two separate and opposing camps. In the cognitivist camp, many asserted that the evidence for genetic or other organic causation (implying an inborn deficit) led inevitably to a pessimistic view of the modifiability of the condition. Some psychodynamicist writers in the USA saw autism as a defensive avoidance of 'refrigator' mothers, and this led to guilt for parents and a psychotherapy which concentrated on the children's 'defences' and 'fears' and neglected their genuine disorder and real developmental delays. In both camps, issues of cause were unfortunately confused with issues of treatment. Nowadays, both groups have moved towards a greater recognition of multiple causation and some recognition that we need to bring together different areas of expertise in order to provide a concerted attack on the problem (Bailey *et al.* 1996). Reid discusses a possible aetiological factor in a particular sub-group of children with autism in Chapter 7. She discusses the difference between the effect of actual external trauma on an ordinarily sensitive very young infant, and the – apparently traumatising – effect of quite ordinary life experiences on particularly hyper-sensitive infants. Other possible integrations arise from the fact that many cognitivists are now more interested in intervention (Howlin 1997: 95). Many psychoanalytic therapists are more aware of the need to take account of the deficits in cognition, the hypersensitivities and the difficulties in what psychoanalysts call 'introjection', the taking in and processing of experience (Tustin 1981a). Alvarez, in Chapter 5, describes her patient Samuel's difficulty in trying to 'take in' the fact of two identical objects. Pundick, in Chapter 12, describes her patient Carmen clutching desperately at her therapist, and Reid, in Chapter 8, speaks of Catherine 'sucking' words in and trying to sort out the difference between foreground and background. Therapists have also had to adapt their technique to take account of the considerable developmental delay present in autism (see Chapter 4).

The Tavistock approach

In any psychoanalytic psychotherapy, therapist and patient embark together on a journey and, although neither can know quite where the journey will lead them, some maps are usually provided by a substantial body of psychonanalytic theory and practice lore. Therapists working with autistic patients have learned that special problems are involved if we are to reach a child who does not understand that he or she is a person and has little idea that their therapist is a human being. In the Tavistock Autism Workshop we have developed techniques of psychotherapy which attempt to take account of the developmental delay, disorder and defensive or deviant structures in patients' functioning. We describe these methods via narrative descriptions of the work with individual patients in the hope of elucidating the unique problems and personality of each one. The struggle to reach severely ill patients has caused us to question and reflect upon every aspect of our psychotherapeutic method and, indeed, upon the nature of human engagement.

The patients

The range of children referred to the Tavistock has led us to think in terms of sub-groups, each of which requires subtle but essential adaptation in the therapist's technique. Some have very strong, even bullish personalities which demand a firm, not too accommodating response if they are to notice our presence. Others impress us with their delicacy, even fragility, and extreme sensitivity and caution are required if they are to begin to tolerate engagement. Tustin (1972) distinguished the encapsulated shell-type child from the more passive amoeboid type. Wing and Attwood (1987) have delineated a differentiation from the point of view of psychiatric description. They have also pointed out that people with autism are similar to other psychiatric patients in refusing to stay put in the diagnostic categories assigned to them. We, too, in our clinical practice, are aware of the need to be open to the possibility, even probability, that as treatment proceeds, the bullish children may reveal vulnerability behind their thick-skinned façades. The hypersensitive children, on the other hand, may well reveal reserves of stubborn determination initially masked by their delicate presentations. Recognition of the existence of different sub-types within the autistic condition, together with increased attention to the defining features of the patient's personality, has allowed us to achieve greater precision in our psychotherapeutic technique. This has led to improved outcomes.

The patients described in this book range in age from two years to young adulthood, and vary in the severity of their condition. The majority received diagnoses of autism from centres other than the Tavistock, prior to referral to us. The treatment offered was from once to five-times weekly psychotherapy, with the majority seen three times a week. The cases illustrate variations in the responsiveness of each child and the variable levels of improvement. Because tragic limitations are imposed on the lives of families, parents are offered help both individually (see Chapter 3) and in parents' groups. We present accounts here both of young or responsive children whom we have helped to get back onto the path of normal development (Chapters 10 and 11), and also of those who are at the severely ill end of the spectrum either in terms of degree of autism (Chapter 5) or of chronicity (Chapters 7, 13 and 15). In the more severe cases, although it may not be possible to effect a major reversal of the process, nevertheless we usually expect to have a significant impact on the quality of the autistic person's life, and on that of the family. Work with very severely autistic patients, furthermore, both informs and illuminates the work with the less severely autistic people. Chronicity brings problems in its own right, and this has important implications for early detection and treatment. The study of the more chronic conditions also throws much light on the course of the condition and, by definition, therefore, on its nature.

Therapeutic technique

Dawson and Lewy (1989: xvii) write:

> Although it is possible that we may never 'cure' autism in the sense of elim-
> inating the primary cause of the disorder, a realistic and worthy goal of
> applied autism research is to devise therapies that ameliorate the secondary
> negative consequences of the primary abnormalities.

Although we do not suggest that the lack of emotional relatedness to others is the primary cause of the disorder, we do think it is the core and primary symptom, and it is towards that area of the patient's condition that we direct our treatment. Early detection of the precursors, at eighteen months, is essential (e.g. Baron-Cohen *et al.* 1992), but it is our view that a study of the precursors of the precursors, – that is, of the infant's state of mind and of social relatedness in the early weeks and months of post-natal life – will confirm the psychoana-lytic and infant developmental view, and that of some autism researchers (Hobson 1993) that, although impairment of social relatedness may not be the core cause, it is the core symptom.

The psychotherapy is informed by three major elements in a child and adolescent psychotherapist's training. All three – psychoanalysis, infant observa-tion and infant development research – involve a study of the nature of interpersonal relations, both in the external and internal worlds. These are applied to the very close observation of the individuality of people with autism.

Psychoanalytic features of the approach

Psychoanalytic treatment involves three major features:

(a) the regularity and consistency of the setting;
(b) the use of the transference; and
(c) the use of the counter-transference.

Developmental researchers and infant observers agree that cognitive and communicative 'skills' arise through *emotional* relationships with caregivers. Like Hobson (1993) and Trevarthen *et al.* (1996) we think that the social impairment is the core symptom, and this is why we work via the relationship between patient and therapist.

The setting

The regularity of the appointments, together with the consistency of the location of the sessions, is important for the recovery of all patients in psychoanalytic forms of treatment, but especially so for autistic patients where a safe, predictable setting is often the first thing which impinges on and attracts them. Like plants which need 'heeling in', they may begin to put down roots and to grow a mind. Parents and teachers must cope with these children for several hours at a time, and every type of contact has its particular stresses and strains. Therapists' particular training involves the toleration and exploration of intense feelings – of anxiety, of despair or of boredom. Their role is to stay with these feelings and not to avoid them. The fifty-minute limit provides a structure which enables therapists to help patients to manage the unfolding of intense and primitive feelings. These feelings may be particularly powerful as they begin to emerge from autistic states of mind, when their intolerance of ordinary human frailty and imperfection becomes more exposed.

The transference

Therapists use the transference – the patient's attitude and relationship to the therapist – as the lens through which to view the patient's world of relationships to others. The patient's changing relationship to the therapist – and, if all goes well, their developing attachment to the therapist – is not seen as a substitute for their relationship to their parents. Rather, it is a way-station on the route back to the important relationships with the real mother and father. Improvements in patients' capacity for emotional communication can make them more accessible to parents' caregiving. It is our experience that it is the emotionality in the contact which promotes change in social relatedness, communication and thoughtfulness. Interestingly, in this context Howlin (1997: 91) has pointed out that training in social skills for people with autism offers some help but does not generalise greatly. It is our view that we are changing deeper structures in the mind, and it is this which supports generalisation.

The counter-transference

The counter-transference is understood as the response evoked in the psychoanalyst by the patient's feelings (see Chapters 2 and 4). Yet the problem with most autistic patients is that of a lack of feeling, a lack of communicative expressed emotion. In general, we can all 'mind-read' others' intentions and states of mind. But when attempting to ascertain intentionality and meaning in the actions of a person with autism we often get a sense of meaninglessness. This experience is disconcerting, alienating, puzzling. It lacks the ordinary ingredients of mutual curiosity and interest. The autistic child either lacks the capacity for, or is not interested in, differentiating animate from inanimate objects; as a result we, in turn, may find it difficult to attribute mental states to a person with autism. Therapists have to be more than psychoanalytic interpreters; we may need actively to 'reclaim' the patient back into the world of human feeling and communication (Alvarez 1992) and to 'demonstrate' to them that the world beyond their private autism is indeed interesting (Reid 1988b). The use of the counter-transference enables the therapist to observe how minute changes in their responses may trigger changes in the patient, which can then be used actively to engage the patient. The therapist must have a mind for two, energy for two, hope for two, imagination for two. Gradually, patients may begin to get interested, not yet in us, but in our interest in them.

Infant observation

The second major strand which informs our work is the naturalistic observation of infants, a core feature of the training of child and adolescent psychotherapists. It is especially important for the study of people with autism, who are impaired in language and communication and whose signals may be faint or non-existent. The training in *emotionally* informed observation of the earliest forms of human interaction – in infants from birth – sensitises therapists to the subtlest, earliest forms of pre-verbal communication (Miller *et al.* 1989; Reid 1997a). Observation is used together with the use of the counter-transference to inform our choice of intervention.

Infant development research

The third strand is the work of infant developmentalists. Their study of the ways in which caregivers amplify and develop their infants' capacity for reciprocity and for entering into the world of human intercourse, informs our technique and sensitises us to the precise developmental level at which our patients are functioning at any given moment. Their work is important for the understanding of how normal development can go awry. Gaze-avoidance, for example, is a normal coping mechanism in early infancy (Stern 1977b) but it may, in the autistic person, have become dangerously habitual. Such evidence may alert us to the fact that even when gaze-avoidance is habitual, it may nevertheless continue to be fuelled by some degree of normal motivation.

Liaison with parents, schools and other helping agencies

People with autism are frequently incapable of distinguishing people from things. A parent may not be asked for help: rather, the child may take the parent's hand and place it on a doorknob. They do not want help, they literally 'want a hand'. They want the function that the hand performs, and the person attached to the hand is incidental. Parents may inadvertently contribute to this downward cycle by second-guessing their child's needs, so that neither child nor parent is aware that an opportunity for a potentially more lively engagement has been missed. To ask for help and to give it are mutually reinforcing experiences, whilst to have one's hand grasped without even a glance at one's face is a deeply dehumanising experience. Such repeated emotionally exhausting experiences can wear away at parents' ordinary human warmth and spontaneity, so that, in the end, the hand may be given reactively and unreflectively without any expectation or demand for anything more. Psychotherapists and teachers, too, note this wearing down of spontaneity in themselves and the effort required to overcome the tendency to take the easy way out. An important feature of our work is the degree of liaison with the children's parents, other family members, and the wider network of schools, nurseries, paediatricians, speech therapists, music therapists and movement therapists. Autism is a communication disorder: living with an autistic child increases the potential for non-communication and miscommunication both within the family and between the family and other helping agencies. Developmental gain, although bringing rewards, may create new stresses. Ordinary psychoanalytic questions of confidentiality and privacy have to be weighed against the need for sharing observation: ways can be found of discussing the patient without betraying the most intimate features of the patient's sessions (see Chapters 2 and 3).

Many families need support to recover from the initial shock of discovering that their child has autism. Joint observation of their child with the therapist during the assessment may support families in finding ways in which they can become usefully firm and begin to make the kind of demands that parents ordinarily make of their children as they leave infancy (see Chapter 2). Feeling responsible for their child's condition can cause some parents to collude with the child's disorder and personality in ways which interfere with the normal development in the child of some capacity for a sense of responsibility and respect for others. This in turn can contribute to an escalation of demanding, intrusive or aggressive behaviour. In other instances, the parents' feelings of helplessness in the face of their child's indifference has meant some children are left too much to their own devices. When not addressed and treated, personality features of impatience and intolerance are in danger of becoming embedded into character. Then states can become traits (B. Perry *et al.* 1995). In some cases this may lead to a personality disorder in the person with autism. Many parents are relieved to find a more robust and ordinary part of their child's personality hidden among the symptoms, or ordinary emotional needs hidden behind strange behaviours. Other parents, blinded by the symptoms and their child's apparent indifference, need help in finding the part of the child that may be enormously needy emotionally and, indeed, hypersensitive rather than insensitive to the feelings of others.

A further note on the question of sub-groups

The main argument of this book is that every person with autism is different. It is clear however, that many of our patients can be grouped together in sub-groupings. Wing and Attwood (1987) found that their classification into Aloof, Passive and Active but Odd sub-groups was useful for planning management, education and services. Our clinical attempts to reach these inaccessible children has led us to similar conclusions and to hypothesise different forms of inaccessibility. We have in fact gone on to conceptualise the existence of sub-sub-groups. We stress, for example, the difference between the *un*drawn passive children (Chapter 4) and those passive children who turn out to be more *with*drawn and so more actively involved in their passivity than it first seemed. We also suggest that there exists a 'thick skinned' sub-sub-group of aloof people, who are somewhat complacent in their autism and who may or may not go on to develop personality disorder. These are very different from those aloof patients with extreme 'thin-skinned' hypersensitivity (see Chapter 7). Reid proposes a new sub-grouping, that of Autistic Post-Traumatic Developmental Disorder. Most of these patients fall into the Aloof Thin-Skinned category, but some are Passive and a few are Active but Odd. This group therefore seems to be on an axis different from that of Wing's and to cut across her sub-groupings. We also suspect that some of our treated patients, although improved, may, because they still have considerable developmental delay in normal functioning, become like those categorised in the Active but Odd group.

Conclusion

We commented earlier that our experience of long periods of close observation and interaction with people with autism – and of the context in which the autism waxes and wanes – not only provides important information about treatment, but also casts light on the nature of the autistic state itself. Early detection is important for the purposes of intervention, but as Charman pointed out at a conference on Theory of Mind at University College London in March 1998, it is also important for understanding the natural history of autism. It is our view that if detection occurs even earlier than the current eighteen-month level, it may lead to a real understanding, not only of the natural history of the overall condition, but also of the individual symptoms themselves. We may learn, finally, which symptoms are primary, secondary and tertiary. How does deficit lead to disorder and disorder to deviance? Where and when do defensive or protective factors enter the picture? How does the trajectory of autistic development differ from that of normal development? Colleagues in France (Didier Houzel), Italy (Sandra Maestro and Filippo Muratori) and Russia (Marina Bardyshevsky) are engaged in pioneering work on early detection in the first months of life and in providing early intervention programmes (personal communications). Adriana Grotta, psychologist, and Maria Grazia Cassola, a child neuro-psychiatrist, in Bologna, Italy, began work with a worrying autistic-like baby and parents at ten months. Their only regret was that they were not given permission by the parents to help at four months! Although in the last ten years children have been referred to us at increasingly younger ages, nonetheless in this country we continue to be hampered by a general but natural reluctance to label children in the first year of their lives, when development is so open-ended and plastic.

In our descriptions of the nature of autism, as outlined in this book, we shall illustrate some of the phantasies and the motivations that accompany the symptoms. Sometimes patients can tell us how they view the change in themselves only after language has developed. Anne Alvarez's patient, Robbie, described having been down a deep well, and being rescued along with all his loved ones. He also described his later struggle against slippages into old autistic habits of mind as a 'climb out of the slippery gutter'. Sue Reid's patient, Catherine, identified 'three dark areas of my mind': one she described as having, in the past, been 'a cold dark dungeon where the feelings inside were lonely'. Such emotive phantasies are not simple after-thoughts, *post hoc* explanations. We think they communicate, however inexpressible and unprocessed they were at the time, something real about the patient's experience of autism and of recovery. We hope that, through the narrative descriptions of patients' experiences in psychotherapy, the reader will have a direct encounter with the way in which each of them, in their different ways, experiences the burden of autism.

Part I

Theoretical and clinical developments

2 The assessment of the child with autism

A family perspective

Susan Reid

In the noisy bustle on the way to the consulting room, created by Sally's parents, two older sisters, older brother, baby sister, au pair and myself, only Sally shows no interest, no animation, says nothing. She is an exquisitely pretty child, with big eyes fringed with long thick black lashes, but her eyes focus on nothing, on no-one.

In my consulting room she stares ahead of her, immobile, indifferent, and then, at some internal cue, turns suddenly and makes for the door. When her father follows her she takes his hand and puts it on the handle. Sally's father tries to pick her up, to put her on his lap, but she resists determinedly, her body rigid, stiff; he tries gently to bend her at the waist but her body will not mould to his and he gives up. I am struck by something incongruous in her delicate features which suggest a fragile, vulnerable creature, and the solid muscular body which takes on the personality of a ten-ton truck. This body accepts no obstacles and acknowledges none; neither people nor objects are negotiated. She moves around as if we and the furniture do not exist. She walks on my feet and registers nothing. She walks into the coffee table, but the impact with it makes no impact on her – she just keeps walking, pushing the table ahead of her, deflected only when the coffee table meets the immovable mass of the desk against the wall. Still she registers nothing – not frustration, not irritation. It must hurt when she bumps into things but she shows no pain. Attempts to get her attention, call her name, play with her, are all ignored; more than that, they are not even registered. She might as well be deaf. Sally seems impervious to all around her, inhabiting a world entirely of her own making.

Occasionally she smiles to herself; sometimes she speaks to herself in a high-pitched, whispery sing-song, but it is not a language known to any of us. Sometimes another member of her family pulls her onto their lap, but Sally goes stiff and refuses to be held. She makes noisy, protesting yells when restrained from walking out of the room, but the cries are dry eyed and stop as abruptly as they start. She seems oblivious to the experience the rest of us share.

Her parents told me that Sally had no language, just this funny noise of her own; she did not play, would not look at anyone. There was a strong wish that I should help her. I felt far from optimistic at this point, since Sally had not even demonstrated the peripheral awareness that some children with autism show. There was, however, one fleeting sign of awareness: on that day I was wearing a large, colourful Swatch watch which Sally, on one of her circuits around the room, stopped briefly to touch and look at. She then gave me a fleeting sideways look and the moment was gone.

Introduction

In this chapter[1] I describe a psychodynamic, developmentally informed approach to the assessment of children with autism which pays particular attention to the experience of the whole family. It is recognised that living with a person with autism can have a devastating impact on all other family members. As in all psychodynamic assessments, the focus is not primarily on diagnosis but rather on attempts to discover the nature and location of the distress in the family. It also explores those therapeutic interventions which might prove helpful. Although a psychiatric diagnostic checklist for autism may confirm the presence and degree of severity of autism, it cannot convey what it is like to be autistic, and it cannot tell us what it is like to live with a child with autism. It tells us what to look for in order to diagnose autism but it does not tell us what to do next. Diagnosis, then, is only a small part of the assessment process as outlined in this chapter. When a diagnosis is discussed, care is needed to assess with the family and other professionals involved, what role this diagnosis might serve. There is an emphasis on observation and on the use of the therapist's counter-transference in understanding how these puzzling children experience their world. This methodology is central to all psychodynamic assessments but is of special importance with non-verbal children. Counter-transference is used in the way first described by Heimann – 'My thesis is that the analyst's emotional response to his patient within the analytic situation represents one of the most important tools for the work ... an instrument for research into the patient's unconscious' (Heimann 1950: 81). These ideas on the use of counter-transference have been further developed particularly by Brenman Pick (1985) and Joseph (1989).

The psychoanalytic observer is interested not only in behaviours, but in monitoring the states of mind which accompany them and which they evoke in others. The observer's changing states of mind (counter-transference) can then be used to guide the observer's own responsive actions and then in noting the child's response to their response. Interest in discovering the qualitative nature of a piece of behaviour requires the use of emotive language. Emotive language is used in all process recordings because we believe it gives a more accurate record of our contact with a patient. We hope to learn something unique about each child, which can take us beyond the limitations imposed by the use of a behavioural checklist alone.

We have found that some adaptations to the assessment technique more usually employed with families with non-autistic children are required if we are to be experienced as helpful to these families. We have also found that some of the elements which form part of the usual psychoanalytically informed assessments need greater emphasis. For example, because autistic children do not project their feelings in the ordinary way, a more active technique may be required of us if we are to make any meaningful contact with them.

The chapter includes a schema: the schema represents my attempt to give a more formal structure to something which has developed organically in response to my changing understanding of what families who have a child with autism seem to need. This approach to assessment is used by the Autism Team in the Child and Family Department at The Tavistock Clinic, and also by members of the Autism Workshop, whose clinical base is elsewhere. These assessments are intended to be therapeutic interventions in their own right.

The primary evidential base for this approach arises from the detailed clinical accounts (process recordings) accumulated over nearly thirty years of my own clinical practice, together with the resources of the Autism Workshop. The Workshop provides a forum for the exploration of autistic phenomena, and has given me access to the experiences, clinical records and videotapes of my colleagues. The unique insights offered by a single assessment can be compared with detailed process recordings from other assessments, and may reveal some recurring patterns across subjects. Gathering this data has informed changes in both our theoretical constructs and clinical techniques as outlined here. We believe these changes have made us more effective clinicians. We are currently engaged in researching the effectiveness of our method. Detailed clinical material is offered to illustrate some of these ideas.

Autism

There is agreement amongst all professionals that autism is one of the most puzzling of disorders. The term 'autism' has been used to identify many different symptoms since Kanner first described early infantile autism in 1943. A considerable amount of professional energy has, perhaps understandably, been directed towards diagnostic systems and schedules, rather than therapeutic interventions: diagnostic schedules such as the Autism Diagnostic Observation Schedule (Lord *et al.* 1989) and the Autism Diagnostic Interview (Le Couteur *et al.* 1989) are extremely important diagnostic tools, and the CHAT (Baron-Cohen *et al.* 1992) is an important contribution to the early detection of autism. Frith (1989) and Wing (1996) have provided an historical perspective on the development of ideas about autism. Trevarthen and his colleagues have made reference to the psychoanalytic contribution to thinking on autism (Trevarthen *et al.* 1996) and Parks (1983) has provided a comprehensive review of checklists and questionnaires. This has been supplemented by Trevarthen and his colleagues in an excellent critical review of medical diagnostic systems since 1978 (Trevarthen *et al.* 1996: 4–26).

The division between those who take an organic approach and those who take a psychodynamic approach to issues of aetiology and treatment has not served families' best interests. Aetiology and treatment have proved poor bedfellows: parents report being advised that, because autism is organic, then it cannot be treated. Here there seems to be a confusion between treatment and cure. Doctors do not refuse treatment to people with incurable physical illness which may alleviate some aspects of their condition or, at the very least, improve the quality of their lives. Patients with neurological damage have been helped to develop emotionally, often with secondary cognitive gains, with psychoanalytic psychotherapy (Sinason 1986). Nowadays more specialists in autism seem inclined to assume multiple causation, and this certainly represents the view of the Autism Workshop.

It seems apparent that there is a need for a more open exchange of ideas between the different professional groups working in the field of autism and some recognition that it is impossible for any single profession to 'own the truth'. It is striking that poor communication is common between the very professional groups that seek to develop knowledge in order to unlock the mysteries of this condition. As child and adolescent psychotherapists we have been as guilty of this as any other profession.

Autism is commonly regarded as a developmental disorder consisting of a triad of impairments: an impairment in communication, in the ability to make social contact and in rigidity and inflexibility of behaviour linked to the impairment of symbolic thinking and the capacity to play. It is the autistic person's deficient awareness of the world of personal relationships that we take as the core feature, and it is this lack of awareness of the members of their family as 'people' who have feelings and ideas, that has a devastating effect on family life. There is a considerable body of evidence, (Wolf *et al.* 1989; Morgan 1985; Helm and Koslov 1986) that caring for an autistic child places very considerable stresses upon family members. For parents to receive a diagnosis of autism for their child can be traumatic, and those programmes which focus on diagnosis alone may be unaware of the impact such a diagnosis may have when some feedback to the family is not also offered. Baron-Cohen (1996) has emphasised the importance of devising appropriate treatment programmes if further research into the early detection of autism in infancy is to be of lasting value. As Newson has written,

> since Kanner first drew attention to the autistic syndrome in the 1940s (Kanner 1943), research in the field has multiplied; but we are still at the point where we are much better at describing autism than we are at knowing how to deal with it.
>
> (Newson 1987: 34)

More recently there is evidence of the desire to bring together assessment and management in autism (Forrest and Vostanis 1996). Newson has recognised the indivisibility of education, treatment and the handling of autistic children – 'with autistic children, anyone who attempts to plan an integrated programme for the child finds immediately that all these aspects have to be taken into account at the same time' (Newson 1987: 34).

Autistic development and normal development

The non-autistic person has the capacity to recognise that the world is an infinitely complex place which is of considerable interest to them. Normal development in infancy is marked by endless curiosity about the world, and by a year most infants can be described as 'into everything'. Early development is marked by the process of discovery, which infant observation (Miller *et al.* 1989; Reid 1997a) and child development research (Stern 1985; Trevarthen 1976) shows us begins at birth. In normal development we can observe babies discovering that they are people and that mummy, daddy, brothers and sisters are also people. People have feelings: they have thoughts and ideas, and can express them. In observing normally developing infants, the drive to communicate on the part of the infant and the wish to make sense of those communications on the part of important adults and siblings, is profoundly satisfying and a source of pleasure to all those involved.

When attempts to communicate are met with some measure of success, then infants have confirmation that they have an impact on their environment: each success tells them something about themselves as a person and also something about those with whom they have been interacting. It is nowadays widely recognised that autistic children are impaired in their understanding of mental states. In normal development most children acquire increasingly sophisticated social and communication skills. They learn to become what Frith (1989) has called 'mind readers', and to use a theory of mind (Baron-Cohen *et al.* 1993). By attributing mental states to others, other people's behaviour becomes meaningful and predictable. Children become increasingly skilful at interpreting other people's behaviour, feelings and intentions, and at reflecting upon their own feelings, wishes and ideas. Out of this develops an 'intentional self' with a capacity for self-regulation and an understanding of how to produce a particular response in other people. This has been described as a sense of agency (Alvarez 1992; Alvarez and Furgiuele 1997). Ordinary children learn to play and have an imaginative life, a rich internal world. They take pleasure in some things and are distressed and made miserable by others. They know how to have fun and they know how to cry. These qualities make people recognisable to one another as fellow human beings.

Listening to families

Families with an autistic child share the experience of living with children who live in a world of their own: mysterious, separate. For parents to feel that they are not really interesting to their children and that they have no real impact on them or influence upon their behaviour, is to feel real despair. No matter how life started out for each of these children and their families, by the time of referral it is usually the parents who are feeling traumatised, desperate and often with little hope and with a damaged sense of personal worth. Autistic children have convinced their family that they are dependent on them only for physical well-being. As one distressed mother put it, 'If I disappeared tomorrow, I don't think he would really notice'.

Having an autistic child can be likened to having a cuckoo in the nest: the autistic child takes more and more of the family resources, but is unable to give anything much back. Other siblings get kicked out of the 'nest' of parental mindfulness and, recognising that their parents are already overtaxed, frequently become pseudo-good assistant parents. Parents' relationships may suffer – with each other, with their other children and with the wider community.

Listening to many families' accounts of life with children with autism has alerted me to a need for change in my own approach to assessment. Each family, to some degree, is suffering from post-traumatic stress. It is therefore important to go slowly, and because of this the usual assessment of a child's needs may now span several months. The assessments are also intended as thera-peutic interventions in their own right; it has become apparent that what emerges over the course of these long assessments, is a microcosm of the thera-peutic process for those children subsequently offered psychoanalytic psychotherapy. The emphasis in this model is on the recognition that each family is unique, and that whilst the children may share a diagnosis of autism, each child has his or her own individual personality.

Technical issues in psycho-dynamic assessments of children with autism

A psychoanalytic approach allows for the discovery of the uniqueness of each child but, with the autistic child, the discovery requires some developments and adaptations in the usual approach to assessing children. The major technical difference is in relation to the amount of activity needed on the part of the ther-apist. With many children it is possible to provide a setting, some toys and for the therapist then to allow things to unfold: here it is right and appropriate for the therapist to be non-directive. The problem specific to working with children with autism, however, at least at the assessment stage and usually a long way into treatment, is that they are not object- or person-related; they seem not to make any kind of relationship; they probably do not give any indication that they recognise our existence, or if they do, that we are different from a table or chair. We may be moved or pushed to different parts of the room, our hand might be used to open a door, or our feet may be walked on with no sign of concern for our discomfort.

Children with autism will often not cooperate at all, may cause chaos in the consulting room and in our minds. They may distract us from listening to parents and siblings, whilst at the same time showing no overt interest in what is going on – not talking to us, not playing, either ignoring us or avoiding us, unresponsive to our attempts to be interested in them. We may then, in our counter-transference, become aware that we have slipped into mindlessness and find great difficulty in being attentive. It becomes only too easy to behave like an automaton, to switch to automatic pilot. This seems to mirror the experiences of many parents. The effort of will involved in sustaining attention to these children allows us to empathise with the difficulty for parents who live with them, sometimes for twenty-four hours a day. How do we communicate with someone who shows no curiosity about us? We must be both interested and interesting, and our role needs to be a more active one than is ordinarily the case with other patients.

Second is the importance of assessing the child in the presence of the parents. Since the primary therapeutic aim is to get communication going within the family in a new way, it is counter-productive with most families to take the child away to another room for assessment, before we have formed a partnership with the parents. We may discover something interesting and important, but to what end? The danger is in becoming merely another 'specialist', whose expert opinion on the child is as mysterious and alien as that of any other 'expert'. Communication would not be opened up and we may unwittingly increase parental helplessness and despair. It seems helpful to be active in offering suggestions about new ways of engaging the child based upon our understanding of the family's own natural style of parenting. If the child makes some response to the assessment, and if the parents are not initially actively involved, then the gulf between the parents and their child may be widened. The therapist's aim during assessment is to begin a new journey and to take everyone with her.

Observation and perspective

Parents come with their feelings about their child, but also feelings about each other: feelings of blame, of hope for a cure, of anger at past failures, whilst also containing inside them all the previous experiences they have had of professional contacts. The pressure on those carrying out assessments becomes enormous. For this reason the importance of an observational state of mind is underlined. As with many aspects of our clinical work, work with people with autism often seems to highlight what is important in our overall technique.

The observational state of mind is a friendly, curious state of mind, non-judgmental, in which the therapist is interested only in 'getting to know the family'. This parallels the situation in normal development for the mother and father of a new baby. In this state of mind it is possible to sustain interest in what is there to be seen and to allow it to have its impact on the therapist. Can they manage the clinic's and the therapist's boundaries? Are they full of anxiety, depressed, or showing no anxiety? How does the child behave? Does the child relate to anyone and if so in what way? In what way does the family and its individual members use this opportunity? What contact do they make with the therapist and in what way, if any, do they seem to use what the therapist may have to offer? For many families it is a relief to have things slowed down; a relief to discover that they are not about to be merely processed, but rather discovered and thought about with whatever time it might take.

Within the initial assessment sessions, we want to see whether we can generate three things in the child – playfulness, friendliness, and curiosity. In order to do this it becomes necessary to build on the shadow of an idea when one perceives it, to fan the flicker of the flame of interest, to build upon, develop and amplify the earliest attempts at play. We try to provide a structure which is firm but flexible, and sufficiently elastic to meet the child's changing needs from one moment to the next. Within one session, and from one session to the next, it then becomes possible to see whether meaning begins to grow out of meaninglessness. Do we form an idea about what the child is doing and why, and does the child begin to do things as if he or she anticipates a response? Does seemingly random behaviour begin to take on a structure? Is it possible to discern the beginnings of intentionality in the child's play? The technical difference in this approach from psychotherapeutic assessments with other patients is that it must be the therapist who takes the responsibility to initiate contact and to lend meaning when it is apparent that the child is not in a state of mind, or cannot be accurately described as having a mind, to do it for him or herself.

The schema

The assessment schema (Table 2.1) is an attempt to conceptualise the stages involved in assessing children and young people with autism. It seems important to include each of these stages in the course of an assessment, although it may not be possible or even desirable to proceed in a strictly linear fashion. Attention to this model helps us in reflecting upon each of the stages. When we deviate from it, it is important to know why we have done so. It is equally important to allow ourselves, in a mindful way, to follow a different course. The child with autism can, and will, activate autistic, rigid, obsessional mechanisms in us, just as they do in their parents and teachers.

Phases 3, 5 and 7 will now be further elaborated, and I shall conclude with detailed clinical material from Sally's assessment (Phase 9).

Sharing observations and learning the child's history (Phase 3)

Using close observation, the assessor can bring a fresh perspective. We can come to know what it is like to live in this family for each member, whilst attempting to retain a link with the world of more ordinary family relationships. It becomes increasingly clear how important it is to hold on to what is 'normal' in the developmental process in order to share this with parents. These confusing children are so patchy in their development and in their achievements that it seems helpful to describe to parents the different levels at which their child is functioning at different points within one session, and how these in turn relate to the normal milestones of development. In this way it becomes possible to support parents in rediscovering their parenting skills. Thinking about the developmental patchiness of the child can also serve to help parents become more realistic about what the child might achieve, and how long this may take.

Some children with autism do not respond well to feeling that the spotlight

Table 2.1 The assessment schema

Phase of assessment	Methodology	Aims
Phase 1 Referral	No reading of reports from other professionals	To prevent premature generalised judgements and pressure for certainty. To view the child in the family through the families' eyes, rather than those of other professionals.
Phase 2 Observation	Observe the child in the family using assessor's counter-transference (feelings as well as formulations)	To avoid premature diagnosis and prescriptive explanation. To facilitate a fluid, open and receptive state of mind in the assessor which respects the uniqueness and complexity of each family.
Phase 3 Sharing observations and learning child's history	Allow spontaneous account of child's developmental history. Attend to healthy development as much as to the autism.	To encourage emergence of a developmental picture not restricted by current generalised opinions about autism. To respect the uniqueness of the child in his or her particular family. To establish that the history is of a child with autism, not an autistic child.
Phase 4 Contact with other professionals	Seek permission for contact. Read reports.	To facilitate communication in the network for a child with a communication disorder.
Phase 5 Containment of possible family trauma	Support each family member in describing the impact of the discovery and/or diagnosis of the child's disorder.	To address the traumatic impact of autism on emotional health of family members.
Phase 6 Consultation	Try to make links between the child's behaviour and the parents' particular response.	To find new strategies to improve the quality of family life (sleep, mealtimes, recreation).
Phase 7 Diary	Encourage parents to keep a weekly diary of the child by recording their contextualised observations of negative and positive changes in the child's behaviour. To illustrate where there is potential for change.	To support the parents' capacity to observe their child and to empower often-demoralised parents to value their own perspective. To provide a home-based record of the possible impact of the assessment.

Table 2.1 The assessment schema

Phase of assessment	Methodology	Aims
Phase 8 Family history	When trust has been established, gather accounts of history of family members other than the child with autism	To recognise healthy development in siblings or to acknowledge where siblings may be in distress. To allow parents to explore how the painful experience of having a child with autism may have evoked memories of previous distressing experiences or losses.
Phase 9a Assessment of child	Individual assessment meetings with the child (usually 3)	To assess balance between degree of autistic pathology and the potential for healthy development: e.g. for an increase in social relatedness, mindfulness and tolerance of change. To assess degree of developmental delay. To assess degree of behaviour disorder. To assess contribution of the child's personality to autistic symptomology, developmental delay and behaviour problems. To assess for sub-group of autism. To assess what, if any, psychodynamic/developmental treatment is appropriate. (family, individual, parallel).
Phase 9b Assessment of parental need	Meetings with parents as a couple and/or as individuals	To assess degree of suffering from impact of living with autism. To discover the degree to which parents are able to support change in the child. To provide opportunity for parents to share their concerns and pressures. To provide an experience of a psychodynamically informed method. To clarify type of support parents may need.
Phase 9c Assessment of sibling need	Meetings with sibling/s individually	To assess degree of suffering at impact of living with autism. To provide opportunity for siblings to share their concerns and pressures. To clarify type of support sibling may need.

Table 2.1 The assessment schema

Phase of assessment	Methodology	Aims
Phase 10 Review of impact of assessment process on child and family	Professional team meeting	To enable professionals to reflect on impact of their observations and interventions on child and family.
Phase 11 Feedback	Feedback meeting/s with parents	To exchange perspectives. To assess degree of congruence. To encourage parents to review usefulness of assessment process. To further empower parents in making choices of treatment plans.
Phase 12 Network communications	Network meetings with parents and involved professionals	To promote good communication in a communication disorder. To exchange ideas and ways of understanding the child from the different parental and professional perspectives. To clarify different roles. To establish mutually supportive structures. To explore possibility of a coherent home, school and treatment plan.
Phase 13 Treatment plan for whoever in family is in need	Meeting with parents	To reach balance between optimal and achievable treatment programmes. To ensure a coherent and manageable package in light of 1) current external professional involvement and 2) resources available in clinic, in family and in professional network.(e.g. escort services). To establish a structure for ongoing assessment of treatment programme.
Phase 14 Ongoing assessment	Termly meetings with parents, assessor and therapist	To exchange therapist's and parents' assessment of child's response to therapy. To reflect on current views of other professionals. To assess need for any change of treatment.

is on them. With attention free-floating on everyone in the family, the referred child is allowed to become aware of us in whatever way they find tolerable. In turn we are freed from any need to force attention on the child. Throughout all this we try to sustain our observation of the child, sometimes needing to be careful to avoid eye contact. Freed from having to do anything but think and feel, we note what the child does but also what he or she does not do. Gradually, we may discover how the world looks through each individual child's eyes. As I watch, I make a commentary on my observations which is intended for the parents' use, but also in the hope that the child's attention may also be hooked. We try to be responsive to how engaged each family member is with what we are trying to do.

Thus the observations that I make during the first and subsequent assessment sessions are in the service of the parents' relationship with their child. I share my observations with the parents in the hope that this will encourage them to observe their child in a new way and to open up communication. I seek to demonstrate that seemingly meaningless behaviour, which has worn them down, may have meaning when we attend closely. It is important that parents, who so often feel impotent with their child, merely ancillary, should be given the key. It is not enough for us as professionals to feel some conviction about a child's capacity to change; the parents need to feel it too. Parents and professionals together can then plan a cooperative programme in which everyone can be clear about how their contributions appropriately differ but complement one another. Observing together, when meaning is revealed, can empower parents and give them hope. As Frith has said: 'It is as if a powerful integrating force – the effort to seek meaning – were missing' (Frith 1989). Our approach to assessment is dominated by the desire to seek meaning where it has previously been absent.

Containment of possible family trauma (Phase 5)

One common factor noted over the years is that, in the early stages of the assessment, few families have shown the ordinary nervousness which most families feel on attending a child guidance clinic for the first time. Rather, they seem to impose their way of doing things on us. We have come to understand this as a reflection of the parents' experience of having their child determine the structure and content of their daily lives.

Children with autism are inflexible and unreasonable so that their families seem to end up fitting in with them and not vice-versa. Emily's parents described how they had turned their whole house over to their daughter. It had become, as they put it, 'Emily-proof'; entirely devoted to Emily's needs so that she was safe to go wherever she liked and do whatever she liked. These parents, with Emily as their only child, had given up going out into the world because Emily simply couldn't manage it, and so their home had become something of a prison. It was the most comfortable, thoughtfully furnished prison they could make, but a prison nonetheless.

The family imprisoned by the child is now a very familiar story. It seems to be a reflection of the imprisonment of the child within the autistic condition. Families frequently become cut off from ordinary society, and the everyday features of family life may become a source of persecution and not a pleasure. A visit to the park or shops can become a nightmare because of their child's tantrums and antisocial behaviour, and where some language has developed, it can be so bizarre as to cause extreme embarrassment. Joe, for example, approached every stranger he met whenever the family left the confines of their home. 'You won't leak down, will you?' he would ask. His mother described how it became a major act of courage for her to face taking him out. 'I can't explain the situation to every single person Joe asks or we'd never even reach the end of our road'. Many parents, in common with Joe's mother, have described the need to develop a thick skin, 'a skin like a rhino', in order to get on with their lives at all.

Without regular daily contact with other families and children, it becomes only too easy to lose any sense of what is 'normal' or 'ordinary', and so the children's abnormal behaviour can become the norm for their families. Gradually but inexorably, parents and other siblings can get sucked into the world of the autistic child rather than the more ordinary situation where it is the parents' task to introduce their child to their world and the world beyond. Parents have told us that they have been advised to get on with their lives, as autism is incurable; one parent was told to put her son into an institution, as 'he will end up in one anyway'. Another was told 'get on with your life, go and have another baby'. Claudia's parents, for example, described how, when their daughter was diagnosed autistic, they were given literature to read which plunged them into depression. They expressed vividly their sense of bereavement; they felt they had lost a daughter, unique, individual, theirs; only to have her replaced by something called 'the autistic child' – 'as if all autistic children were just the same', said her father. A child 'with autism' emphasises first and foremost that this is a child, with a unique personality, special to their family. In time, parents like Claudia's, whose lives have become entirely focused on their child, may well need support to allow space for other things in their lives and, possibly, even another baby. But parents need time to mourn the 'normal' child all parents hope for, and to come to some realistic appreciation of their child's potential for development.

Diary (Phase 7)

Parents are asked to keep a diary at home, noting at the end of each week any changes they see in their child, whether these are for better or worse. This serves several functions. It encourages the continuation of observation at home and may support parents in the struggle to keep their child in mind. It emphasises the partnership that is essential between therapist and parents if the child is to sustain any changes that are seen to emerge. In the early stages of the assessments a common feature is that many parents seem to find it very difficult to remember their child as a baby, in any detail. Despair and exhaustion make it difficult to remember and note current changes. The diary supports the development of memory and emphasises where there is a potential for change. The weekly diary can be discussed in the next meeting, and links made between the parents' observations of their child at home and what can be seen in the current session. This also supports and enables parents to tackle problems at home. Disturbed nights, lack of family outings and chaos at mealtimes are familiar to many families. Respecting the parents' own observations of their child supports the possibility of a real dialogue. It aids thinking of ways in which a family might change things at home, based on what we have seen together, using the style of parenting which is unique for this particular family. Some parents find it impossible to remember to keep the diary. We take this as a significant reflection of the family's capacity at this point in time, and as an indication of where further support may be needed.

Individual assessments (Phase 9)

It is important, within this model, not to begin any individual assessment, whether of the child or of the parents' needs, until we have made a bridge between parents and their child. When the parents feel some hope that their child's behaviour has meaning, then it can be helpful to conduct an individual assessment. Trust is established on the parents' part that this individual assessment will be used primarily to further helpful interactions between them and their child, as well as inform us in making recommendations about future treatment. We explain that having the focus of the therapist exclusively on the child, it becomes more possible to see whether any glimmers of interest on the child's part in 'joining the world' can be expanded. It is then possible to link such movement to whether or not individual psychotherapy might be helpful.

The assessment process – more about Sally

I have chosen Sally because, although her response to the assessment was especially quick and dramatic, the process none the less reflects the major elements which are features of the work with these children. In my first encounter with Sally, I had felt very much in agreement with the referring psychiatrist who described her as 'profoundly autistic'. Over the following sessions I learned more about Sally's history; in her first two years of life her family were struggling to cope with a family tragedy. I learned that Sally did not relate to other adults or children but maintained a rigid control over a world of her own. She would not eat meals with the rest of the family but helped herself from the fridge. Her speech had not developed and although she occasionally mumbled the odd word, or even phrase, they were never repeated. Sally's parents expressed guilt and remorse, feeling that they had neglected their daughter during these important years. They wanted to know if they had caused her difficulties. It was easy to sympathise with the terrible experiences they had had as a family and I said, simply, that it would have been a difficult situation for any family to deal with, and that Sally may have been the sort of baby who was particularly vulnerable to their difficult circumstances. I emphasised that my interest was in trying to see if I could help Sally join the loving family who so much wanted her to be part of them.

The next meeting

They were late for this meeting, and whilst her parents were apologising, Sally had walked across to a dolls' house which I keep on the far table in my room. As soon as I saw that this had gained her attention, I stopped talking to her parents, explaining why, and turned to Sally to say that I would bring the dolls' house to the small table in the middle of the room. She showed some irritation with this interference. None the less, I put the dolls' house on the table around which her parents and I were seated. Mr and Mrs A began telling me about what had been happening with them since I saw them, and as they were talking I saw that Sally had taken two small plastic people from the house, standing them side by side; opposite them she put a rather strange figure which she had brought with her. This was, in fact, the head of a plastic ornament which her parents explained had been broken long ago but which Sally had held onto. The part of the ornament which remained was a round shape with a rather simple doll-child's face on the front. It was flat, but the eyes were prominent: I said that maybe Sally was showing us something about what was happening now with two people who were sitting and talking to one person, who was very busy using her eyes. Sally made no observable response to this but was chattering away quietly in her own private language.

The parents continued to tell me more about what had been happening. One of the things that emerged was that Sally had begun to like to look at herself in the mirror, and Mrs A wanted to know what I thought about this. I said that I thought that it could be a good thing that Sally was showing an interest in herself, and I explained that many children like her have little sense of themselves as separate beings and of their bodies as being separate from those of other people. Mother went on to tell me that Sally now comes into their bedroom and looks at herself in the mirror, that she will then move away from the mirror, move closer to the mirror, put her arms up, put them down, lie on the bed and look at her reflection, and sit up and look at herself from that position. Mother was worried that this could easily become stuck and repetitive as so many things had done in the past. I agreed that it could be bad for her if she just sat for ages doing the same thing time after time and day after day with no variations. I therefore commented that if she was interested in the sight of herself coming closer and going away, they might play around the mirror with her. I suggested a game of playing Mummy in the mirror with Sally, Mummy gone; Daddy, Mummy and Sally in the mirror together, and various combinations, leading to a rather ordinary peekaboo game around the idea of the faces coming and going. We spent some time discussing how to play in a way that would feel acceptable to Sally and how difficult it was to get it right. I encouraged them not to be pushed away by her, which is something she had done in the past, whilst at the same time not pushing *themselves* into *her* world, but to try and keep it as light and playful as they could bear, and to be determined not to let her slip off too quickly into a world of her own.

The conversation with Sally's parents had turned to the sleeping arrangements at home. All the while they were talking I was also carefully watching Sally and what she was doing. I noticed that when Mother was talking about the sleeping arrangements, Sally picked up a little bed, peeling off pieces of the green foam mattress on it. At one point she briefly put in one of the dolls before removing it again very quickly. Mother had been telling me how their au pair had taken to having Sally in her room because Sally always woke the baby up in the mornings. There was a new development since I had last seen them – Sally had come out with some words. Their au pair had been firmer with Sally, telling her that she must stay in the room with her and not go out and disturb the baby, and she had therefore shut the bedroom door. At this Sally had screamed, 'Let me out, let me out', time and time again. The parents expressed their pleasure and amazement at this new development.

On seeing Sally again on this occasion, I was struck by what a beautiful-looking child she is. I was struck by her big eyes with thick, thick lashes. Up to this point in the session she had used her eyes to make contact with no-one. I told the parents that I would now like to try and engage Sally in some play and suggested that they might like to watch and think about what was going on, too. I opened the toy box, which I keep in the room for such sessions, and took out a bag of dolls, saying that I thought we would find more people for the house. I opened the bag and held it towards her, being careful not to look at her directly. Sally peered into it and put her hand into the bag, then she took the bag from me and emptied the dolls on to the table. She still had not looked at me. However, I took this as sufficient encouragement to try and engage her in play.

I began to search among the dolls, saying that I was looking for a doll who looked like Sally. Sally had put her hand into the pile and picked up a doll which Mother immediately recognised as resembling their au pair. She then took up another doll, a mother doll, stood them side by side and began some of her high-pitched chattering to herself. As I watched her, her head moved from one to the other and I could see that she was examining them very closely. So I said that I thought that Sally was looking closely and noticing the difference between the skin colour of the two dolls, perhaps thinking about the difference between her au pair's skin and her own. This was also stimulated by Sally looking at her hand and staring closely at the texture of the skin. She then rummaged among the dolls and picked up a mother doll who was holding a tiny cloth baby in her arms. This had been left from another assessment session, not with Sally, but Sally stood staring at this mother doll as she held the baby doll. I felt as I watched Sally that she looked at it in the sort of way that was not mindless but rather suggested to me some feeling that she might be thinking about it. I therefore said that I thought she was thinking about the mother doll with the baby doll in her arms and that she was noticing the way in which the mother held the baby doll. Mother, Father and I had had a brief discussion at this point about what seemed to help Sally and what did not, stimulated, I thought, by the fact that Sally had started to show some interest in the things in the room. I therefore said that I thought Sally was showing us that she felt she knew what baby-Sally needed: that she needed to feel held safely and then perhaps she could begin to grow.

Sally opened the arms of the mother doll, closed them round the baby, opened them and closed them, and then discarded the doll that the mother was holding and rummaged around on the table and chose a little pink rubber baby. Mother had been telling me that Sally likes to take her clothes off, and in fact, when my box had first been put on the floor, Sally had lifted up her skirt to sit on it. Mother had expressed surprise that Sally had not removed her knickers in order to sit on the box, saying that this is what she usually does. I asked whether she felt that Sally masturbated against things or whether it was the skin-to-object contact that she sought. Sally's mother was thoughtful and said she thought it was the second, that Sally liked to feel everything against her skin. I therefore said to Sally that she had chosen the little pink doll because this was like the Sally who liked to be without clothes, who liked to be with just her skin. She picked the pink doll up and tried to put it into the mother doll's arms. She managed to do this in the kind of way that suggested that the mother doll couldn't hold her and I therefore said that the little pink doll was Sally and she was showing us that she wanted to feel held and safe but she didn't seem to feel able to find a way of doing this.

I should say here that before Sally became interested in the dolls she had made several bids to leave the room, and had to be restrained by her father. From the point at which I introduced the other dolls, however, Sally's attention was absolutely riveted, as was mine and her mother's and father's.

Sally moved the pink doll into different positions. I said that she was still trying to find a way to feel comfortable and safe. The baby wanted to be close to the mummy doll but couldn't seem to find a way of feeling close and comfortable. She then put the doll into the mother doll's arms in a very comfortable-looking way but with the doll upright against the mother doll's body. I said that this was how she felt comfortable; now she felt held. On several occasions then, she showed how the baby doll somehow slipped and dropped and fell, with the mother doll not holding onto her properly. I said that she knew what she wanted, she knew what she needed but she often couldn't find it. She was showing us that she often felt herself to be in nobody's mind; she felt dropped and lost and unheld. She then picked the doll up and placed it again in a very comfortable way, this time lying in the mother doll's arms as a baby might do when being cradled, perhaps just before being put to the breast. I said that this was another way in which mothers held their babies and she had probably seen Mummy holding their own baby like this, and that perhaps this was how she also felt *she* would like to be held, to feel close. I then added that I thought perhaps when she felt understood by me, she did feel held like this.

To my astonishment, Sally then lifted the little pink rubber doll up and put its face against the mother doll's face in a suggestion of a kiss. I was very moved by this, and said that when she felt held in mind she felt comfortable and good and it made her feel loving, and then the baby-Sally wanted to kiss the mummy and be close. Her own mother, who had been watching all of this closely, had begun to weep quietly. She watched her daughter playing, occasionally stroking her hair and kissing the top of her head tenderly.

Sally then showed us again how the little doll fell through the mother doll's arms; she rummaged amongst the other things that I had put out on the table, which included rubber animals. Her hand went to the lion, to the little lion cub, to the pigs, and to the piglets. I said that she was choosing all the pink, skin-like animals, like the pink-skin baby, and she was saying something important to us about how she felt that these were all alike in a very important way, that they had no covering, no clothes, just their skin, and that Sally felt the need to have that kind of closeness, skin to skin.

The play continued. Again, the mother doll dropped the baby doll, and this time, when Sally replaced the little rubber doll, she stood it on the mother doll's arms so that the baby doll was taller than the mother. I said that she was showing us that sometimes when she didn't feel safe and held, it made her need to pretend that she was bigger than she was, bigger perhaps even than Mummy and Daddy, to feel that she was the biggest, most powerful person in the family. When I made this comment about her need to be so omnipotent, she returned the baby doll to the mother doll's arms. It was apparent that we were all struck by the obvious meaning in what Sally was doing and by the fact that every time I spoke or did something, her eyes flickered and flicked upwards towards me in the quickest of sweeping looks before she cast her eyes down again to the mother doll and the baby.

I have to say that I had not anticipated anything like this in this assessment session, since my first meeting with the family had seemed most unpromising in terms of Sally's wish to make any contact. I think that because she had seemed so profoundly uninterested in contact, the impact that this meeting had on her parents and myself was particularly strong. Her mother wanted to know immediately if Sally would be offered psychotherapy, and also to know whether Sally would ever, as she put it, 'get back to normal'. I said, as I always do, that I didn't know how far Sally would get back to what she had called 'normal', but I too had been impressed by Sally's evident availability to this way of working, and all our hopes had been stirred.

When it was time to go, Sally didn't want to leave. I repeated that she would be coming again the next week to see me, but she clutched the mother doll in one hand and the baby doll in the other and her grip grew strong on them. I said that she was showing us all that the mother doll and the baby doll were very important to her and that Sally was frightened to let them go in case she never got them again. I added that I would keep them here in the room and that they would be here for her next time. Sally, however, would not give them up. Her parents understandably became a bit panicky and felt tempted to just grab them from her. However, they were quick to accept my suggestion that we just give her a minute and try to talk with her about her anxiety and fears.

Then I talked to Sally about her feeling that she had found something important here, not just the mummy and baby dolls, but all of us thinking together about her: Sally began to cry and there were real tears on her face. I put out my hand and she put the baby doll into it, hesitated, and then took it back. I said that she wanted to trust me but she couldn't quite do it, couldn't trust that she would be able to come back again, find the mummy doll and baby doll and then discover some more about how she was feeling. Eventually, Sally allowed me to take the dolls from her hand and her father picked her up to leave. She leaned over her father's shoulder, her arms outstretched, and cried loudly with tears spilling down her face. As she cried she turned towards me and called out, 'Bye, bye, bye'. This moment was full of pain for us all, but it was a new experience for the parents with Sally, who ordinarily seemed so impervious to everything around her. Although I think they were relieved at this emotional moment that they had shared with their daughter, who seemed human to them, as they said, for the first time, it was also very painful. I encouraged them, rather than cheering her up or calming her down, to actually talk to her about her distress; about how upset she was, and why, and to remind her that we would all be together again the next week. I explained that I thought by talking to her about how upset she was and recognising it, they would actually then be making her feel held in just the kind of way she had shown us that she wanted to be held. They left trying to do as I had suggested but finding it hard not to jolly her along.

There is only space here to say that the following assessment sessions confirmed that Sally was not completely locked in her autistic world. Her wish to make contact and to learn how to play developed until, in her final assessment session, she announced, 'Gonna be happy', lifting her arms up in a delicate, beautiful movement that suggested a plant seeking the light; I could scarcely believe my ears or eyes. She began four-times weekly therapy soon afterwards.

Conclusion

This approach to assessment pays particular attention to the impact of living with a child with autism on the family as a whole, and on each of its members as individuals. It is recognised that the resulting stresses can have serious implications for mental health. The reciprocal impact of each family member on the referred child is also observed, allowing for the discovery of those situations, approaches and attitudes which seem to facilitate and encourage more engagement for the child with the family. Any strain in the parents' relationship, and likely undermining of their effectiveness as parents, is also given due attention. Space is given for siblings to express their feelings, wishes and needs.

We are increasingly working in a climate influenced by limited resources and a consequent pressure to do short-term work rather than long-term intensive psychotherapy. Sometimes families are referred to us only for assessment, because they live too far away from the Tavistock Clinic to make longer-term treatment viable. In such cases we try to find local resources, where appropriate, to continue the therapeutic work. For other families there may be a lack of internal resources and external supports which make intensive, ongoing therapeutic work inappropriate: here we might direct more of our energies than usual into working with the professional network and offering regular six-monthly reviews for the parents. We are therefore challenged to try to make the most of therapeutic assessments for each family.

The willingness to take the time to get to know a family and to puzzle over things with them seems to be of particular value to families where there is a child with autism. The lack of any apparent epistomophilic instinct (Klein 1932) in the child appears to gradually erode the belief in the value of questioning and discovering in the adults who care for them (teachers and psychotherapists are also very aware of this danger – of switching to 'automatic pilot'). Genuine interest in, and respect for the difficulties and hard work involved in parenting these children can help to revive the battered spirits of parents and siblings and generate hope. With the experience that these children can change, many parents find the internal resources and external supports to engage in ongoing psychotherapy.

Using the model outlined in this chapter helps us to make a realistic assessment of both needs and resources – of the child's capacity for change and the support for such change in their family. Involvement in the assessment seems to make our approach and ideas more comprehensible to many parents. They can then engage with us, and with other involved professionals, to create an integrated home-treatment-educational package, which supports those aspects in the child and in the family, which are open to change. Our experience shows that some of these fascinating, but puzzling and often tragic children, can be helped by our approach.

Note

1 An earlier version of this chapter was given as a paper to the study weekend of the Association of Child Psychotherapists in 1992, and another version appears in the *Journal of Clinical Child Psychology and Psychiatry*, 1998.

3 The significance of trauma and other factors in work with the parents of children with autism

Trudy Klauber

Introduction

This chapter[1] addresses the central significance of trauma and post-traumatic stress in the experience of parents of children with autism, and in the work which professionals offer to them. This is not to suggest, in any way, that trauma is the cause of autism; it is rather to suggest that the experience of having and living with a child with autism inevitably carries trauma with it. With trauma in mind it is important to note that parents' capacity to parent can easily be disturbed or disrupted by post-traumatic stress and high anxiety, and that the same phenomena can and do impede some parents' ability to work closely with professionals.

I have also come to understand that work with parents of this group of children and young people can start with practical help, especially around eating, sleep patterns and toileting, in which parents can begin to restore their own confidence in their role as parents. From practical success, some parents are interested and eager to explore other aspects of their situation. Some make spontaneous links with inter-generational issues and their relationships with their own parents. Others begin to look, spontaneously, at their own history and its representations in their internal world, seeking to understand more about how such a structure may have been affected by the autistic child and may further affect the capacity to parent with confidence.

Wherever there is a disabled or disturbed child, and a history of medical or psychological intervention, parents are under considerable stress and there is a common perception of the professional worker as critic and even as persecutor. This is often the case, whatever the overt content of interactions. Parents, who feel extremely anxious, despairing and hostile, often communicate their emotional states by projection, not through words. In the face of projected anxiety, hostility and despair, it is often difficult for the worker who feels overwhelmed by the emotions generated within herself to hold on to thoughts or to avoid being drawn into hasty and judgmental action. One such action is to jump to conclusions about, for example, who or what in the family, caused what, and to whom.

Inevitably, thinking about such work brings in questions about the aetiology of autism. It is not the subject of this book, but these issues do impinge, because parents are so preoccupied with what caused their children to be so different from the norm. The tendency for gross splitting and polarisation of views about causation is unhelpful, and can be the cause of acute and chronic distress to parents who are also seeking a way forward for themselves, and help for the optimum development of their children (Kysar 1968, 1969).

It is easy, when working with such parents, to confuse the effects of the child's autism (on the child itself and the family) with its causes. Particularly in the USA in the 1940s and 1950s, there was a tendency for clinicians all too often to use the evidence of their meetings with families as a diagnosis of the aetiology of the disturbance. They did not take into consideration that the phenomena which they observed might have been the *consequences* of trauma and loss; the result of having and living with the referred child. Simplistic links between parental pathology and the child with autism have never been part of the approach to autism at the Tavistock Clinic (Reid, this volume: Chapters 2 and 7).

Elsewhere, Tischler, writing in the 1970s (1971, 1979) reacted strongly against the parent-blaming inherent in Kanner's view (1944) of 'refrigerator mothers'. He propounded a much more subtle and complex model, which found it impossible simply to blame mothers or parents. In fact, he wrote that workers in the field themselves were also responsible for some of the difficulties in furthering the question of aetiology. They did not recognise their own bias, towards research, towards cure, or in believing mothers to be responsible for not meeting children's normal needs. He also stressed that workers were not always able to acknowledge their own emotional difficulties, which could include an excessive identification with the suffering child, mother or father, leading to paralysing pity, condemnation or both. Some workers' over-sensitivity to suffering, he felt, clouded their judgment and could lead them to act out. He emphasised a need to understand themselves in order not to confuse the patient's pathology with their own, and to work in an unhurried way, particularly in the collection of base data.

Tischler's comments are highly relevant to those who strive to offer a contribution to a differential diagnosis, seeking to reason out and offer the best treatment options, and, in terms of this chapter, in trying to think about effective help for parents in the difficult job of parenting their atypical children. In that context, it is necessary, I suggest, to make conscious and articulate our preconceptions and our clinical ambitions, fears and fantasies, so that they do not excessively impede our way towards understanding and containing highly traumatised parents. This need for receptive flexibility in the worker implies the need for much mutual support and training for those who choose to do this work.

Tischler's paper, 'Being With a Psychotic Child: A Psycho-analytical Approach to the Problems of Parents of Psychotic Children' (1979) poignantly discusses the issues of the quantity, quality and duration of loss, the frustration and strain involved in giving birth to, and living with, a psychotic child, which are such, he suggests, that they constitute chronic 'ego strain' or 'strain trauma'. This aspect of trauma in the parents' lives links with the impact of the trauma on the professional worker, who attempts to intervene and help, and the worker's subsequent impact on the parents again.

A pattern has been established for quite some time before we are likely to become involved in assessment or long-term work. Tischler writes:

> We meet them [parents] at the end of a long process of suffering and of partial adjustment. Their chronic-severe-trauma-in-adult-life leads to intrapsychic repercussions and adaptive processes, which depend on personal and interpersonal, including marital, factors at different psychic levels.
>
> (Tischler 1979: 30)

In short, by the time we meet them the parents have already lived with the child and a crazy way of life for a long time. I concur with Tischler's view, and have found vivid examples of what he describes in working with families where there is a child with autism. The autistic child's fear of change or difference may have become the parents' fear, or may echo a fear they already had. Their adaptation to routines which never challenge or question the status quo may be as rigid as the child's, as may their avoidance of any upset, large or small, for fear of the consequences. Whole families may become trapped in the same system, clinging to predictability and routine at the expense of all spontaneity. Seeking help may indicate *some* wish for *some* change, but it may, of course, indicate a wish for 'cure', for an instant, miraculous and complete change without any conception of a process of development over time.

In the earliest stages of work, it may not be evident that parents will have difficulty in managing the normal ebb and flow of hope and disappointment in treatment. It may be that hope rekindled following an optimistic assessment is so intensely painful that it is unbearable, since hope is hope and not instant cure. Situations can develop where progress is greeted with great joy, but the tiniest setback, perhaps after a very good week or month, can be experienced as such a blow that the parents may not be able to recognise that there was any progress before. Indeed, they may even feel that they have gone right back to the beginning or that there has been actual deterioration. For them there is no such thing as a sense of proportion.

Parents who have lived with disturbed children become worn out with the effort of trying to understand, encourage and stimulate. The response of some is to become entangled, over-close and intrusive, so that there is no space. Others distance themselves or give way to despair. Many are worn out, tired from too many sleepless nights, from gargantuan temper tantrums and the absence of limits and boundaries. They lose the will to establish parental authority or the imagination to envisage the possibility that they could. They feel they are ineffective and of no significance to their child, who might cling but shows no particular appreciation or special affection. Ideas about what is good for or bad for children, or why boundaries, limits and firmness in a very ordinary way, are useful, are not there.

Children with autism do not help their parents to be good parents in the ordinary way by the apprenticeship which so many children and parents go through. Seeking help from professionals may be experienced as a minefield filled with the fear of judgment and criticism, compounded by the dreadful stirrings of the memory of noticing something was wrong, seeking diagnosis and help and encountering the all-too-common professional disputes and dogma which surround work with autism.

Trauma and post-traumatic stress

Garland (1991) has described post-traumatic stress phenomena in some of the people who survived disasters. It is particularly interesting to consider her ideas in relation to the parents of children whose diagnosis is along the autism continuum. Post-traumatic stress disorder is defined in relation to experience of an event which is outside the range of usual human experience and which would be markedly distressing to almost anyone. Such events include serious threat or harm to one's children. One thing which is certain, is that parents of a child with autism have been subjected to a massive, private disaster of just this kind. Their private tragedy is made painfully public in every encounter with professionals. I would suggest that the traumatic event or events which can reactivate at any point are:

1   traumatic events of the pregnancy, birth or early infancy
2   unrelated traumatic events afflicting the family during those vulnerable months
3   the moment of realisation that there is something wrong with the child compared with others
4   professional diagnosis
5   the loss of the expected 'normal' child
6   the constant daily strain of living with bizarre, avoidant, strange or totally uncommunicative behaviour.

Garland suggests that post-traumatic stress disorder is suffered when severe trauma activates and widens the 'fault lines' already present within the personality, so that pathological processes which might never have developed come into being. The traumatic event is experienced unconsciously as dangerously intrusive and terrorising. The fear of intrusive terror creates an unconscious need to avoid reminders. For some parents, the trauma linked with the child means that the child itself can be the unconscious reminder. Parents also, not unnaturally, become phobic about contact with professionals, who may be experienced concretely as bringers-back of the trauma itself. The ability to give detailed histories or to remember events in detail may be severely impaired. There may be intense psychological distress at exposure to environs or events which symbolise or resemble an aspect of the traumatic event. Our own and other clinics, other professionals and we ourselves can become equated with the trauma in an actual, concrete experience, capable of being suddenly evoked in a consultation, without warning.

A rather different aspect of post-traumatic stress disorder phenomena is the need some sufferers experience, once in touch with the trauma, to go over and over the same ground, describing the same events in the same vivid detail week after week.

One couple I worked with had a son who had an autistic episode at eight months old. He had contracted meningitis, at ten days old. They spent every week for a year, when they did not avoid attending, describing in great detail the events of the days when he nearly died, and what the doctors did to him. They conjured up a dreadful Casualty/Emergency Room video in my mind which I could not turn off.

Diagnosis is profoundly shocking for parents; the diagnosis of autism is particularly traumatic (Reid, this volume: Chapter 2). There are many professionals who deliver the diagnosis without offering follow-up appointments to help parents take in what it means. Some professionals underestimate the impact of throwaway remarks about the nature of the condition, about the child's likely need for behavioural training and special schooling, about the institutional life of autistic adults or that the aetiology of the condition is organic and unchangeable.

All those who work in this field do need to think a lot more about their impact on parents, not only in diagnosis, but in earlier consultations of different kinds. I have heard quite a lot about the early months and years when, for example, either false reassurance or excessive concern have an awesome power over anxious parents. They are easily blinded by a professional view which differs from their own. Some, who do not want to notice, will cling to reassurance that a sleepy or passive baby is fine and 'will grow out of it'. Where they have been genuinely concerned to notice something about their child, for example, an absence of social referencing, no babbling, early single words disappearing again or strange, unplayful manipulation of toys, and they then meet a professional who does not take them seriously, the vulnerable will lean on the professional judgment which goes against their own accurate observations. Parents are always very anxious about what could go wrong with their children, and are sometimes too easily convinced that they are being over-cautious or fussy.

One trauma can pile on another. First, noticing something wrong and seeking advice. Second, waiting for and receiving the professionals' judgment. For some there may have been yet other kinds of trauma, connected with the pregnancy or birth, personally for either parent or within the extended family. The devastating, private tragedy can rock a family's universe.

When parents relate their experience of diagnosis or of encounters with other professionals about their child, the psychotherapist may easily become identified with a generalised idea of 'professionals' who bring shock into the parental consciousness. The psychotherapist then, by talking about diagnosis or history, can become identified with the trauma. As such, she may be hated, abandoned, stood up (sessions missed) or treated with sudden, deep and apparently inexplicable hostility by parents.

When trauma is re-experienced in the consulting room, there is also, of course, the possibility of understanding its meaning, and of parents being helped to move on, to become more realistic and to be able engage or re-engage more closely and clear-sightedly with their child. These considerations may help the professional to be less ready to judge and more able to stay with the terrible, painful tragedy with which the parents live. Hope of work on trauma may raise the worker's own hopefulness, which is essential if one is to be able to go on, to be supportive and to keep some sense of proportion.

The parents' distress may at times be vented on professionals. The psychodynamically trained may be able to use these 'transference' feelings of engendered upset in order to understand what is happening and further the work. The implication for the worker is that she will be exposed to experiencing some of the traumatic anxiety or fear, and will need to be mindful of the parents' fear that it will ricochet back at them with no-one able to give it a home and to process it.

Mrs C and Molly

Molly, aged four years, was referred to me by the developmental paediatrician who was puzzled about this 'odd' little girl and felt that her mother, Mrs C, was excessively anxious. Molly herself was anxious and controlling. She had an eccentric appearance, emphasised by her little glasses, protruding eyes and a rather old-fashioned look. She was physically very small. She looked intelligent and sounded as if she should be articulate, although she had great difficulty with anything more advanced than toddler talk, particularly with her parents. She was very clinging and easily distressed or provoked to tantrums. Her stubbornness was legendary. She drew endless pictures of monsters with rows of sharp teeth, and used the activity as a way of absorbing herself completely. The drawings were always the same, although she had an undoubted graphic talent. She could suddenly become transfixed by her own toes, as if they were more important than anything else. She seemed to become timelessly stuck to them. This was her most obvious autistic feature, along with intense resistance to change and the use of language (like drawing) to wrap herself in, rather than primarily for communication.

Her bowel function was monitored by gastro-enterologists, she was monitored by the growth clinic, had been seen by a neurologist and had been tested for chromosomal abnormalities. None of the more or less intrusive tests or investigations assisted in finding a diagnosis. Results were all negative and the specialists offered nothing more than follow-up appointments to monitor the situation. Mother was in a rage with all the experts who put her through so much anxiety and gave nothing back. She appeared, superficially, to be accustomed to the appointments, so that she scarcely mentioned them. When I began to see her regularly, I was the one to suffer repeated shock and disruption as she cancelled her appointments with me with virtually no notice, in order to attend one clinic or another. There were many times when Molly the child disappeared in the midst of Mrs C's torrent of talk about the range of symptoms, tests and questions. Her outspoken hatred of doctors did not impede a compulsive need to seek further assistance, in order to get answers, despite the consequent upset for Molly and her parents of each investigation.

The series of Molly-related traumas for this family began during the pregnancy when there was a threat of miscarriage which, for four weeks, left Mrs C terrified and consciously struggling not to think about the baby who might not survive. The birth was difficult and long. The baby was rather passive and looked slightly odd to mother. Mrs C could only begin to describe her experience with Molly when she could compare it with what it was like with her next baby, Joe. Molly was difficult to soothe and scarcely looked at her mother. At around eighteen months, mother was worried about Molly who seemed detached, switched-off and developmentally delayed. There followed a year or so, when the parents felt they were constantly taking her to hospitals and doctors, who mentioned first one syndrome then another. Mother protested vigorously at other parents' comments on Molly's size, her facial features or her behaviour, whilst herself keeping Molly under such microscopic examination that the normal responses of a child of her age were scarcely noticed; everything seemed significant and strange, and could not really be thought about at all.

After Molly began psychotherapy with a colleague, Mrs C grilled me about what happened in her sessions. What did the therapist think? Was Molly using them? Could she use them? Had she made progress this week? This was in addition to questions about what I had said during the assessment. What did I mean by autistic features? Didn't I mean autism but was not saying so? She had seen a TV programme on Asperger's Syndrome. Was that it? A dinner party discussed dyspraxia; had they or we overlooked that? Why did Molly look away when mother tried to read a book with her? Why couldn't she do up her buttons? Why could she do them sometimes while protesting that she couldn't? Was she deliberately naughty? Why couldn't she understand the concept of number? Other children knew how to play, why couldn't Molly?

After the first holiday break in her psychotherapy, both parents were in panic because Molly seemed so stupid that she must be brain-damaged. Her speech had regressed to baby talk and her toe-gazing and hand-flapping had returned. The holiday had been awful for both parents, who had been filled with despair which led to acrimonious recrimination. The on-off quality in Molly's abilities and interests was terribly difficult for her parents to think about; it felt provocative and drove them mad with fear.

In our sessions, they began, slowly, to process the holiday, and to see it in terms of Molly's anxiety when school and psychotherapy terms ended. Molly's anxiety and her regression became meaningfully linked. They could observe how quickly Molly picked up again when the routine was re-established. They could also begin to think about the effect of their own close scrutiny of Molly on themselves and her, and they could begin to talk about the unbearable difference they felt in looking at her compared with the ordinary way they could look at Joe and their new baby son, Charles.

Mrs C then mentioned her own elder sister, who had considerable difficulties as a child, at home and at school, and had psychotherapy throughout most of her child and early adult life. Mrs C, the clever, younger sister, felt she was neither allowed to make demands on her parents, whose time and energy were taken up with her sister, nor to be angry and protest about it. She felt she had to be well behaved. She felt very different from her sister as well as guilty and resentful about her parents' neglect of her. Her rivalry with a sister who had such difficulties had become confused with her fears for Molly in a very unhelpful way.

Her anger with professionals seemed also to have unconscious links with her conviction that, at the next appointment, they would reveal the real truth about Molly, a diagnosis of permanent handicap. When she herself had a minor medical investigation, she made little of it, smiling at me benignly when I persisted in wondering about her anxiety. She revealed, a little later, that she had felt she was riddled with terminal cancer and that the doctors were hiding it from her just as she hid her fear from me. She had little sense of a relationship where the rational and irrational aspects of her fears could be distinguished from each other.

Mrs C came back week after week, while her husband was unable to attend, busy at work and often away. She talked of hopes dashed and renewed fears, complaining of the lack of support from her overworked husband, clinging to her weekly sessions with me. Her critical self was projected into her absent husband, whose questions and doubts she quoted extensively in sessions. She complained, in addition, of his reserve, of his inability to talk about his feelings and his insensitivity to her difficulties in coping with three young children. She was more able to verbalise her anger with her husband and other professionals she had encountered, than with me, which left her uncertain about my strength in bearing what she brought, and made her less able to use the sessions during the rest of the week, in order to manage her doubts and her fear.

The difficulty in seeing Molly for who she was is obvious, as is the impact of a traumatic past on a traumatised present. There is much work to be done on the impact of the inter-generational transmission of unworked-through trauma in families. Patterns repeat themselves and the child is muddled up with figures from the past internalised in the parents in such a way that he cannot easily be seen as separate, as himself with his own personality and his own needs.

Slowly, as I survived the onslaught of Mrs C's anxieties and questions and her fears about my health and stamina, she could begin to listen as I verbalised some of her fears, and we could distinguish fearful fantasy from actual evidence. It was also possible, because of my discussions with Molly's therapist, to link Molly's personal view of herself, as inferior and incapable, with mother's worst fears. It was even possible to think about how Molly's beliefs about herself might actually be impeding her attempts to try to use her natural curiosity and intelligence. Mother did begin to try out a different perspective. She began to describe, with pleasure, some small but significant developments. There were two joyful landmarks: the day Molly joined her mother and brother in putting a few bricks into a Lego castle, and the time when she took her first bicycle ride without stabilisers, and expressed her longing for her father to come home and see. Molly had been given a bit more freedom and space in which to enjoy new activities and to begin to explore her own agenda.

The emotional switchback described above is linked with most parents' fears about the nature of the disability. There is always the pull, as Mrs C demonstrates, towards believing in concrete, unchangeable damage (despite the absence of evidence to confirm the possibility in very many cases). Hope is so fragile, and setbacks in development feel like regression or deterioration.

Every step forward in learning or relating reminds parents of the gap still to be narrowed. There is still so far to go. And it also reminds them that the child is not like the others. The difference is somehow underlined by any evidence of progress.

It is important to mention the impact of 'statementing', meetings with teachers, annual reviews or follow-up appointments. All of these, no matter how well handled, are traumatic. Temporary setbacks within psychotherapy, too, are also frequently experienced as confirmation that progress has been illusory.

What is developmental and what is not

It is the task of the parent-worker to monitor honestly the signs of real hope and improvement, along with evidence to the contrary. Parents in these circumstances, like Mr and Mrs C, very often feel that progress has not been made, and they do need a guide in reading the clear evidence that it has. They need someone who will be able, for example, to interpret what is really developmental, but looks like the opposite. For example a formerly blank but so-called 'happy' child who becomes more overtly distressed about change, *is* developing. The emergence of babbling in a previously silent child can appear to be meaningless or mindless noise to parents because the child is not a toddler. It needs to be underlined that babbling is actually a prerequisite for the development of coherent language. Babies start with babble, and children who have not begun the development of language will start there, no matter what their chronological age.

Some of the children have highly developed skills or interests, but within very narrow limits. Some are more pervasively developmentally delayed. Many seem to be more able on some days than others. This is a very confusing picture for anxious parents.

Children on the autism continuum have not been utilising their lifetime in the same way as their healthy peers (Alvarez, this volume: Chapter 4). One part of a coherent developmental model needs to include the idea that when children are helped to emerge from the autistic state of mind, they will inevitably be behind their peers. Activities, play and language which appears to belong to a much younger age group will be appropriate; the children will need to go through earlier stages of development before they reach later ones. An autistic child of four years of age, who begins to drop toys and to show pleasure when they are retrieved, having never done such a thing before, is not demonstrating evidence of mental handicap, but of developmental progress, even if it is delayed. A child who has never really looked at toys, who begins to do so, and to explore them with her mouth is doing something normal babies do. The appearance of babble, an interest in peekaboo games or in scribbling, where they have never occurred before, are all signs of hope. It is very easy to be confused when children are much older than they ought to be when such things begin.

The worker's own developmental model must be coherent – with a working knowledge and experience of the steps within the stages of acquisition of language, play and interaction. Then parents can be helped to see what is hopeful and how they can build on what is developing in therapy sessions and in school. (The training in infant and young child observation which is integral to child psychotherapy training is a considerable advantage in such work.) The model will ideally also include a recognition that some 'activity' does not contain developmental potential for encouraging curiosity and playfulness, but is being used as ritual, to blot out the possibility of anything new, interesting or anxiety-provoking coming in (Alvarez, this volume: Chapter 5).

The quality of life for all the family

Before working collaboratively with parents on establishing play and playfulness at home, it is often essential to work on improving the quality of life at home. Children with autism, and other atypical children, can evoke powerful feelings of protectiveness in their carers and they are often babied in their families. Some parents may have largely given up trying to engage the child. In other families the child is pandered to. Its every demand is met unquestioningly, apparently for fear of being cruel or rejecting to a handicapped child. This leaves little time or potential space in the mind of child or parent, for fun, play and development.

When parents describe their daily life, it often becomes apparent that the child has wreaked havoc in terms of everyday routines. Nobody else's needs or preferences are taken into account. Many parents have given up hope of even the semblance of normal life. They do not go out with the child because her behaviour is so embarrassing in public places; or they do not go out without her because that would be to shirk their responsibilities. The child cannot be left. The abnormalisation of life grows like a cancer, to the detriment of the child's own developmental potential as well as to the mental and physical health of other members of the family. What is so often hidden within the submission to the tyrannical demands, is guilt about hatred of the disability and of the child herself. How can one admit to sometimes feeling hatred for a disabled child who looks like an angel? How can one be firm in the face of the tragedy displayed on her face?

Explorations around the feelings the child arouses in parents and siblings (who are often helpful reporters of their mixed feelings) can lead to change. Many parents become more consistent in setting firm limits and boundaries, particularly if they can really see that it has importance for the child's cognitive and emotional growth. They can be helped to normalise the abnormal and to have hope and expectations for the child. There can be enormous relief as family myths are dispelled about the impossibility of resisting the whims of the tyrant-child.

Children with autism need not raid the fridge on a whim or sleep when and where they choose. They do not need to take over one bed and then another during restless, disturbed nights for the entire family. They do not need physical access to their mother's breasts or hair as the whim strikes. They do not have the right to break into handbags and pockets, or to eat only from other people's plates. Unless limits have been set, one cannot tell whether the child can understand, or whether they, like other members of the family, will actually begin to feel better when normalisation is set in motion. Some element of this kind of work is always a feature, and is often productive in itself, as well as providing a route to other areas of exploration.

The introduction of such changes takes time. Lying behind certain parents' passivity in the face of tyrannical behaviour, is the sense that, fundamentally, the child does not understand. They are enacting a belief that this child is so different he might be an alien; a changeling for whom they are responsible and whom they consciously accept and unconsciously may resent or sometimes hate. The child also may, in his silence, easily represent hated aspects of his parents' selves or their internal parental figures, which can further contribute to the inconsistency to which he has been subjected.

Mr and Mrs S and Sasha

Mr and Mrs S represent the most extreme example I have encountered of submission to the will of a child with autism, their son, Sasha. The work with them also illustrates how moves may be made from one level to another. What began as a long, slow process in helping them to understand and to stand up to their son's tyranny, moved on to an exploration of the trauma which father had experienced in his own childhood and still lived with, and later still became a psychoanalytic exploration of the links between the parents' difficulties in using the work we did and the lack of benign but firm authority in their own internal parental figures.

Sasha was referred at five years old, and his parents soon revealed how they suffered in the face of his total domination of their family life. They felt it was only possible to show their love for him by allowing him to do as he liked. He grazed the house, eating and drinking what and when he chose. Bottles of drink were opened for him, he took a sip, and then poured away the rest when he saw the gap at the top of the bottle. He ate only the crusts of baby rusks, discarding the unwanted middles. He would eat only one brand of biscuits, which he named 'cofi', taking one biscuit from a newly opened packet, then spilling the rest and grinding them into the carpet. He had his own words for a number of things, which his parents used without thought. At night, he would fall asleep lying across the bottom stair, which was the signal for his exhausted mother to take him to bed. At that time, he slept with his mother in his parents' bed, and his father had a mattress in the living room. He had several baby bottles of milk provided every night.

In his parents' relationship with me, while Sasha had individual psychotherapy with a colleague, there was neither negativity nor complaint. Whenever I told them of my holiday arrangements, or smaller, unavoidable changes, Mr S would intone 'No problem', and smile broadly. He and his wife would present me with excessively generous gifts just before each break began, while we all knew that holidays from therapy and school were the most excruciating torture.

Initially the work of thinking about setting some limits on the situation seemed to be a hopeless task. Neither parent apparently believed that Sasha could understand anything. They thought he was severely learning-disabled. They were also terrified that if they refused him anything that he would run amok. Chaos did not break out when we worked on not buying the bars of soap he demanded, but within two weeks soap was replaced by sweets. The 'poor' boy had to have something.

It seemed abundantly clear that Sasha understood quite a lot, and was able, quite often, to communicate clearly. His parents often seemed to misunderstand his behaviour or to find it meaningless. For example, in the evening he would stand on the window sill looking out to the road, even occasionally saying 'Dadad', while he waited. When his father came home from work some hours later, he would hurriedly hand Sasha some chocolate. There was no connection in father's mind between the window sill vigil and Sasha's longing for his father's return. His father truly could not imagine that the boy was waiting anxiously for him. Mr S could not imagine that he held any significance for his son; he attributed Sasha's behaviour to a habit he had developed, and continued to feel persecuted and guilty when he came home.

My work with Sasha's parents allowed some brief moments of comprehension that Sasha did seem to understand them, and would probably respond to the setting of some order and limits. They were astonished at the ease with which he took to his own bed and to mealtime routine. Mr S began, at first rather mechanically, asking Sasha to bring his spectacles to him, and was fascinated but scarcely believing when he did so.

Mr S could not stick to routine within his own life or his working week. He let work spread into weekends and evenings and no-one knew when he would come home. It was partly this which impelled Sasha to stand guard at the window anxiously waiting for hours on end, and it was one of the triggers which brought out the tyrant within him. When father's working life was most hectic, or anxiety-provoking, Sasha would become most irrationally demanding and would scream for hours on end. Each time he got what he demanded he screamed louder and longer for something else.

Over many sessions it became possible to look at the pattern of what was happening and to suggest that the things which they gave Sasha were anti-developmental. I suggested that they were repeatedly poisoning Sasha's ability to learn to distinguish between hunger and appetite for good things like his daddy, feeling safe, wanting dinner or using toys for exploration and play, and that what he demanded simply stuffed his mouth, filled his hands and filled up any spaces where healthy anxiety or need might find a place.

They began to manage some better regulation. They also reverted back to old ways whenever Mr S became manically busy at work, or there was any kind of family crisis. This frantic activity on his part was not only linked with a conscientious need to build his business and to provide for his family, but also had other roots and significance. He kept a distance between himself and Sasha, in whom, I felt, he located his own deprived self and his own difficulties in knowing what was good for him. He was ever-busy, mostly driving his car between meetings and getting caught in traffic, just as Sasha filled up his time and occupied himself with the stickers and drinks which he demanded.

Sasha's psychotherapy stopped after a couple of years. I continued with the parents, since it seemed to be so important to establish some kind of clarity at home and in their minds if Sasha were to be able to free some space in his mind for more ordinary relating and learning.

Three years on there was some space in the sessions for explorations beyond the routine of life with Sasha. Mr S's own childhood was marked by feelings of abandonment by his own father, who, he said, scarcely came home until very late. He was said to be out working, or with his friends, leaving Mr S's mother to look after the four children alone. Mr S described hours of childhood spent playing soccer, hating to go in to his put-upon mother and sisters, even when he was hungry or when it was too late to play more. He pinpointed a sense of loss and disruption during childhood as well. The family moved once, from a much-loved village to a town, and then, when he was twelve, his mother and sisters were sent away to a large city, while he wandered disconsolately, locked out of the house by the aunt who was supposed to look after him in his mother's absence. Once the family was re-united, he was sent away to school where he felt isolated and different from the other boys. Then the whole family moved to England when Mr S was twenty-one, and he had to find work instead of going to university.

Mr S's sense of loss felt so overwhelming he could not think much at all. He kept himself so busy, out of the house, out of the family, and sometimes out of his own mind, that little could be addressed. At home Sasha was left abandoned, waiting for the father whom he feared might not return. Holiday interruptions to my work with them were smoothed away. 'No problem'. Sessions on return would be filled with stories of the chaos, of family life in shreds as they failed to manage the demands of Sasha and could not, at all, recall any of the thoughts we had shared together about the sense of loss and upset which accompanied the breaks in our routine.

While this link with father's past became more clear, so did Mr S's continuing contribution to maintaining the status quo with Sasha. When Sasha was offered a special holiday play scheme which he clearly enjoyed, for the full length of one summer holiday, his father could only let him be there from very late in the morning to early in the afternoon – well inside the offered number of hours. He felt he was abandoning poor Sasha, who would suffer in such a place of exile. His childhood experiences, still so alive within him, were located in his son and managed there. But Mr S had a sudden realisation about his irrational action: bringing Sasha home early was actually causing considerable upset both to Sasha and to his mother, who had to put up with being physically punched and shouted at by the bored and confused boy. Mr S had managed to look at what he was doing and to put it right. They had their most peaceful summer holiday to date.

Mrs S carried with her a belief that all men were rather weak and needed looking after and, in her presence, Mr S continued to explore his own internal difficulties. Sasha began to do more coherent drawing at school and to learn to write his own name. He seemed a little more content, and to be listening to his father, who began to help him by telling him in advance about his whereabouts and what the family plans were for evenings and weekends. Sasha began to ask one-word questions which seemed to indicate that he wanted to know where Daddy was going or what Mummy was doing. He began to link two or three words together, and one day read the word 'Safeway' as the family car passed a local supermarket.

Mr S's capacity to look after himself, and particularly to allow his wife and me to know about his fears, made him simultaneously more overtly frightened and more steady. He constantly returned to the preoccupation that he had to look after everyone and everything, which seemed to be a way of projecting anxiety and preventing it from invading him. I began to be perceived as stronger and the therapeutic relationship became more robust and realistic.

Within the process of moving from work on improving the quality of this family's life, a space had grown for working more analytically and in the transference.

One day Mr S was more assiduously courteous to me than usual, and then described his deep depression and inability to get down to any work. I suggested he did not feel I was of much help. He denied this, saying how much better his thinking was. I felt fobbed off. He complained that his suppliers were overcharging, letting him down, and that customers who got special treatment were not paying him what they owed. I said again that I thought he was angry about people who did not supply decent goods, or pay their dues, linking it with his anger with me for not making the depression go away. He said Sasha had been unsettled and violent at school, and was hitting his mother. I linked Sasha's anger and violence with his father's feelings about myself, the therapist unable to supply the quality of interpretation and support that would sustain him during the week. Mr S said he could not stop Sasha. I said that I thought his own politeness with me denied considerable anger, located in Sasha, for free expression. I thought that so long as he could not acknowledge that he did feel both needy and angry himself, our relationship would continue to feel superficial and relatively ineffective and might be one of the sources of his continuing depression.

The excessive politeness and care with which I was treated was masking an image of a relationship with a feeble and demanding maternal figure who had to be cared for without complaint. This figure, separated from any more paternal or masculine decisiveness, seemed to mirror, in the session, the weakened mother and unconcerned and absent father of Mr S's childhood memories. In such a situation, Sasha was frequently abandoned and in panic, as his father repeated a pattern of absence from home himself, and enacted the anger (which his father masked and denied with excessive courtesy) against Mrs S and at school. Mrs S, like her mother-in-law and her own mother before her, put up with it. The session seemed to bring the situation more into the open, and, I think, indicated the beginnings of an experience with me of a more robust relationship, which they could begin to internalise and use in their own relationship as a couple and as parents, with Sasha and in Mr S's work.

Conclusion

Children with autism shake their parents' confidence in their parental capacities. While easy and rewarding children are able to make their needs known and to respond positively and appreciatively to the nurturing and thought they are given, the difficult and often unrewarding aspects of parenting children on the autism continuum can increase anxiety in parents and evoke a powerful, unconscious fear of destructiveness. The absence of reassurance that things are going well enough can lead to self-doubt and an over-reliance on, and fear of, professional experts. Such a situation can create the uncertainty and anxiety which may pull parents down and pull couples apart.

It is very easy, as child development research experiments show (Murray and Trevarthen 1985), to set up a downward spiral between parents and child where the 'dance' between them, to quote Daniel Stern (1977) becomes a series of missteps on either side; where mutual monitoring so easily becomes mutual, suspicious watchfulness or turning away. These powerful dynamics operate very strongly in autism, with conscious and unconscious feelings of responsibility in parents often evoking unnecessary guilt and fear.

Any work with parents needs to be highly flexible and responsive to individual needs. It often entails the slow nurturing of positive experiences between parent and child which may have become much reduced over time. Parents need to build their own sense of potency as parents, and to be able to report on their developing attempts to observe their child more carefully and to develop a more meaningful and contained relationship with him.

They need to learn or re-learn, first-hand, of their importance to their children as interested and interesting companions in play and exploration, within a reliable and friendly relationship. In this way, Alvarez's thinking (1992) about the importance of developing potency in strengthening the egos of deprived and disturbed children, is equally important for parents whose flattened sense of their capacity to parent their children needs bolstering and strengthening as well.

The need for the worker to feel unhurried and able to consider the different levels of work which are possible or necessary (Rustin 1997) goes hand-in-hand with the necessity to hold in mind the traumatising experiences of having and living with a child with autism, which may activate, in any of us, the 'fault lines' which Garland describes. Wherever the work begins, the relationship with the parent-worker affords opportunities to internalise stronger and more sustaining experiences. These may allow parents to be both more realistic and more hopeful in facing the painful struggle to help children with autism to develop to the best of their potential.

Note

1 Parts of this paper are published in a paper for the *Journal of Child Psychotherapy*, 24, 1, April 1998.

4 Addressing the deficit

Developmentally informed psychotherapy with passive, 'undrawn' children[1]

Anne Alvarez

Introduction

Several newspapers recently reported the results of new findings on the condition known as Persistent Vegetative State: in half of the patients diagnosed with PVS, sensitive approaches by carers had succeeded in producing evidence of communication, awareness of identity, and of pleasure in being alive. The Director of the Royal Hospital for Nervous Diseases declared that the word 'persistent' should be removed from the diagnostic label. Chronic autism is something very like a persistent vegetative state of the mind. Yet clinicians, parents and teachers have been able to arouse animation, movement and development in some previously emotionally deadened children. In the Autism Workshop, we believe we have built up experiences of finding ways to reach these children – sometimes by meeting them wherever they are, at other times by tugging on the lifeline of human communication to get their attention and interest. I want to look at some of the issues involved in this process, and to think around issues of deficit (in this chapter) and disorder, deviance and personality (in the next), in an attempt to clarify only a few of the many mysteries and challenges inherent in working with these children.

Alexander Luria, the great Russian neurologist, declared that scientific observation is not merely pure description of separate facts. Its main goal, he said, is to view an event from as many perspectives as possible (1987). This chapter examines the tragic 'event' of autism from three perspectives:

1 clinical findings from the interaction between therapist and patient during long treatments: that is, the observation by the psychotherapist of the child's responses, then of the therapist's own feelings and responses to the behaviour of the child (the observer as the observed) – and finally the child's response to her responses, and so on;

2 modern developments in psychoanalytic theory and technique which involve less attention to the uncovering of repressed material and more emphasis on the containment (in the interactional here-and-now) of lost parts of the personality;

3   findings from research in infant development – findings which illuminate
the precursors – and the precursors of the precursors – of normal
social/emotional/cognitive development.

All three perspectives involve the use of a two-person psychology. The type of
information thus gained is vital for treatment, but it may also supply a fuller
descriptive psychology of autism than that provided by a one-person psychology
which simply lists symptoms. Such classificatory diagnostic work is important,
but it may be that, however multi-axial its approach, it tells us only a part of the
story. A relational approach involves a study of interpersonal and intrapersonal
relations, in particular of infantile ones, and of the stage of development of
emotional communication. None of this implies a comment on initial aetiology
(see Chapter 1 of this volume for some discussion of the issue of aetiology).

This chapter mostly concerns the treatment of a particular sub-group within
the larger group of children with autism: that is, those who seem more undrawn
than withdrawn, whose lack of social responsiveness seems to be marked more
by deficit and indifference than by aloof or active avoidance. (There are some
overlaps with Lorna Wing's views [1987] on the 'passive' sub-group. The
patients described in this chapter are largely of the more indifferent type, and
they also have especially severe autism.) The 'aloof' (Wing and Attwood 1987)
children, on the other hand, raise quite different technical problems beautifully
explored by Tustin (1981a) in her discussion of 'shell-type' children, and I will
not discuss these here (see Chapters 5 and 9 of this volume). It is important to
add that the element of deficit may exist even in aloof children. Many cases are
mixed: if a child is aloof for too long or from too early on, there is extreme
developmental delay and deficit in normal functions (see a description of
Samuel in the next chapter). Many severely autistic children may have no
language at all; worse, they may never have babbled playfully. It may be a real
achievement in the therapy when the non-speaking child begins to play with
sounds, to make sounds which are more contoured, to begin to engage in what
Trevarthen calls the 'pre-music' of 'pre-speech' (Trevarthen and Marwick
1986). The technical issues for the psychotherapist are important: how can we
reach a child with no language? How should we talk to such a child?
Furthermore, if the child's social/cognitive deficits result in a situation where
he cannot manage two-tracked thinking, i.e. to hold two ideas in his mind at
once, explanatory interpretations of the kind, 'You seem very upset, and
perhaps that is because ... ' may be far too complex (see a discussion of the
therapeutic implications of Bruner's [1968] research on the development of
two-tracked thinking in normal babies in Alvarez [1992]). The therapist's
comments may need to be simplified and one-tracked; yet at times even a
simple and sympathetic, 'You seem very upset' may be too much: many children
with autism, as is well known, cannot manage the I–You distinction, and it is
often better simply to identify a feeling, without bothering to locate it in one
person or the other. For example, rather than 'You are upset', it may be better
to say, simply 'It is very upsetting when ... ' This places the feeling somewhere

in the middle of the room – a bit removed from the child, in a sort of shared but safe place at a comfortable distance. At this level of impairment, thinking about one thought at a time may be quite enough to ask, and loading the feeling onto the child, in his direction, may at best produce total incomprehension; at worst it may flood and overwhelm him.

The normal baby is now known to be born hugely precocious socially (J. Newson 1977: 49). To paraphrase Bion (1962), there is always at birth at least a *preconception* of a living (and thinking) human object, or to quote Trevarthen (1978), of 'live company'. Braten (1987) proposes that there are, within the central nervous system of the normal neonate, circuits which specify the immediate co-presence of a 'virtual other'. With experience of the actual other, the sense of other becomes progressively more elaborated. Subjectivity, these authors suggest, is inherently intersubjective, inherently dialogic, but experience fills in the outline. Bion's version suggested that without an adequate realisation in experience to meet this preconception, an adequate *concept* of this living, thinking human object may not emerge. Yet the traces of a preconception or of a pre-object may still be detectable in children with autism, and it is on this foundation that the treatment may build.

Method of observation

I have argued elsewhere that to examine the autistic child while ignoring the interpersonal dimension between child and therapist may be like listening to music while tone deaf, or comparing the scent of two roses without a sense of smell (Alvarez 1992). The musician buying a new cello insists on playing it first in order to assess its tone and resonances. Hamlet, mocking Guildenstern for imagining he can play *him*, says of himself, 'and there is much music, excellent voice, in this little organ, yet cannot you make it speak'. What is studied is a living changing relationship, a song, not a still life, and a duet, not a solo. If one forgets this, autistic patients have a way of reminding us. Several of my own autistic patients have done certain things only when my attention has wandered for a moment, never when my attention has been fully on them. I have had to monitor my responses as well as theirs, and try and remember what I just did and just felt or failed to feel and do. They do not declare an interest in us openly, but they do find their own methods of eliciting interest and even mindful attention. Mark, an eleven-year-old, could go on engaging in his repetitive rubbing of the table, walking in circles, rubbing the table, walking in circles again, for half an hour at the far end of the room while my gaze was on him. The moment my mind and my gaze wandered away from him, or simply the quality of my gaze changed (if I became a bit absent-minded), his circle changed to an oval which brought him into my field of vision. Thus he got my attention back! Then, and only then, did he return to walking in his circle. The signals of the 'undrawn' children are very faint; the signals of the aloof children are often extremely indirect or delayed. In either case, the therapist may need to use all his powers of observation in a highly vigilant manner (see Tsiantis *et al.*

1996 for a full discussion of the ways in which therapists use their feelings as an essential tool in their work).

The triad of symptoms

Wing and Gould's huge study of 35,000 children in Camberwell confirmed that Kanner's original set of three symptoms did continue to form a triad (Wing and Gould 1979; Kanner 1943). The three classic features of autism –

1   severe social impairment (there was an important change in wording from Kanner's 'severe autistic aloneness');
2   severe communication difficulties, both verbal and non-verbal;
3(a) absence of imaginative pursuits including pretend play,
3(b) with the substitution of repetitive behaviour

– all these imply a notion of impairment. Rutter suggested that all of the symptoms could be accounted for by a cognitive deficit common to all of them (Rutter 1983). Subsequent attempts by authors such as Frith (1989) and Baron-Cohen (1988) to explain the psychological features in the cognitive deficit make use of a sort of one-and-a-half-person psychology, which asserts that what autistic children lack is a theory of mind. Their ideas are of great interest, but the half-person that may be missing in their somewhat over-cognitive theory concerns everything else that goes into personal relations besides cognition and rational inferences about other people's states of mind. Hobson (1993) has pointed out that the concept of 'persons' is more fundamental than either the concept of 'bodies' or the concept of 'minds', and argues persuasively that the essence of autism is severe disturbance in intersubjective personal engagement with others. It is interesting that it is no longer only psychoanalysts who place feelings at the centre of cognition, as part of its very structure (Bion 1962; Urwin 1987): feelings, especially feelings about other people, are thought by developmentalists (Trevarthen 1980; Murray 1991) and contemporary brain researchers (B. Perry *et al.* 1995; Schore 1996) to be not incidental or additional to cognition, but at its very heart. It might be better to agree with Hobson and say that what children with autism lack is not a theory of mind, but a theory of person – a sense of the interesting otherness of the world.

It may be interesting, therefore, to look at each of the three major symptoms from a perspective which involves both psychoanalytic object-relations (Klein 1959) and infant development (Di Cagno *et al.* 1984; Stern 1985; Miller *et al.* 1989). Could the absence of a theory of mind then be conceptualised as the *presence* of a theory of an unmindful or uninteresting person? (There is no aetiological implication here: it is the child's inner world of figures and representations that are at issue. Many psychoanalysts use the term 'internal object' rather than 'representation', as the latter may be sometimes taken to imply an exact copy of external figures, whereas the former carries no such implication. Internal objects are thought to be amalgalms of both inner and outer factors.)

If we think of the first and most general symptom: looked at from a purely descriptive one-person psychological and behavioural view, 'severe social impairment' may seem to be the equivalent of Kanner's 'severe autistic aloneness'. Yet 'aloneness' is closer to subjective experience, and may open the way to further questions. Does the child feel alone? Are there different ways of being alone? Is something invisible keeping the child company? Is it that she does not turn *to* other human beings, or is it that she does not feel drawn *by* them? Is she *with*drawn or *un*drawn? (One child may seem withdrawn and avoidant – another may seem undrawn and indifferent. This chapter is concerned primarily with the latter type of child.) Also, what does it feel like to be *with* her? And, perhaps most important of all, under what interpersonal conditions are there variations in this feeling of aloneness or social impairment? Does it vary with changes in the other person's responsiveness to the child, for example? In a model of the mind which involves a two-person psychology, the mind contains not just a self with particular qualities and orientations and possible deficits; it also contains a relation to, and relationship with, what are called 'internal objects' (Klein 1959) or 'representational models' (Bowlby 1988), and these too may contain deficits. That is, the child's 'theory of mind' may be inadequate, but her 'theory of person', both for others and herself, may also be deficient. A more personal, interpersonal and intrapersonal view of autism carries the implication that the self is in an emotional, dynamic *relationship* to its internal representations, figures, objects – however skewed, deficient, or odd this relation may be. If she treats us as a piece of furniture, she may be seeing us as something like a piece of furniture, but she may also *feel as though we are like* a piece of furniture.

The first symptom, social deficit, may therefore need to be addressed, both in terms of the deficit in the child's sense of self and in her lack of sociality, but second, also in the lack of sociality of her 'internal object', internal figures, inner representations of persons, or her theory of mind. She may seem uninterested in other people, but she may also have failed to build up an inner image of a figure who is interest*ing* or who is interest*ed* in her. The second symptom, communication difficulties, may require definitions which include a description of what kind of internal listener or responder the child is addressing or failing to address. Why does she not speak? Toward whom or what is she failing to communicate? This will therefore raise questions about the kind of developmental level on which the therapist's communications should function. The third symptom, the question of play, is more complicated, because it contains two elements: first there is the lack of imaginative pursuits and pretend play, which, like the first and second symptoms, involves a deficit, so we can wonder about the absence of a playable-with or playful object; but the second element, that which replaces imagination, the terrible symptom of repetitive or stereotyped rituals, may have as much to do with disorder and deviance as with deficit, and I shall return to this subject in the next chapter.

Therapeutic implications of deficit in the internal object: waking the child to mindfulness and amplifying preconceptions

First example

The following case material is a condensation of several chapters from Alvarez 1992.

Robbie, an autistic patient, showed behaviour which seemed to be the most unrelated and asocial I had seen outside the back wards of psychiatric hospitals. Yet it was possible to ask the question: towards what kind of human figure or near-human figure or pre-human figure was he relating or failing to relate? His own answer when he was eventually able to put it into words, was 'a net with a hole in it'. That of course is not a very human, useful or magnetically attracting object. My endless therapeutic problem was: how was I to become dense enough, substantial enough, condensed enough to provide him with something or someone who could concentrate his mind? Simply waiting receptively and too passively for him, in his infinitely dispersed and flaccid state, would have taken a lifetime. And in fact, until I belatedly became clearer about my task with him, one of my earliest and illest autistic patients, it did.

His own image for what finally got through to him was a kind of lifeline. Robbie was a profoundly empty and lifeless boy, but one day, soon after his treatment was finally increased from once-monthly treatment to five times weekly at the rather late age of thirteen, he described excitedly (I could not tell if he had had a dream or a very vivid phantasy) how a 'long long long stocking' had been thrown down to him in a dark pit where he said he had been for a very long time. This stocking enabled him and all his loved ones to come out and go 'flying over to the other side of the street'. He himself had always had a lost, rag-doll quality, and spoke in apathetic, wispy, listless little phrases; but here he came dramatically, verbally and musically to life. The implications of some kind of lifeline were inescapable. Robbie was socially impaired and indifferent because, I think, he had given up. There are interesting questions here concerning sub-types of autism: I came to think that Robbie was not hiding: he was deeply lost. With the more actively withdrawn shell-type children, where there is a self in hiding, we have to be far more careful not to be intrusive, and to respect distances, as we shall see elsewhere in this book (Reid, this volume: Chapters 2 and 7). Every autistic child is different, and is different from one moment to the next, but concern about intrusiveness would have been something of a luxury at Robbie's profound level of psychic emptiness. My function seemed to be to reclaim him as a member of the human family because he no longer knew how to make his own claims. He had stressed the length of the rope/stocking; and this exactly corresponded to my continuous feeling that I had to traverse great distances – distances created both by the degree of his unresponsiveness and by its chronicity: he was a very long way off, and he had been there a long time. He needed to be recalled to himself. I chose at the time the word 'reclamation' to describe the situation. Wasteland does not ask to be reclaimed, yet its hidden potentiality for growth may flourish nonetheless when it is reclaimed. I had begun to notice that Robbie at times could be awakened to himself and to me when I spoke in particularly lively or urgent tones. (Robbie later often spoke of the time when he had been sent away to the country to strangers at eighteen months [when his descent into deepest autism seems to have begun] as the time when he had died.)

The chronicity itself may need to be addressed, long before luxurious questions such as the child's original reasons for having autism can be dealt with. Neither earlier psychoanalytic explanations which would have seen his unresponsiveness as defensive autistic withdrawal, nor others which might have seen it as a passivity resulting from a projection of active ego functions into others, seemed appropriate to his level of deficit. It seemed that his internal figures were as empty of life as was his sense of self. Perhaps Robbie had a predisposition to autism (Rutter 1991) and perhaps two early traumas were the final straw (see Reid, this volume: Chapter 7). But years of autism bring further consequences in their train. A weak sense of the reality of other people may get weaker, and the child may lose ever more interest. Malnutrition, or a state of starvation, is a condition vastly different from hunger. In thinking about Robbie's lifeline story, I gradually became aware that I was often overwhelmed with powerful feelings of urgency about his nearness to psychic death; at other moments it was all too easy to forget about this and peacefully allow my mind to slip dangerously away, just as he had. Subsequently I had to learn to think about how to translate the original dramatic emergency rescue operation and the panicky moments of urgency on my part, into something more like a steady regime of regular, vigilant, intensive care which does not panic but must not be too slack. I had noted, early on, that I often found myself moving my head into his line of vision, or calling his name, in response to his rag-doll emptiness. I now think it is possible to respond to the child's needs to be found down his dark pit (or in the case of other children, to be found in their bland and all-too-comfortable permanent resting-place) and his need to be reached, by working on oneself to provide a tighter, tauter ongoing attention. This need not always involve moving one's head or raising one's voice, but does have something to do with the level of intense attention necessary (perhaps like the primary maternal preoccupation described by Winnicott [1960]). In a way, the cognitivists were right to criticise psychoanalytic therapists for imagining that explanatory interpretations about the past could help such very impaired mindless children. We have had to learn that less attention to the past and more to the present, with careful attention to the quality of the relationship in the living here-and-now, does seem to pay dividends and to begin to repair the social deficit both in the self and in the internal object.

I have previously suggested a possible link between the 'reclaiming' activities directed to desperately ill patients, and the more normal 'claiming' and 'awakening' activities engaged in by ordinary mothers of ordinary babies (Alvarez 1992). Klaus and Kennell (1982) studied parent-infant bonding by filming mothers' and babies' behaviour in the delivery room for ten minutes during their first contact after the birth. Each mother at first examined every part of her newborn infant. At the same time, she showed intense interest in waking him in an attempt to get him to open his eyes, and this was verbalised by nearly three quarters of the mothers: 'Open your eyes, oh come on now, open your eyes', or 'If you open your eyes I'll know you're alive'. After one baby in a similar study finally opened his eyes, his mother said 'Hello!' to him seven times in less than one and a half minutes (Macfarlane 1977: 53). (In videos by the developmental researcher Lynne Murray [1991] the voices of normal mothers show an unmistakeable note of coaxing or of invitation, as in 'come on, give us a smile'.)

Brazelton *et al.*'s study (1974) describes what the mother does when she is invited to engage in a period of interaction with her young baby (the babies studied were aged from 2 to 20 weeks). The things she does in order to engage her baby's attention in the first place are quite different from the things she does after it has been gained, when she is then attempting to sustain it and maintain it. At the first stage she reduces interferences from within and without, by making him comfortable and by containing startle reactions. She moves her head into his line of vision to get eye contact. At the next stages, although avoiding overloading, she nevertheless starts explosively to get his attention, and alerts, amplifies, emphasises, accelerates her speech and caresses in order to keep his interest. When his interest flags, she exchanges one activity for another, or alternates alerting with soothing, always improvising. This is 'live company'. I think there may be lessons to be learned for work with children with attention deficits and communication disorders, where deficit is also in the internal object. A more active approach need not therefore imply seducing a passive patient into life when what he should have had was help to be able to come alive for himself: rather, it may involve something more like calling an almost comatose patient into life. I will discuss in the next chapter the problems when the symptom is over-determined, where deficit is accompanied by secondary gains, and genuine incapacity and indifference is exploited by passive complacency. Several other chapters will also address these issues (see Bungener, this volume: Chapter 14, for a description of a patient who did project her intelligence and capacity for thought into others and who turned out to be not at all as slow as she appeared). These mixtures and complications are the stuff of clinical work.

In the Tavistock Autism Workshop we have learned nowadays to be more gently active, to try to get eye contact where we can do so tactfully, maybe even occasionally to 'chase' the child a little, without being too intrusive. Finding the right distance, psychologically and physically, is all-important – not too far away to reach him, but not too close to scare him off. Most of this sensing of distance, of tone of voice, speed and pitch of speech, comes quite naturally to people when they speak to tiny babies. It does not always come so naturally when one is speaking to a ten year-old child who seems to be rejecting or ignoring all our friendly overtures.

I hope it is clear that we are not suggesting that the 'cause' of cognitive deficit or emotional apathy, or both, in a baby is in the caregiver. But a baby who is born apathetic, or who is drifting away, for whatever reason, from human contact, may have required a tauter pull on the lifeline than would a more vigorous baby. He may have had what psychoanalysts would call weak introjective and projective processes, that is, a weak ability to take in and learn from experience, and a weak capacity to get rid of uncomfortable feelings or distress by protest and other normal interpersonal and expressive means. What we are suggesting is that the conditions for recovery or improvement, regardless of what combination of factors may have set the child originally on an autistic path, may nevertheless lie in the area of promoting a capacity for interaction at the appropriate, possibly very early, developmental level, so the ordinary inter-actional exchanges so vital for mental life may be set in motion.

Second example

I want to give an example of an interaction with a three year-old autistic girl, Angela, where her seemingly unsocial ritualistic preoccupation with doors did seem to hold the seed of at least a preconception, but not the concept, of a living object. Angela's mother was a single parent and said that she herself became very withdrawn from her baby towards the end of the first year of Angela's life when her marriage was breaking up. After several months of her own withdrawal, she realised that Angela had become far more attracted to, and obsessed by a lamp in the living room than she was to her mother. In the first session Angela was very absorbed in opening and closing doors on a dolls' house which my colleague and I had provided. By the second session, I began to feel sure that her absorption was not as mechanical as it first looked. She appeared to be studying the house through the doors, and I wondered, was she checking for symmetry or fascinated by three-dimensionality, tunnels, or what? She was clearly, in her confused urgency, not getting the answer to her 'question'. In the end I suddenly thought of peeking back at her through the tiny window on my side of the house. She smiled with delight, and threw herself on her mother as though to celebrate, and this sharing of her joy delighted all three of us adults. We underlined Angela's wish to share her pleasure with her mother. There are important issues here: first it is important, during an assessment, to discover the child's capacity to respond; at the same time, it is equally important to help parents to learn how to engage the child better, without making the parent feel responsible for the child's original autistic condition (see Reid, this volume: Chapter 2). Angela's needs were not being clearly expressed. In this situation the child and parent can fall or drift further and further apart. If Angela was looking for something, she didn't quite know or remember what it was. She was in a state of pre-expectation, rather than expectation. Like Klaus and Kennell's, and Brazelton *et al.*'s mothers calling their babies into contact, I think for a moment I provided a realisation of a preconception, not of a concept. I met a pre-need, not a need. The child needs repair to his ego defects

(Sandler and Sandler 1958) but also to the defects in his internal objects. Everyone concerned with the child may need to be sensitised to respond to, amplify and focus signals which are weak, delayed or highly immature. In many cases, as we have said, individual help for the child would not be the treatment of choice, and work with the child in his family is carried out instead.

Communication deficit – getting on the right developmental wavelength

The above examples show how difficult it is to separate out the three symptoms of sociability, communication and play. Trevarthen has studied 'pre-speech', and 'pre-music' dialogues between mothers and their actively participating babies. Apparently, 'motherese' is high-pitched, initially in an adagio, later in an andante rhythm, and the dialogue has certain rhythms in common in every language (Trevarthen and Marwick 1986). Can these findings about the nature of early dialogue be of practical use to clinicians in our understanding and treatment of the autistic child's communication difficulties? I think that they can: therapists have had to rethink how they talk to these children in order to repair the communication deficit. (Note Reid [1990] reporting the fact that she often sang to a very withdrawn, frozen and traumatised toddler with autistic features. She was drawing on her experience of infant observation with profoundly moving results.) I myself had a rather strange experience with Mark, the eleven year-old autistic boy with the table-rubbing and walking ritual. I had begun to try to reach him on early rhythmic levels, talking and tapping my feet in time to his ritualistic walking. He had seemed lit up by this, and begun to improvise himself a little, and even to follow my rhythms occasionally. He had become freer, and according to his parents, happier. But the first time I ever spoke in an even freer real 'motherese' happened without plan. I was talking to Mark about the fact that his family was moving out of London and how he would lose his twice-weekly treatment, but that his mother had promised to make the long journey about once a month. It was very painful for me because he had recently become so much more reachable, and for him because he had suffered an enormous setback only the Christmas before when he had lost his previous therapist. I mentioned his coming back after Christmas, and then my notes read

> I seemed to go into this baby talk – the way you talk to babies or animals, and I said, softly and coaxingly 'Would you like to do that, eh? Mark???' (i.e. come back to see me after Christmas). I was looking right at him and he had been listening closely. To my astonishment (because in the year he had never uttered a word to me), he suddenly whispered loudly, looking intently at me, 'Yesss.'

A week later (by now he was spending much less time in his rituals) he was holding a little toy rabbit which I had handed him, and he kept repetitively but rather playfully turning it away from him. I had been lending words to the rhythm of the turns, occasionally speaking on his behalf, occasionally on the rabbit's. My notes read

> I have to keep my voice alive or his activity goes dead and mechanical. At one point, I spoke for the rabbit whose back was turned from M. and said, 'Oh, *please* look at me ... !' Mark himself swung around and looked at me, very shyly but profoundly. It was very moving.

He thought the plea came from me, and of course he was a very confused child, with whom it was rather foolish to make the play too complicated, but my mistake taught me something. Trevarthen suggests that the baby's sensitivity to certain rhythms and pitches is innately laid down in his brain, and when one sees these children light up and pay attention the moment the voice of a colleague or parent changes to 'motherese', one feels Trevarthen and Marwick (1986) must be right (see also Steiner's [1987] discussion of the work of Ivan Fonagy – an authority on psychophonetics – on the importance of intonation in proto-communication).

Deficit in playfulness

I have already mentioned the way in which the therapist may join in on the child's private and unsocial activities, by tactfully lending accompanying rhythms to something the child is doing. The child with autism may not be ready to become interested in other people, but he may be enabled to become interested, first, in their interest in him. The developmental level has always to be taken into account. The child may not be ready for ball-throwing games. He may not even be ready for ball-rolling games. He may, indeed, not even be ready to pass a ball to us, but he might, slowly, accept one into his hands, and after a few weeks of this, be prepared to offer it back and eventually to play a turn-taking game. He may not engage in pretend play with doll families, but he might persist in lining the dolls up, and some shred of meaning and an immature but powerful sense of agency may accompany the behaviour. We have to approach him where he is and move on from there. It will not help if we see his limited doll play only as an irreparable impairment in pretend play. But it will also not help if we are too neutral or too containing and passive in our approach to his severe developmental delay.

Summary and conclusion

This chapter discusses a contemporary approach to the psychotherapy of the child with autism: the developmentally informed use of the psychotherapist's feelings to repair the deficits in the self and in the internal world of a particular sub-group of severely autistic children marked more by indifference than by avoidance. The deficits concern social, communicative and play functions. Infant development research has illuminated certain precursors of social/

cognitive development, and it is important that the therapist tune his or her response to the appropriate, possibly very early, developmental level at which the child is functioning.

The work described here may seem a long way from the classical description of psychoanalysis as the analysis of transference and resistance, and its accompanying technical rule of abstinence. But psychoanalysis itself has moved a long way. I cannot consider in detail the developments in psychoanalytic technique, theory and meta-theory which are important for the work of the contemporary child psychotherapist. These include

- less emphasis on interpretations which invoke the past as an explainer of behaviour, and more attention to the patient's need and functioning in the here-and-now
- the supplementing of the theory of sexuality with a greater attention to, and respect for, the 'higher' side of a person's nature (conscience, capacity for symbolic thought, creativity)
- the development of a meta-theory which is more relational, less reductionistic and mechanistic, and more able to accommodate novelty, growth, change, and the mentalness of mind
- the supplementing – in the theory of the therapeutic action of psychoanalysis – of the lifting of repressive barriers with a process which involves, by means of analytic containment, the extending of the boundaries of the self to include the regaining of lost, split-off and projected parts of the self (Joseph 1975).

However, in the case of the highly impaired children described here, these lost parts of the personality may be under- or undeveloped, and this raises problems which may at moments take the therapist beyond even these more modern psychoanalytic advances. At moments when the child's lack of social responsiveness is arising from massive deficit, rather than from active avoidance, when his introjective and projective processes function weakly and inadequately, and furthermore when he has poor language and imagination, then interventions must reach the child in a 'language' or form that is appropriate to the (possibly very early) developmental level at which he is functioning. At other moments, when the child is more present and aware, and his behaviour has more intentionality and motive, more ordinary psychotherapeutic work may take place (see other chapters in this volume). I would maintain that the work with these children remains both developmentally and psychoanalytically informed. Getting a balance between, on the one hand, attempts to focus and engage the child, to turn preconceptions into concepts by being developmentally attuned and therefore more active; and on the other hand, leaving him space to have his own experience once he is enough *in himself* to be able to do this, is a perpetually difficult task. It is by no means simply a question of playing with the child.

Note

1 Earlier versions of this chapter were published in Italian in 1993 under the title 'An Interactional Approach to the Psychotherapy of Autism', in *Richard and Piggle*, Rome: Il Pensiero Scientifico Editore, and in English under the title 'Addressing the Deficit in Children with Autism', *Clinical Child Psychology and Psychiatry*, 1 (4) 525–37, London: Sage.

5   Disorder, deviance and personality

Factors in the persistence and modifiability of autism

Anne Alvarez

Introduction

There is a delta in south-eastern Alaska where a tiny change in the temperature each spring – from zero to only one degree – melts a huge glacier. The tiny change brings great cascades of ice, sometimes twenty storeys tall, crashing down. It brings movement, too: everything is churning. It brings silt down the delta, and seawater back into the bay. The result is a massive wheel of fertility, a huge botanical and biological stew of wildlife and plankton.

Like that glacier, some forms of autism do respond to relatively small changes in emotional temperatures, in the child or in someone else relating to him: this may bring in its train huge cascades of emotion which the child may find difficult to regulate. In other forms of autism, the 'deep freeze', as one patient of mine called it, may be much slower to thaw. Some children swing wildly back and forth between frozen states and a churning, highly intemperate and over-emotional condition. The emotionality always seems more human and healthy, but therapists have had to learn that certain sudden retreats to frozen unfeeling may also serve healthy, protective or regulatory functions. Samuel, a patient of mine, was a very tense boy with severe autism, and at times he seemed full of a barely controlled, almost frenzied excitement; but I was nevertheless astonished, some while into treatment, when I found that, even at his most happy, friendly, cooperative and less autistic moments, his heart was racing like that of a terrified wild bird. I never learned whether it was racing in the same way when he was off in a corner absorbed in one of his repetitive behaviours and out of emotional and social reach; I certainly got the impression that sometimes these behaviours did serve to calm him; they were a bizarre and dangerously addictive, but nevertheless effective form of self-soothing.

Sinason (1986) has distinguished primary mental handicap from secondary handicap. She points out how handicapped people may so over-identify with the image of themselves as handicapped, that they give up the struggle to be intelligent, and may produce extra handicap in themselves for a variety of psychological motives. What is it about autism, particularly the symptom of repetitive behaviours, which is so persistent and also so deadly in its effect on normal development? What enables some children to emerge from autism? In the previous chapter I discussed the element of deficit and developmental delay in the triad of symptoms: in the present chapter I want to discuss three other factors:

1 disorder – in particular, disorders of excitement, sensitivity and reactivity;
2 deviance – with particular reference to the repetitive behaviours; and
3 personality and personal motivations.

What role do these three factors play in autism – in particular in the degree of secondary autism? I shall also discuss some of the ways in which the psychotherapy may address these factors in the person with autism.

Some possible primary disorders: arousal and introjection

Psychoanalytic clinicians were among the first to comment on the problem of excitement and excitability in children with autism. Tustin (1981a) described the children's difficulty in 'filtering' experience, their states of unbearable ecstasy: she described a child completely overwhelmed by the yellowness of a yellow flower. Meltzer *et al.* (1975) suggested that they were bombarded by stimuli. American researchers have explored what they have called unusual levels of arousal in children with autism (Dawson and Lewy 1989). This work adds another dimension to the psychology and the psychoanalysis of autism. It reminds us that the positive or negative content of experience is only one aspect; another is its intensity. Many children with autism seem to be as disturbed by positive experiences as by negative. Questions of intensity, overload, oversensitivity and over- and under-stimulation are very much the subject of study in infant development research and infant observation. They relate to the question of how, or for that matter, whether, experience can be taken in or introjected.

Some American investigators suggested that children with autism were in a chronic state of over-arousal, while others suggested they were fluctuating between states of over-arousal and states of under-arousal. Dawson and Lewy (1989) suggested that autistic children have a deficit in modulating arousal. They attempted to explain why a problem in modulation (or what developmentalists call regulation) should lead to difficulties with people; they explored a complex interacting non-linear causality where a primary deficit or disorder may lead to self-reinforcing situations and then lead on to secondary disorder. I shall go on to suggest there are even tertiary disorders. Munday and Sigman (1989: 17) suggest that a baby who does not interact enough – because he finds emotional experiences with others too exciting or disturbing – may not receive the kind of lively attention which is so necessary for 'the neuroanatomical and neurochemical substrates of behaviour'. They quote the effect of social isolation on primates, and one might also add the recent research showing that trauma and deprivation effect both the minds and the brains of babies, and that therapies of different kinds repair both their minds and their brains (B. Perry *et al.*

1995; Schore 1996). Self-deprivation in an over-sensitive baby might be predicted to produce similar effects on the brain. Mundy and Sigman are not suggesting that parents fail to offer what their babies need: rather, that a self-isolating baby deprives himself of emotional/social experiences which are necessary for normal development to proceed.

To return to the question of how to understand Samuel's racing heart, or what Dawson calls 'arousal' and its effects. Avoidant behaviour and frustration have been shown to be associated with increase in heart rate, but in infancy, the orienting response and attention to the environment are associated with *decrease* in heart rate (Tronick 1989). Samuel seemed to want contact with me at such moments – to be orienting towards me and attending to me, not avoiding me, but yet, at the same time, he was very disturbed by it. Dawson and Lewy (1989) stressed the importance of therapies which take into account the question of what is the optimal level of stimulation for a child. Many of these children are thrown into a terribly turbulent universe when they relax their guard. I think this may be more characteristic of what Wing and Attwood (1987) termed the 'aloof' sub-group, (or what Tustin [1981a] called the shell-type child) than of the more floppy indifferent child (see previous chapter, and Wing and Attwood (1987) on the 'passive' sub-group).

Samuel was a boy whose severe autism was of the aloof type. I began treating him on a three-times weekly basis when he was four years old. He rarely looked at, or related to people, except to throw them the occasional fleeting, wild, and sometimes angry glance. He had no language, did not play and had shown little interest in toys or in ordinary functional objects. He seemed interested mostly only in the flowing of water, or in his own reflection in any shiny surface he could find. If left to his own devices, he would stare at a running tap or spin the wheels of toy cars for an hour or so. Everything he did was punctuated by his most frequent ritual: he stared fixedly at his hand, which was formed into a rigid, rather grotesque claw. He often got into a frenzied, almost hypnotised state as he carried out these repetitive activities. Gradually, as he began to spend less time in these states and to show more interest in me and in objects in the room, I introduced toys that I thought might be suitable for whatever extremely early developmental level might be revealed in his non-autistic moments in the sessions. When children become less autistic, a tremendous developmental delay is almost invariably revealed.

Disordered arousal and introjection: lowering the intensity

After about six months' treatment, Samuel, who had hardly ever stopped to look at anything in the room, finally became interested in a little blue cube-shaped brick. Much work had to be done in helping him to 'filter' even an experience as apparently simple and easy as gazing at a brick. Some weeks later, he noted that there was more than one brick, and began to pick up two at a time. He would look at them briefly as though for a fleeting second he was examining and enjoying their symmetry and the way he could put the two cubes neatly together, and then he would suddenly squash them together and make them explode in the air, as though they had erupted. He would be over-come by the same sort of disturbing excitement whenever he came close and looked into my eyes or at my face. Then he would suddenly dash away, carry out his hand ritual, and lay his face close to the open section of the window. At first, I thought he had returned to the old autistic state of mind, but I began to understand that he was often still in touch with me at such moments. I began to suspect that he had simply gone over to the window to 'cool down'.

After another six months, he had slowed down somewhat, and could study the shapes of the bricks very closely, build towers, and post some into appro-priate holes in shape-sorter toys. I wondered how this had come about, and what might have been the major preconditions. I did not have the impression that the explosions were simply the result of an enraged attack on twoness (as in Bion's [1959] concept of 'attacks on linking').

Samuel was, I think, having difficulty in coping with excitement, and also with the comprehension that twoness could be available to him *in time* – that there was enough time to look at both bricks, not precisely at the same instant. In fact, from the way he first began to look at my face, I gained the impression that he had never learned how to scan, which is how most people manage to sustain eye contact. In the beginning, he never met my eyes for more than a peripheral fleeting instant, but when he did, his gaze was too strong, and then he would have to tear his eyes away, just as babies do in the early days of life before they have learned to scan (Stern 1977b). He needed a temporal container which could help him to find out how, not to make do with one, but to have two in sequence, one at a time. I did not ask the question of myself or his family at the time, but I wonder now whether he had ever played passing an object from one hand to the other, which as Bruner (1968) has suggested is important as a reflection of the developing concept of twoness. I heard of a baby in a recent infant observation who tried this out immediately after a feed, when the father had suggested to the mother that the baby could hold her own spoon while the mother fed her with another. First the feeding spoon held by the mother went in his mouth, then the baby's own, in a kind of turn-taking. About ten minutes after the feed was over, the baby began to pass an object carefully from one hand to another: it seemed possible that the baby had been able to take in, and was practising in order to internalise, some idea that two people could have agency, and each could wait while the other had his turn. Bruner suggested that such coordinations are based on earlier coordinations, e.g. the acts of sucking and of looking in the early days and weeks of life. But coordinations of sensory modalities were difficult for Samuel, and patience was foreign to him, too. I had to work hard to slow him down sufficiently to help him to conceive of a universe which could exist comfortably in the dimension of time.

Disordered arousal and introjection: tuning in to the right band of intensity

In the later stages of Samuel's treatment, when he had learned to enjoy playing ball with people, there would sometimes come a moment when he would suddenly throw the ball at me very viciously. The ball was large and fairly soft, so there was no danger to me. I began to notice that if I threw it back too gently afterwards, perhaps in an attempt to contain and transform the violent emotions fuelling his throw, he would seem deflated and disappointed. If I became somewhat strict because it had gone near something breakable in the room, he looked persecuted and upset. Yet if I threw it back as viciously as he had, but in a humorous, slightly dramatised and hammed-up manner, he loved it. In the same way, if – again after some years of treatment – he resorted to his ritualistic hand movement, or teetered dangerously on the edge of a table in his socks, but in a now provocative and irritating way, my response had to be very precisely calibrated. I found that if I did not feel irritated or disappointed and simply commented calmly that he was trying to irritate me, he redoubled his efforts. Sometimes – but not always – he may have heard an edge to my voice and sensed the hypocrisy in it. Also, if I asked him to stop in a tone which conveyed too much undigested irritation, he became embittered, and again redoubled his efforts. At such moments, I think he felt I was colluding in a nasty power game. The point I wish to emphasise is that even the non-hypocritical, non-forced, genuinely friendly response on my part could disappoint him profoundly if it was too light and too calm. Yet if I dramatised and hammed up a humorous, warm but genuine exasperation, in the manner of, 'Oh no, not that boring hand again', he would yelp and roar with laughter and delight, and seem somehow wonderfully invigorated. The bitterness would go out of the situation, and he would often stop his ritual and resume a more social activity. I became certain that if he were to feel really understood and really heard – if the ice were to melt – it was not only a question of my getting the emotional content right, but also of reaching the right level of intensity. I am convinced that his powerful vitality required a loud enough or big enough answer.

Greenspan (1997) has very interesting things to say on these therapeutic issues. He makes an important distinction between regulatory 'factors' which distinguish one (normal) infant or child from another, and regulatory 'disorders'. He suggests the former can be seen as constitutional/maturational factors, such as, for example, sensory over-reactivity (to sights or sounds for instance). These may or may not lead to regulatory disorders such as difficulties in paying attention to other people, to behaviour and thinking difficulties. He suggests that the therapist should try to help such patients achieve adequate levels of sensation (and therefore adequate experience of emotion) which 'should make their relationships more salient and meaningful'. He states that the clinician may need to create a more 'compelling interpersonal environment. They may for example energize their voices and up the intensity of expressed affect to involve the other person more fully in verbal interactions' (*ibid*.:

389–90). Marina Bardyshevsky (personal communication) has observed that autistic-like babies in a Russian orphanage seem to have a very narrow band of level of stimulation through which they can be reached. I have discussed elsewhere the need for 'reclaiming' activities with certain passive patients who have lost the hope of and memory of the pleasures of human contact (Alvarez 1992a). But Samuel's treatment suggests that the converse is not necessarily true – that is, that over-reactive patients do not necessarily need simple soothing. They may need levels of stimulation which, although not too high, are sufficiently high.

Primary disorders: continued arousal, regulation and introjection

Greenspan (1997) points out that it may be premature to concern oneself with the autistic child's difficulty with abstract thinking, if the difficulty is a prior one, namely a difficulty in taking in information in the first place. There has been much work done by psychoanalysts (Bick 1968; Meltzer *et al.* 1975; Tustin 1981) on the failure by autistic children to communicate their emotional states to another through processes of projection. Perhaps as much attention now should be paid to their difficulties in taking things in (what psychoanalysts call introjection), and how therapists can facilitate this process.

Stern (1974) refers to the slowness of tempo and grossness of exaggerations of mothers' behaviour towards their infants. He says this probably matches closely the range of infant preferences and tolerances of rate and degree of stimulus change. The slowness of the tempo, along with the exaggeration, may enable the infant to maintain the identity of the mother's face across its various physical transformations and thus facilitate the acquisition of a stable face schema. Normal adult facial expressions flash very rapidly and conceivably could present the infant with a discontinuous sequence of faces (*ibid.*: 192). I do not have the impression that Samuel was likely to have been particularly rushed by his caregivers in early infancy: I can imagine, however, that he had an intolerance – that he himself was simply unable to slow down and quieten enough as a baby to use what was available to him. I often felt that my room was too small, my voice too thin, the world too puny for his vast but enormously compressed vitality. The developmental research is helpful, I think, not to determine the causes of autism, but to alert us to therapeutic strategies for autism.

Oliver Sacks (1995) has described the problems of Virgil, the fifty year-old Olkahoman, blind since the age of five, who had his vision restored forty-five years later. At first, he had no appreciation of depth or distance. Street lights were luminous stains stuck on window panes and the corridors of the hospital were black holes. Moving objects, such as his cat at home, or a human face greeting him with mobile features, were impossible. He could manage the details of the cat – tail, back, head; he was used to taking it in sequentially by touch – but could not grasp movement at a glance. I suspect that Samuel's years of gaze-avoidance and his extreme myopia may have made him a bit like Virgil.

When he did start to want to look at the world, he wanted desperately to see everything in one glance. Gradually, something began to change and his eye contact became more sustained. His vision improved, and, incidentally, I heard that his glasses' prescription had approached the normal. I guessed that he was finally using his eye muscles. I had indeed often slowed my face and speech down when he began to explore objects, and because he hated being interfered with, one had to pace one's interventions very carefully. Even so, his new curiosity cost him dear, and he began to look exhausted halfway through a session.

In the previous chapter I stressed the importance of approaching autism, for purposes both of description and treatment, from a psychoanalytic object-relations perspective, that is, via a two-person psychology, involving a close study of the patient's internal object representations and relationships. I also emphasised the need for the therapist to tune her responses to the appropriate developmental level. As I became ever more awed by some of these patients' wild swings in levels of arousal and excitement, I have also come to think that the developmentalists' concept of 'regulation' provides an essential supplement to the more usual psychoanalytic concept of defence. Defences are meant to stop someone having an experience (or at least feeling it), whereas a regulatory function may allow the experience and the feeling through, but under bearable yet sufficiently demanding and interesting conditions. Regulation may thereby assist important introjective processes. The question of who – the self, the internal object, or an external figure – does the regulating is another matter (see Tronick below).

Secondary disorders

All three of the symptoms of deficit described in the previous chapter – deficit in social engagement, in communication and in play – tend to be accompanied by disorder. Instead of looking at faces, the child grabs wrists, instead of asking for what he wants, the child may use echolalia (Rhode, this volume: Chapter 6); instead of play, the child engages in repetitive behaviours. Lengthy descriptions of these many disorders and of the related therapeutic strategies may be found in other chapters of this volume.

A particular secondary disorder: repetitive behaviour as a form of self-regulation

The third symptom in the triad of autistic symptoms is different from the first two described in the previous chapter. Not only does it refer to the element of deficit (the lack of imaginative pursuits and pretend play), it also contains a second element. The replacement of imagination with repetitive or stereotyped rituals has more to do with disorder and deviance than with deficit. Rituals differ from the other symptoms: they define what the child does, not what she omits to do. They replace far more than pretend play: they replace ordinary social life and communication. If we observe these children with autism closely, the timing and context of the occurrence of rituals can begin to give us clues to the function they fulfil.

Tronick (1989), like other modern developmentalists, points out that the normal infant is far more active and less helpless than previously thought. He points out that infants have two major and different methods of controlling and regulating their emotional states: first, by the use of 'other-directed regulatory activities', such as cries of anger or distress, they can signal to the caregiver that they need help; and second, by the use of self-directed regulatory behaviours. He points out that the infant is not solely dependent on the caregiver to help him control unpleasant feelings; he has several coping behaviours available: looking away, self-comfort, and even self-stimulation. Looking away can reduce infants' heart rates during stress, and thumb-sucking can calm their distress. Tronick labels these ways of coping 'self-directed regulatory behaviours'. Psychoanalytic workers would need to decide whether such activities were healthy reminders of previous experiences of good care-giving which maintain mental contact with the world, or whether they were unhealthy and dangerous in allowing the child to descend into a too compellingly private and cut-off universe (see also Mike, in Reid, this volume: Chapter 7).

It is not difficult to see the child with autism using his rituals to calm himself, especially when he is trying to move out of autism into a new experience. I have seen Samuel's rituals increase on such occasions. When he first began to look at me, he would alternate these looks with looking at his hand. Or when he began to try occasionally to talk, he would make his old familiar autistic moaning, whining sound, as though he was running along a launch pad or diving board before making his leap into the unknown world of language. Suddenly, as though out of a primeval swamp of sounds, something would take shape. Here it did seem that a repetitive behaviour was being used for purposes of regulation. He was touching base before making the adventurous leap into the unknown which autistic children so resist.

The other person as a regulator of excitement and facilitator of introjection

Around the same time that Samuel became interested in the bricks, I provided a new toy, a series of ever larger, brightly coloured plastic rings on a tapering pillar. Samuel loved it, but hated the fact that the perfect shape could only be achieved by placing the rings on it in exactly the right sequence. His solution to the problem was to hurl the pillar away contemptuously, and build a tower of the rings in any order he chose. I made many interpretations – about his impatience, his hatred of order and ordinality, of the difference between big things and small things, of rules – but these often only confirmed him in his hatred of such undigestible otherness. At other times, I tried to make reality more palatable: he would sometimes try to build the tower if I would hand the rings to him in the right order, holding my breath and making suspenseful comments before each ring went on: 'and ... the purple one, and ... the blue one'. I suppose what I was trying to do was to bridge the previously intolerable gap with something which, instead of threatening boring emptiness to this wildly impatient but also desperate little boy, contained a promise. There was also a certain sort of pleasurably teasing torment which, because it was playful, was just bearable. For him, simply doing the task was too frustrating or else too boring, too flat, too emotionally even. Yet the high curve of suspense, as long as it were neither too high nor too low, seemed to hold him: it seemed to catch and harmonise with his own tortured inability to wait and to tolerate sequencing, but also to modify it by making it into a game.

Musicians and music therapists describe a particular dynamic shape in time, for example ta-ra-ra-BOOM-de-ay, as anacrusis. Perhaps Samuel was having a rudimentary experience of that nature. Bion wrote that we have to learn to modify reality, not to evade it. But perhaps reality sometimes has also to be modifiable by us and even to modify itself. Animate, living objects are constantly both self-modifying and being modified by the infant. The typically developing baby has experiences of reality as both unmodifiable and modifiable. There is some evidence to suggest that Samuel's autism was present in early infancy. His difficulties with attention span and eye contact, which may have been constitutional, seem to have been accompanied by a vast impatience with the otherness of the world. I suspect that all these factors together – and they are certainly extremely difficult to separate out – may have left him closed to the ordinary modulating and regulating life experiences which enable cognitive and emotional development to go forward. Extremely early onset can set the child with autism on an ever more divergent path of development. A child with less severe autism may allow a therapist to approach such anxieties and intolerances via interpretation, but I learned that my verbal interpretations often needed to be accompanied by other activities when Samuel was functioning at very early, sometimes just post-natal developmental levels, and in very desperate states.

Sometimes the therapist may need to hold out strongly for non-autistic, non-ritualistic ways of calming down. Subsequent to the early period of Samuel's rejection of me, there came a period when he would seek my lap as a place of refuge from his agitations or frustrations, and even make a lot of very close eye contact while he was there. He was, however, a very sensual child, and as time progressed I began to feel that, as he was now sufficiently interested in face-to-face contact to be willing to accept it from a few feet instead of a few inches, he should be able to begin to use a small chair which I drew up next to mine. It took about six months to persuade him to use it! He felt rejected at first, and, as so many of these children do, tended to retreat to autism. I found I had to function as a sort of traffic policewoman: on the one hand, stopping his physical intrusions; on the other, beckoning him, at the same instant, to the chair, while my voice suggested that we could have a 'talk'. He had begun by then to engage and to enjoy playful proto-conversation, but he seemed to have no idea that he could do the same thing at a slight distance. (Typically developing infants learn to extend the distance at which they can make face-to-face contact

in the early months of life [Papousek and Papousek 1975].) In a way, by beginning to refuse to offer my lap, I was addressing an activity which was in the
process of becoming a disorder, with the accompanying danger of leading on to
more deviant behaviour (and tertiary disorder?). By deviant, I mean that the
normal infant's desire for the caregiver's lap can, in the autistic child, become
solidified and embedded into something which may, in these often highly
sensual children, become intrusive and anti-social. It can also become anti-
developmental and stand in the way of other important achievements such as
speech. In offering the chair and the talk, I was addressing the deficit or developmental delay in his understanding that more distant contact was still contact
of a kind and pleasurable. In other words, I was introducing the concept that
frustration need not imply that alternative forms of living were unavailable. I do
not mean to imply that frustration on its own was not important also for
Samuel's development, nor that I saw my task as a placation of his intolerance. I
mean that at some moments, when his desperation and despair were very great
and when he could not conceive of survival without recourse to autism, then I
had to ensure that he understood that there was an alternative.

Repetitive behaviours as forms of deviant development (or tertiary disorder?)

Repetitive behaviours are not simply linked with disorders of regulation. There
are motives for, and consequences of, such activities. Can psychotherapists' felt
perceptions in the counter-transference, when we sit for long enough with such
children, teach us anything about the rituals? Deficit requires repair, but what
do we do about disorder? And what if something more than disorder is
involved? The problem is that, as the child grows older, these 'bad habits'
become more and more ingrained, more and more a way of life, and may
contribute to autism as a chronic condition. Then, 'persistent' and 'permanent'
labels of 'persistent vegetative state' seem almost appropriate. The chronicity
can make the child even more unreachable, partly because normal development
is interfered with by the persistence of this symptom, but partly also because the
rituals gather to themselves more and more motivations, both normal and
pathological.

Motivations and processes involved in repetitive behaviours

Needs and ordinary motivations: do people with autism need their rituals?

Those of us who started working with these children psychoanalytically in the
1960s had to make use of what we had in the theory. We tended to suppose at
first that the child's autistic rituals arose as a means of defending against anxiety,
which of course is sometimes true (see Reid, this volume: Chapter 7). But the
nature of autism, and its difference from neurosis and psychosis, made some

psychoanalytic authors rethink the over-generalisation of this model. Meltzer *et al.* (1975) pointed out that the rituals in autism were used in a far more primitive way than rituals in obsessional neurosis, and they rejected the model of defence against anxiety. They thought something much deeper was going on, and recommended that the therapist mobilise the suspended attention of the child to bring it back into contact. Tustin (1981a) referred to evasive or avoidant reactions, but preferred the term 'protective manoeuvre' to that of defence (50). She felt that the rituals needed to be tactfully discouraged. Both Tustin and Meltzer refer to primal or catastrophic depression. We have found only a few patients with that type of 'black hole' depression. Depression, like the regulatory problems around positive excitement described above, is profoundly different from anxiety. Although not all the patients described in this book are suffering from a hidden depression, they do all suffer from deficits in using ways of getting ordinary psychological needs met, for example the need for pleasurable social engagement, the need to feel safe, the need to communicate. Unfortunately, the rituals begin, however inadequately, to offer a partial fulfilment of such needs. This may be one reason why autistic rituals are so difficult to shift: not because they are defensive, but because they are protective; they offer, however inadequately, just enough rewards. Cigarette smoking provides no nourishment, but, addiction aside, it satisfies a universal need to put something in the mouth. Tustin pointed out that the autistic object was used to keep out stimuli, but we need to add, it also brings something *in* – and we ignore the latter element at our peril. We cannot remove the child's ritual without providing something – usually very quickly – in its place. Robbie, an autistic patient, dreamed he was hanging from a cliff by a piece of grass. He had a repetitive ritual of touching walls, which he later explained, when he had recovered somewhat, was to see 'if the walls were still there'. Later he described a lifeline which was pulling him out of a very deep well. A lifeline is not a defence against anxiety, because endlessly falling or drowning is not the natural state of a person. Until I reached him with the lifeline of intensive treatment, he had to make do with the ritual wall-checking. Dry land, stable earth beneath our feet and firm walls around us are what we expect, and limited securities and equilibriums, gained from slipping into old familiar habits, may be better than nothing. (Guimaraes Filho has suggested that ritualistic preoccupations with 'autistic objects' [Tustin 1980] can be seen as something similar to a form of imprinting gone wrong at very early sensitive periods [1996]).

Sometimes the children behave as though they love their ritualistic objects, or admire them. When Samuel looked at his reflection in the mirror, he sometimes gazed with utter love or wondrous admiration. This seemed better than his previous hypnotic preoccupation with running water, because he was showing exploratory curiosity, and a new and positive interest in his own being. In other cases, however, it often seems as though ordinary attachment processes have gone horribly awry. The child may be attached to his autistic object for social needs, for comfort and a secure base. Also, it may begin to be used in the service of meeting some ordinary sexual needs.

Ordinary secondary motivations

Difficult issues are involved when we come to distinguish between the original causes or motives for the rituals, and the later uses to which the rituals may be put. They may be used in quite non-autistic ways, socially related ways, e.g. to express aggression by using them to provoke, irritate, hurt or disappoint another. Ordinary psychological defences and protective manoeuvres may contribute to the causation of the ritual at any particular moment (see Chapter 7 for a discussion of defensive protective reasons having a possible more primary function).

Deviance continued: addiction to the rituals

Tustin's (1980) concept of the autistic object was a revelation to psychoanalytic clinicians trying to find meaning in the repetitive rituals of their autistic patients. She showed that such objects were not full of symbolic meanings relating to live human figures: rather they were used *instead* of such figures to shut meaning and life out. It is interesting how much is implied in Kanner's description of rituals as the result of an 'anxiously obsessive desire for sameness'. At some moments, the rituals may indeed be carried out anxiously; at others, they are carried out in a rather lazy, comfortable, even complacent manner; and sometimes they seem quite desultory, not even comforting. The ritual goes on, although there seems to be no obvious motivation for it at all. Dawson and Lewy's (1989) research underlined the point that children with autism do not get bored and seek novelty. The normal human mind gets bored with sameness; we cannot stare at any object, especially something as over-familiar as our own hand, without becoming restless for new visual input. At least the faces of other people do unpredictable things: the mouth moves, the jaw works, eyes gleam and dull, constantly surprising us. This is one reason why we, and normal infants, can enjoy examining them. The spun wheels of a toy car are not used by the autistic child to send it off travelling across the room – they go nowhere. Hands stared at don't talk, neither do they talk back. Yet these children do seem to get what Reid calls 'stuck' to these objects (Bick [1968] termed these 'adhesive relationships'). When you are interacting with living human objects they are not perfect mirrors; they talk back, move, surprise; by definition you cannot easily get stuck. Autistic objects are dead ends and, while the child's original motive for turning to the object may gradually fade, the melodyless behaviour lingers on. The child may possibly turn to the ritual in a defensive way, but as he continues with it, it may lose that function and run on and on, because it does not get turned off. Frith (1989) says these children lack a switching-off mechanism. Why does the ritual not get switched off? Can we help these children to learn to switch it off and switch on to something else? The therapist needs to be highly alert to her own feelings of boredom in the counter-transference, not necessarily because the child, too, is aware of becoming bored by the activity (although sometimes that is the case) but because he may be bored, but not know that he is bored, or, if he does, he may not know how to stop. The activity becomes, at its most minimalistic, simply a way to keep on going.

My experience with my patient Robbie suggested that a particular repetitive preoccupation could begin as a way of managing some state of disturbance or of emptiness, or, sometime later in his treatment, even as an object of genuinely fresh interest. But the fuel which afterwards kept it going was neither the disturbance nor the emptiness nor the novel interest. It was something else. Like bronze, the rituals had a way of keeping their shape even after the cast is removed. Once the mould is cast, the binding agents may be of a different order altogether and not amenable to being analysed away by simple explanatory interpretations referring to whatever causal agent may have first set the activity in motion. The repetitive activities at times act like a drug – they have a terrible pull and power. I had to remember not to use particular words which could push Robbie over into the gluey mental world of his ritualistic talk. It was like walking on marshy ground: I had to try to keep to the tussocks. If I slipped, we were both lost in the swamp. His rituals had a pull like the power of the force of gravity, or like huge suckers. I had to confront this force before it took hold. In addition, lazy desultoriness and stickiness could move on to strange excitements.

Strange excitements as a *consequence* of repetitive behaviours: tertiary autism?

We have written elsewhere in this volume (Chapters 1, 2 and 5) about the particular importance of the use of feelings aroused in the counter-transference in understanding these children. There is a further reason why an emotive clinician's language is needed to give an accurate description. It has to do with the clinician's perceptions of the qualitative nature of the rituals themselves at certain moments: that is, the perception of some disturbing qualities which occasionally become attached to the rituals. There are times when abnormal excitements, thrills, frenzies, and even sexual arousal may attach themselves to the rituals and may play a large part in their perpetuation. It is important to remember that a young person with autism, who has little connection to the outside world of human relationships, may be hit particularly hard, for example, by the arrival of puberty and of greater sexual feeling. He may feel rather like a car with an engine revving frantically but with no clutch to transmit the power to the wheels and so move it forward. What happens then to the torrent of sexual feeling? The ordinary outlets of interpersonal relations, and the usual adolescent peer group flirtations, gossip, and sexual experimentation are unavailable. It seems as though a river of energy and feeling is dammed up, and must turn on itself in whirlpools, eddies and strange currents, and even, in places, spread too far afield where it rests eventually in stagnant pools.

Kanner (1943) referred to the fact that certain actions and rhythmic movements were accompanied by an ecstatic fervour which strongly indicated the presence of masturbatory gratification, but this observation has, to my knowledge, never appeared again in the psychiatric literature on autism. Psychoanalysts like Tustin (1981a) and Meltzer *et al.* (1975) did comment on the fetishistic quality of the play with some toys or objects. Robbie, in anxious moments, could lick the inside of his lower lip apparently for purposes of self-soothing; but at other times he gave himself over to it, he licked it with a highly sensual pleasure, and the expression on his face at such moments was unpleasantly lascivious and somehow triumphant.

The understanding of abnormal sexual acts, or fantasies with abnormal sexual content, has a long history in psychoanalysis. The understanding, however, that abnormal fantasies may express themselves more indirectly, not through the content but through the form of verbal presentation, is a relatively recent formulation. Joseph (1982) called it 'chuntering'. She was discussing adult borderline psychotic patients, but her work also applied to other sorts of patients: she showed the strange states of excitement some of her patients got into when they appeared to be talking about depression. Other features and phantasies, however, revealed that their repetitive complaining conversations, especially if they could get her to join in, were producing excitement, even sexual excitement for them. I had to learn to become very alert to the way Robbie's repetitive, apparently anxious and concerned conversations could so easily shift into states of high sexual excitement, especially if I was too slow to see the warning signs. For example, he would occasionally arrive in a clearly agitated state, telling me that someone at work had shouted at him. He would repeat this over and over. By now we both understood that he was not simply telling an upsetting and frightening story, he was also 'turned on' in a sexual way by the experience and the idea of someone being angry with him. He was both frightened and excited, or, to be precise, he was frightened/excited. Sometimes he even had an erection when he repeated the story again and again. But it was not simply the content of the story or the idea that was disturbing and exciting him, it was also the way in which he was living out a type of aggressive sexual phantasy in the telling of it to me. He would be half glaring, a little frightened of me, but also frenzied and thrilled by the way his repetitions were penetrating my mind. After all, Robbie had no ordinary outlets for sexuality – penetrating voices in his ears and high emotional registers seemed to provide necessary excitements but no real release. It was necessary to show him that although it was true that he was in part trying desperately to communicate his upset, he was not simply desperate, and he was by no means simply engaged in a straightforward communication. He was, instead, engaged in an apparently normal conversation which turned out to be designed both to excite and enrage the listener, so that Robbie could get the original irritability to begin all over again in them. If I missed the excitement and simply betrayed irritation, a highly sensual grin would show me I had gone wrong and had played my part in escalating the process into a game of mutual verbal over-stimulation.

It was also important to note when he himself enjoyed talking to me in an ordinary way. And, just as it was important to show him when he had clearly sensed my distaste for the bizarre quality of the talk and my consequent dislike of it and even of him at such moments, it was also vital to show him that he felt I liked him much better when he made an effort to speak to me in a straightforward way. This treatment has been described at length elsewhere (Alvarez 1992a). Now, when I read my earlier discussion in this chapter of the ways in which, a few years later, I tried to help Samuel, a much younger patient, to find forms of exciting and lively engagement with me, as distinct from his ritualistic or provocative activities, I think Robbie, too, needed to be offered more options. My refusal to collude with him produced sanity, but often only a dulled-down sanity. More recently I have tried to help him too, to discover a third, more lively option – with some considerable success. I have tried to keep the tempo and loudness of our conversations up and not let it flag. He seems to love keeping up.

For a more detailed discussion of ritualistic autistic language, see the chapters in this volume by Reid, Rhode, Youell, and Klauber.

Personality: normal, disordered and deviant

I suggested at the beginning of this chapter that it may be useful to distinguish between primary and secondary autism. Primary autism may involve original or very early sensitivities or deficits; secondary autism may refer to the symptoms and behaviours which the child develops to cope with his sensitivities or deficits. Both may be tractable to treatment. The secondary autism, however, seems to be particularly influenced by factors in the child's personality, particularly the balance between the strength of the intact, non-autistic part, as opposed to the autistic part of the personality. People with autism are more than a collection of symptoms – they are always mysterious, often fascinating and certainly challenging. But each has their own unique personality, needs, preferences, will and demands, and these deserve as much study as the symptoms themselves. Indeed they often amplify and colour the symptoms. The floppy, passive autistic child may be as he is partly for constitutional or other reasons, but he may sometimes use his natural passivity or apathy for other more ordinary motives. As a teacher of one of these children said of one very passive child, 'Sometimes he is very knowing'. The aloof child with his jaw or shoulder set against contact may find contact difficult and unbearable – again for mysterious reasons – but anger, disappointment and despair may feed these reactions against psychologically life-giving social engagement. Strength of character and will can feed the symptoms, but it can also change sides and work on the side of normal engagement with the real world.

The interactions between illness and personality are not always easy to sort out. Some children seem to be autistic out of a helplessness which they cannot change without assistance; others seem to prefer their autism because they dislike the alternative; others seem, quite simply, to be happy in their autism and be all too comfortably ensconced in it. Samuel's impatience, excitement and difficulty in staying with an interesting (for him) new activity, may have been in part genetic. However, he also seemed to feel that he really should not have to wait. On the first occasion when his mother refused to allow him to bring crisps into his session with me, he backed away across the waiting room, not in anger but in utter disbelief. He also paid a great deal more visual attention both to her and to me on that occasion than ever before, when crisps had ruled! Such episodes raise the question of character and will as well as of personality.

Behaviour disorder in autism: are there sometimes elements of personality disorder?

Demanding, greedy behaviour, resistance to discipline, resistance to toileting, wild running away, climbing, sexualised intrusiveness – all such behaviours may lead, in some children, to ever greater disorder and eventual deviance as the years go by: the processes of development may become even more skewed. In a small group of children there is sometimes a certain sort of chilling quality in their gaze: unlike those who appear to see through people, these regard other people with a clear but cold eye. Such persons may give up the worst of their autistic symptoms, but character problems in the form of an almost psychopathic lack of warmth, or of demanding and intrusive behaviour, may remain. Major alterations in character formation may require many years of treatment, difficult but not impossible to provide in the National Health Service. It is very much worth the effort where it can reduce heavy pressures on families and carers, and help the patients themselves to learn to become more friendly and to feel more likeable. They begin to feel that they can win attention, affection and liking through less forceful methods. Left untreated, features of personality disorder and character formation can be very worrying in adulthood – another argument for the importance of early interventions which take account of the whole of the person with autism.

Summary

This chapter draws attention to some factors additional to deficit, which may enhance or reduce the features of autism. The factors include:

1 Primary disorders of arousal, sensitivity and regulation;
2 Secondary disorders such as repetitive behaviours (these latter may be fuelled by

   (a) normal needs and motivations, including defensive and projective processes;
   (b) addictive processes; or
   (c) strange excitements, and

3 Personality.

I have discussed how some of these elements may contribute to tertiary disorders and deviance. I have also tried to show how psychotherapy addresses the ways in which any of these factors acts to enhance either the autistic or the normal non-autistic part of the person with autism. Subsequent chapters will provide much more detailed examples of the often dramatic struggle between the two.

6 Echo or answer?

The move towards ordinary speech in three children with autistic spectrum disorder

Maria Rhode

In her recollections of her autistic childhood, Donna Williams describes the experience of being echolalic:

> 'What do you think you're doing?' came the voice. Knowing I must respond in order to get rid of this annoyance, I would compromise, repeating 'What do you think you're doing?' addressed to no-one in particular. 'Don't repeat everything I say,' scolded the voice. Sensing a need to respond, I'd reply, 'Don't repeat everything I say.'
>
> (Williams 1992: 3–4)

Later, she writes:

> mirroring, as with the matching of objects, was my way of saying: 'Look, I can relate. I can make that noise, too.' ... echolalic children ... in their own way ... are trying desperately to reach out and show they can relate, if only as mirrors.
>
> (Williams 1992: 188)

Framing a reply, on the other hand, would entail understanding the meaning of what was said, and 'I was too happy losing myself to want to be dragged back by ... understanding'.

Ellen Stockdale-Wolfe, a psychologist who has described 'from inside' the experience of being autistic, experienced mental auditory and visual 'echoes' of other people's words and actions (Stockdale-Wolfe 1993). Oliver Sacks recounts how a Parkinsonian patient responded to L-Dopa by

> seeing tiny figures and faces all around her, and hearing voices, which suddenly appeared and disappeared in all parts of the room; she also became uncontrollably echolalic, repeating anything one said to her in a shrill screaming voice hundreds or thousands of times in succession. Haunted by hallucinations and echoing indefinitely to external stimuli,

Mrs I. gave the impression of a hollow, untenanted, ghost-filled house, as if she herself had been 'dispossessed' by echoes and ghosts.

(Sacks 1976: 224–6)

Echolalia is a typical feature of autistic disorders, though it does not occur in all children with autism. It can be a stage in their development of more normal speech. Even when echolalia as such is not present, children with autism often speak in a flat voice or a sing-song, or repetitively recite stories (Shulman 1997). Others seem preoccupied with echoes or piece together their utterances from bits of songs or videos. They lack a voice of their own (Reid, this volume: Chapter 7).

This lack of a voice of their own seems to be part of their lack of a sense of identity. Psychoanalytic writers have tried to understand this. Meltzer (1975a) has written of echolalia as an example of the mimicry characteristic of children with autism. Bick suggested that they behaved as though stuck to the surface of another person, with whom they could therefore feel identical (Bick 1968). Tustin (1972: 68) wrote: 'other people's words may be repeatedly echoed so that the delusion is maintained that these "not-me" words are part of the subject's own mouth and have thus become "me"'.

Psychoanalysts from Freud onwards have described the mysterious process of identification, by means of which someone may behave as though they really were the other person with whom they are identified (Freud 1905, 1917, 1919; Klein 1946, 1955, 1961; Bick 1968; Meltzer 1975b; Rey 1988; Tustin 1994). This may occur in many different ways and for many different motives, and can be helpful or detrimental to development. When normal development is not impeded, the good qualities of role models can be internalised so that they become an integral part of the child's own personality rather than something simply to be imitated.

Children with echolalia seem to have got stuck at a stage (a normal stepping-stone) where the identification with the voice of important people is superficial, unprocessed and undigested. The sensory qualities of the voice may be attended to rather than the meaning of what is said (S. Klein 1980). In more ordinary forms of identification with the voice of reproving or encouraging adults, mimicry has given way to something more digested in which the authentic voice of the child can be heard. A mechanical directive such as 'don't touch' becomes a more reflective 'mustn't touch'. This development implies a degree of understanding which may then be available for generalisation to other similar situations (what Bion [1962] called 'learning from experience').

The three children described in this chapter shared a particular preoccupation, an anxiety about damage which seemed to contribute to a difficulty in coming alive and in finding a voice of their own. The echolalic speech, when attended to closely, gradually yielded clues as to the kind of anxieties which seemed to inhibit more normal speech. As the therapist and child began to understand together what these anxieties were about, the echolalia began to give way to more ordinary forms of communication. (Obviously, many other factors, known and unknown, affect the development of echolalia. This chapter addresses only one element in the construction of this very complex symptom.)

Jonathan: the broken mirror

This seven-year-old boy had come to therapy producing words with blurred outlines that were difficult to recognise as separate units. Sometimes his blurred speech would be interspersed with clear statements, which generally sounded like accurate imitations of adults he knew. Occasional instances of straightforward echolalia occurred during the early months of therapy: he echoed my words whenever they were concerned with something frightening, particularly with the loss of something from his mouth such as a sweet. Tustin (1972) has described what a catastrophe it can be for children with autism to realise that the sensation-providing feeding object is not part of their own mouth.

Quite soon this pattern of speech was replaced by frenetic, anxiety-saturated outpourings (see Youell, this volume: Chapter 13). Although the content of these outpourings was very evocative, I had to become used to being unable to comment on it: Jonathan did not let me get a word in edgeways. Instead, I focused on the emotional experiences that his mode of speech conveyed so vividly: overwhelming anxiety; everything in a whirl; complete obliteration. When most of our time had been used for work on the feelings that were being communicated, Jonathan might then be able to respond positively when I asked him, 'Are you ready to think about this now?' For quite a long time, however, my suggestions would get woven into the fabric of one of his later productions: the boundaries between us remained blurred, and the experience of chaos he associated with being separate was presumably kept at bay. Working with him was like being in a hall of mirrors, so that I often doubted whether my thoughts about him were well founded or delusional. If I thought that together we had managed to recognise a pattern that made sense, he would undermine this by saying, 'You thought of that.'

The notion of shared reality, of an agreed order, could not be taken for granted. Often Jonathan turned the room upside down, and then triumphantly asserted that this was the right order of things. 'Adults can make babies', he said, 'but I can make an adult'. On the other hand, when communication did feel possible, his relief was immediately followed by alarm. It was as though he had won through against all odds to a position of getting me to collude against the world, rather than feeling that agreement could be based on shared experience.

The echo in the ghost-house

On one occasion Jonathan went on a rampage that turned the room upside down, without making his usual immediate assertion that this was a superior alternative order. Instead, he found the resources to address the chaos. 'There's nothing there', he said; 'just an echo'. Almost at once, however, this seemed to overwhelm him. His eyes became unfocused, and took on the vacant look that had earlier been characteristic of him and that rarely appeared now. He said, 'I'm in the ghost house'.

Children in therapy can feel about the room as they do about an imagined maternal figure (Klein 1932, 1961). A room, for any of us, can feel full of possibility, potentiality, a sense of being fully lived in, furnished with comforting presences. At other moments of depression, it may seem bleak, sinister or simply hollow.

For Jonathan, an echo meant there was no answering life in the room. Instead of an answer, he found echoes. Instead of living inhabitants or comforting presences, he found ghosts. This incident made me wonder whether his echolalia was an expression of these ghostly echoes: as though the voice coming out of his own mouth were the same as the ghostly voices he found in the room.

The origin of the ghosts: life-and-death rivalries

Jonathan did not behave as though he felt there was a place for him: it was as though all available space were filled up with something else. He did not seem to believe he could assert his presence constructively. The only alternatives appeared to be killing or being killed in the battle for space. In Tustin's words, 'such children feel in competition with a swarm of rivalrous sucklings who threaten to crowd them out or crush them to death' (Tustin 1990: 49). In contrast, Klein (1961) related a patient's pleasure in music to the notion that the musical harmonies represented harmonious relationships between the mother's children.

Mother and brother

We gradually learned that Jonathan's particular tragedy arose from the mistaken belief that anything he could have must be stolen from a sibling who was not just the mother's child, but an essential, intertwined component of her very being. Getting anything for himself meant destroying both mother and brother. It also meant destroying mother's capacity for lively reflection about him.

He told me over and over again about the Disney cartoon of Robin Hood. Bad Prince John, the usurper of his brother's kingdom, was drawn breaking a mirror that belonged to a baby snake. The resulting fragments were arranged over the baby's head as though they were thoughts within a speech-bubble. Sir Hiss, Prince John's snake counsellor, reproached the prince: 'You broke your mother's mirror!'

In the many repetitions of this story, Jonathan referred interchangeably to 'your mother's mirror' and 'your brother's mirror'. The rhyming words no doubt made it easier for him to express the idea that mother and brother were indistinguishable. This implies that if the child himself acquires anything, it must be by usurping the brother's position. The right order of things is overthrown, and the mother's capacity to see and reflect her baby is shattered (the mirror). The baby is then in no position to see himself accurately and to learn to think properly (the broken fragments of mirror above the baby's head).

Jonathan's torrent of stories had the dual effect of communicating to me his overwhelming anxiety and of effectively shutting me out, so that I could not impinge on him as a separate person. His device of taking up any comment of mine that did get through and weaving it into his own 'web' perpetuated the blurring of boundaries between himself and others that had earlier been expressed by his blurring of words. When this confusional entanglement (Tustin 1981a) diminished, Jonathan was faced with the fear that his active presence had a disastrous effect on the maternal figure ('I'm in the ghost house'). This disaster was experienced in terms of eliminating a brother whose presence was felt to be wiping him out in the first place. It is interesting that a schizophrenic patient treated by Segal (1950) for a time experienced a mental echo, which turned out to be the internal mocking voice of dead father figures whom he felt he was triumphing over by getting better.

Britton (1995) has suggested that patients whose primitive, non-verbal communications were not received by the mother, or may not have been understandable because they were too faint or distorted (Alvarez, this volume: Chapter 4) may ascribe the blocking of these communications to the 'third party' in the triangle of mother, father and child, while remaining attached to the mother in order to survive. Similarly, children with autism may not realise that the person they are with may be mentally preoccupied: instead, they can mistakenly feel that a physical obstacle is blocking their pre-verbal communications (Rhode 1995).

Jonathan's mirror drawing suggests that the 'third party' whose presence is felt to have such disastrous consequences may sometimes be a sibling rather than the father. When this third party is felt to be usurped, the mother-figure's reflective function is damaged (the broken mirror) and so is the child's capacity for thought. Britton (1989) has shown how the capacity for thought depends on the developing child's capacity to see things from the point of view of care-giving adults who support each other (prototypically, the parental couple) as well as from his own. When this goes wrong, it is as though the child had not been able to make sense of seeing a live mother talking with a live father or sibling, and to learn that this is partly how meanings get made.

We learned that Jonathan's solution was to give up his own separate identity, which he supposed to be so damaging, and to speak instead in the ghost-voice of the imagined legitimate child he felt he had eliminated. This is similar to Freud's descriptions (1917, 1919) of people who identify with someone they are frightened of having damaged. This can serve to avoid any feelings of guilt, however unrealistic, and also to maintain some kind of contact with an important person who might otherwise be feared to be lost (Rey 1988). When Jonathan was so filled up with someone else's identity, there was only room for him to speak in the echo-voice of the supposedly damaged sibling rather than in his own. If I did manage to understand his communications, he would become anxious about having 'got through', that is, about having eliminated his supposed rivals. He would then retreat from owning his feelings ('you thought of that'), leaving me wondering who was echoing whom in a hall of mirrors.

This oscillation between anxiety and guilt, between feeling dispossessed and feeling a usurper, meant that Jonathan found progress difficult to maintain. It took a long time before he could own his good capacities and loving feelings, and speak consistently in his own voice.

Anthony: victim or giant

Unlike Jonathan, this highly intelligent, extremely withdrawn six year-old boy was not echolalic, but he was preoccupied with echoes. His solution was the obverse of Jonathan's: Anthony embraced the identification with a powerful, damaging figure whose voice he adopted.

In the stairwell on the way to the therapy room, he vocalised and listened for the echo, as though, like Jonathan, he wondered whether there was just an empty echo, or an alive, transforming presence. He took virtually no notice of anything I said, but he did hum occasional snatches of songs, or repeated fragments of what sounded like nursery rhymes or videos. His voice sounded as though he were imitating somebody else: he had a repertory of different voices, including a deep, gruff voice saying 'naughty child'. This voice on one occasion said 'fee, fie, fo, fum'. Anthony joined in when I completed the rhyme, and listened when I spoke about the scary giant who wanted to eat Jack for climbing the beanstalk. Indeed, he spent much of his time standing on the desk by the window, being a giant looking down on me, and trying to arouse jealous curiosity in passers-by. He repeated 'jealous' when I talked about this, but mostly he muttered about Super-Ted, a cartoon character who could fly and rescue people. Overtly, he was taking up an all-powerful position. In fact, his balance was extremely precarious, and I had to be constantly alert to make sure that he did not fall. While standing by the window, he sometimes used the cord of the blind to saw painfully at his mouth until I stopped him: both horizontally, as though he were cutting the opening into his face, and vertically, as though cutting his face in two down the midline.

Although initially he made no direct contact, Anthony enacted dramatically his terror of falling. He repeatedly slid head-first off the desk onto an armchair, demonstrating that he could get over the gap between them. As he did so, he clutched at the drawstring cord at his waist and pulled his mouth into a painfully distorted shape. He looked tortured, and in turn inflicted tortures on the dolls, who were dismembered, thrown through the air and clamped in the opening of the toy-box; and he cut deep, ugly gashes in the fairly thick sides of a plastic beaker.

I understood Anthony's cruelty as an identification with the cruel giant. Like Jonathan, he was caught in a false dilemma: whether to suffer obliteration, or to make his presence felt by identifying with an implacable, murderous figure. Though he often chose the second course, the possible consequences deeply distressed him. Before the first holiday break, he drew the curtains, darkening the room. 'Dark, dark, dark', he said. 'No more lady, never, never, never'. The intensity of feeling was overwhelming. When Anthony did feel driven to speak, he spoke in the words of King Lear mourning Cordelia.

While his hopes were still faint, the solution was to be the powerful giant. Anthony repeatedly enacted the part of the giant lying hidden under the couch: a menacing voice being the only sign of his presence. On one occasion, however, he retired under the couch clutching his genitals. I suggested he might need to make sure they would remain part of him, so he went under the couch to be a hidden giant making frightening noises. He promptly emerged from his hiding place: looking straight at me, he said, 'Will-ll-ll-lly noise'. His voice was more resonant than usual, and he moved his tongue vigorously from side to side in his mouth.

Anthony was emphasising the strength of his voice and the potent movement of his tongue in his mouth as though these were attributes of the giant he was being when he hid under the couch. (In contrast, Jonathan's mouth when he was echolalic was occupied by the ghost-voices of supposedly damaged siblings.) Meltzer (1986) has written of the mouth as a 'theatre for the genera-tion of meaning'. A familiar example would be babies who explore objects by mouthing them; this kind of activity can be significant in language development (see Bartram, this volume: Chapter 9). Anthony's communication was still very strange: in reality, voices and words are not 'willy noises'. Nonetheless, he was using real words, linked to our shared experience. This moment became part of a shared language between us. Whenever I said something about the scary giant, or about Anthony's need for a place of his own, he would respond: 'Will-ll-ll-lly noise' as if to remind us both.

The development of a strong voice

Holiday breaks were always very disturbing for Anthony. In the run-up to one, he temporarily took a big step backwards, and reverted to listening for the echo in the stairwell, something he had not done for many months. In the room, he stood high above me on the desk, speaking in a robotic computer voice: 'Those – answers – are – all – correct. You – are – a – GENIUS'. I suggested that before a holiday, he could not trust that I would be strong enough to help him, as though no-one and nothing, material or mental, could be strong enough to withstand his approaches. I said that perhaps he could not believe that we could each have a voice, as well as a complete body; I reminded him how he had once demonstrated that we both had hands by clapping his hands together with mine and saying 'Gimme five!' He turned to me and responded, 'Gimme five!', speaking in his own voice. Then he came 'down to earth' off the desk, and maintained good contact for the rest of the session.

Two weeks later, he held two beakers together, rim-to-rim, and pulled them suddenly apart. He filled each one in turn, and showed me that they held water properly, unlike the plastic beaker into which he had cut gashes and which now leaked. He said, 'Lady crying', and put the plastic beaker inside the dolls' house, precariously balanced between table and chair. I said he was showing me how important it was that he and I should both be all right when we were separate: we both needed to be able to hold things inside, like the beakers he had pulled apart, and not to be cut or leaky or crying.

Anthony verified that the beakers were full by vocalising into them without eliciting an echo; then he took a drink from one of them, and gave me the other. I said, 'One for Anthony, one for Mrs Rhode', and he responded, 'Anthony and Mrs Rhode'. It was the end of the session, and he growled ominously in the giant's voice. In the following session, the last before the holiday, he again filled a beaker for himself and one for me, and found a little sponge for each. That day, he managed to sustain a verbal interchange: he answered appropriately in his own voice, and volunteered his summary of the way I had coloured in the holiday chart: 'Red for clinic, green for holiday'.

Most of the time, Anthony tried to keep himself and me safe by being a giant under the couch or a genius high above me, instead of playing on the floor like the child that he was. His identity was not yet well founded, since his internalised mother-figure (represented by the plastic beaker on which he had visited his own painful experiences) was leaky ('lady crying') and so could not support him and stop him from falling. On the other hand, when we could both be separate and intact (as in 'gimme five' and the two full cups each with a sponge) the echo disappeared and Anthony could speak in his own voice.

Daniel: coming out of 'Wonderland'

This nine year-old boy exhibited varying types of echolalia in different contexts as his therapy progressed. Like Anthony, he developed his own identity as his trust in the survival of a firm, receptive person increased.

Daniel came from an extremely deprived background. His mother was affectionate but extremely fragile, and subject to unpredictable episodes of extreme violence. He conformed to the criteria for autism of DSM-IV in that he was reported not to be developing normally before the age of two. His teachers at a school for children with severe learning difficulties referred him for assessment when he was nine: they had recognised that he showed all the symptoms on the 'Is this Autism?' checklist. He was echolalic and was felt to be ineducable. Any change or interference produced a major tantrum, in which he tore his clothes or the wallpaper, and bit his hand, which had become badly scarred. He was preoccupied with shapes, and obsessively drew houses, though he could not draw a person. On the other hand, he had made great progress with toilet training since settling at school, and he inspired enormous affection in his teachers, as he has in me.

From the beginning of his assessment and throughout his first year of once-weekly therapy, Daniel attempted to relate and to communicate, but always under threat from an invisible presence in the corner, which he looked at sideways with a terrified expression. After his second session, he looked into a recess and said 'Monster'. Often when he spoke, it was softly or indistinctly. Asking him to explain was no use, but if I could guess what he meant, his speech became clear. For instance, very early on he hummed something indistinct out of which emerged words that sounded like 'Cruella deVille'. When I talked about the horrible, cruel lady who wanted to kill puppies so that she could have their skins, and how difficult it was for him to be sure that I would not be like that, he sang, 'Cruella deVille, Cruella deVille', quite clearly, with one 'Daniella deVille' interspersed among the Cruellas. This suggested that he was confused between a bad aspect of himself and frightening figures in external reality.

In his first assessment session, when I had met him together with his teachers and a female colleague, he was preoccupied with making W shapes ('double-you'). When I saw him alone, he talked about 'two Ladies in London'; now that my colleague was gone, he made V-shapes (half-Ws) instead. He took from the dolls' house a dresser with a mirror, and held it up to the right side of his face as he lay on the couch. He then he sucked his left thumb, pressing against his left eye with his fingers, and looked over his right shoulder with a haunted expression, as though expecting to be attacked by the monster in the corner. I explored the possibility that the absence of my colleague (my other half) had stirred a primitive anxiety in him that he, too, might lose his other half (in his case, one half of his body); and spoke to him about feeling that he needed his thumb in his mouth and the pressure of his fingers on his eye in order to be sure that he had a right side and a left side, a right eye and a left eye. Tustin (1981a) and Haag (1985) have described how some children with autism can feel split down the middle of the body when they realise that the feeding mother-figure they depend on is a separate person rather than a part of their own mouth.

Daniel protected himself from the catastrophe of losing half of his body by the device of turning to sensations in his mouth and his eye that he could generate himself (Tustin 1981a). The alternative seemed to be a life-and-death struggle with a Cruella deVille who wanted his skin for herself. Before a holiday break, he misinterpreted the impending separation in those terms: 'Poor mouth. Poor skin'. He had not yet established the idea of a separate nurturing person who could go away and come back. Material from the third term illustrates this as follows:

Daniel brought a little bottle of lemonade along to his session. He tapped on the closed lid of the bottle, emphasising that it was shut. When he unscrewed the lid and drank, a plastic ring remained on the neck of the bottle. He passed this back and forth between the bottle and his mouth. When it was on the neck of the bottle, he showed me that his empty mouth was open in the shape of a hole. When the ring was in his mouth, he looked at the bottle fearfully, as though expecting attack. Once all the lemonade was gone, he threw the bottle into the bin and shrank away from it.

The shut lid of the bottle seemed to represent a frustrating barrier to immediate gratification; Daniel appeared to feel that it was bitten off in the process of drinking. The lid was perhaps also a physical manifestation of a mind unreceptive to his feelings (these two aspects of the frustrating boundary could be teased apart in later work). Tustin (1972, 1990) has described the difficulty in taking things in that may arise in such a situation. Her patients David and Ariadne, like Daniel, felt that they literally 'took' their qualities and accomplishments from parental figures, who were damaged as a consequence and could not provide internal support. This links with Anthony's oscillation between the positions of victim and giant.

Whose words?

Daniel's fear of despoiling me and of inviting retaliation applied to the possession of words as much as to any other desirable quality. This was illustrated during his second year of treatment, when he was coming twice a week.

While repeating some words I had just said to him, he tore shreds of paper off a sheet and put them in his mouth as though he were going to swallow them. This seemed to demonstrate graphically how concretely he experienced internalising my words as having torn them off me.

Some months later, he parted from his escort with an echolalic repetition of my words: 'Let's say goodbye to Sarah'. He then began the session by retaining a mouthful of Coke for a long time without swallowing it, just as he had retained and regurgitated my words without properly assimilating them.

The process by which the mind grows through assimilating nourishment is a mysterious one. Disturbances like those which Daniel showed can have a bearing on learning difficulties in non-autistic children. For instance, a ten year-old anorexic girl recited French verbs while eating sweets out of a bag. Her memory was perfect until all the sweets were gone, after which she could remember nothing. It was as though, like Daniel, she could not know what she had taken in for fear of having depleted the source of nourishment.

Although Daniel did speak communicatively within the sessions, he could not explain himself unless I showed that I could understand something of what he meant. This counteracted his fear of ripping my words off me, and he became able to own them himself, as in the exchange about Cruella deVille. Technically, it can therefore be helpful for the therapist to demonstrate familiarity with nursery rhymes, children's stories, videos and so on: this would not be so necessary with non-autistic children.

After some months of work, echolalic speech occurred only at the beginnings and ends of sessions. For instance, if his escort prompted him, 'Say goodbye to Mrs Rhode', Daniel would turn to me and repeat, 'Say goodbye to Mrs Rhode'. But it was striking that something intermediate between echolalia and true internal speech could now be used to bridge the gap between waiting room and therapy room: he would take my hand and volunteer in a voice that was obviously not his own, 'Let's go to the room'. It was as though by linking hands we formed a 'double-you', with my words coming out of his mouth.

Surviving the tantrum

After a year of once-weekly work, Daniel had learned to read and was forming friendships with other children. However, he still had to be given his own way almost all the time if a major tantrum was to be avoided that would seriously have disrupted the school setting. When his sessions could be increased to twice weekly, he was able to show directly his intolerance of frustration and the resulting aggression. Within the framework of the sessions, he could articulate these complete sentences, spoken in a baby's voice: 'Give – me – that – pen!' 'I – want – it – NOW!' 'I – want – to – bite – you' 'Don't – you – dare – stop – me!' However, when it was time to separate, and fears about possible consequences were no longer counteracted by my physical presence, he reverted to echolalia.

This points up the need for stable people to depend on, who could remain steady in the face of his threats, so that existing as a separate person need not remain confused with being destructive, and he could retain a secure sense of self. This in turn made it possible for such a confused child to be clear about his own contribution to events and relationships, instead of experiencing them purely as a reflection of himself.

For weeks, Daniel worked on establishing that his own face remained steady when he moved his mirror reflection around at dizzying speed. He was differentiating between a self he could experience subjectively and the self reflected in the eyes of an unstable other. The alternative was to become lost in a mad mirror world which he called 'Upside Down at the Clinic.'

These concerns reached a crisis during a week in which a bereavement of my own made me less steady than usual. Daniel enacted being in the mad mirror-world: he held the mirror while spinning round and round in a swivel chair, sucking his thumb and pressing on his eyeball. After repeatedly encouraging him verbally to stop, I moved to hold out my hand towards him. He shouted 'No!', mistakenly fearing that I was attacking him, and threw the mirror to the floor where it broke into tiny pieces. This felt both like a desperate counter-attack and like freeing himself from imprisonment in the 'Upside Down' world.

For the first time, he went on the rampage in the room, much as Jonathan had done. The contents of his box were scattered everywhere, chairs were overturned, blankets and cushions ripped off the couch. This continued in the next session. I experienced vividly the fear that he would create mess faster than I could clear up; that he was too big for me to handle; that we would be lost in chaos together. Before I was able to formulate this, I tried telling him to stop. He obviously – and rightly – took this as a sign of weakness, of my inability to tolerate what he was communicating. He reacted by desperately biting the cushion on a chair; his piercing screams resounded through the clinic after each bite, as though he were the person being bitten. When I managed to talk about the terror of being lost together in a place dominated by destructiveness, and reminded him that we would find his escort afterwards, he calmed down enough to allow me to clear up. He was still sobbing in terror when we found his escort, and recovered very gradually as she and I talked. Finally he gathered himself together, and produced a complete sentence in his own voice: 'I'll be all right'.

Daniel returned the following week noticeably buoyant. He pointed out that there was a separate clock and a light on either side of a door in the passage (compare Anthony's two beakers).

In the room, he sat on the swivel chair and said, 'Alice in Wonderland'. I said that was a strange place where he went when he was frightened, and that perhaps he could try to come out of there. He looked at my watch, which he had been interested in for some while; he had broken a watch of his own which had been a present from someone he loved. He said, 'Pauline's watch!' His pronunciation of this, with a long 'i', made me think there was a pun involved; I asked, 'Do you mean "poor lion's watch"?' He repeated this several times in agreement; then said, 'Lion King'. I suggested that he couldn't believe it was safe to come out of Wonderland and grow up, in case that meant the Daddy dying, as in the story of the Lion King, and me not being strong enough to help, like last week. He looked straight at me, and said several times and with obvious pride, 'Young man'. In the waiting room after this session, he said 'Goodbye' to me in his own voice.

Many oscillations have followed between withdrawal into Wonderland, and tantrums if I asserted my separate existence by saying 'no'. The tantrums were increasingly manageable, and Daniel could begin to envisage growth that was not destructive to a nurturing figure. He no longer swallowed torn-off bits of paper: instead he sucked water from a sponge, and showed me that the sponge was undamaged afterwards.

Tantrums were no longer followed by word-for-word echoing of what I said. Instead, Daniel's echolalia evolved to encompass what sounded like a conversation between three people rather than two. For example, instead of 'asking' for a drink by saying 'Would you like a drink?' as though I were speaking to him, Daniel might ask to walk independently by saying 'Don't hold him on the stairs', as though a third person were talking about him to me. This is a stepping-stone further on the way to owning a wish.

Discussion

Each of these children seemed to feel that having a voice of their own was at someone else's expense. All were acutely sensitive to other people's moods, and to the possibility that they might be responsible for causing damage (Meltzer *et al.* 1975). Bad aspects of themselves were easily felt to invade the outside world (Cecchi 1990), as in Daniel's confusion between Cruella and Daniella deVille. They had no concept of natural, gradual development: instead they oscillated between usurping and being usurped, between helplessness and omnipotence, between losing bits of themselves and snatching bits of other people. Like Tustin's patients David and Ariadne (Tustin 1972, 1990), they did not feel that they acquired capacities by identifying with a nurturing person: instead, their capacities were felt to be concretely 'taken from' others, in a way that reversed their own prior experience of helplessness.

Anthony's material suggests that he felt that having a voice himself meant appropriating it from me. Though he did speak expressively when he was desperate ('no more lady'), this became more solidly established when he could develop a notion of separateness that did not involve damage to either of us (the two cups).

Similarly, Daniel became able to think of himself as a young man after realising that his tantrum did not in the end overwhelm me, and that his escort and I could come together to support him. This helped him to distinguish his own destructiveness when he was frustrated from unpredictable violence in the outside world; to distinguish Daniella deVille from Cruella deVille.

This leads me to speculate on the nature of these children's interest in mirrors and reflections. (Anthony, like Jonathan and Daniel, was fascinated by mirrors, though I have not described any of this material.) As Alvarez (1992a) has emphasised, mechanical mirroring is different from creative transformation. It is important that links are felt to be maintained between the mother and her husband and other children (Britton 1989). This prevents the kind of *folie-à-deux* that Jonathan feared, but without blocking the mother's receptivity to her child. Hamilton (1982) has suggested that when this balance is not achieved, the child may feel trapped in someone else's view of him, like Daniel in Wonderland.

A baby needs to see himself reflected in the mother's eyes as being loveable (Winnicott 1967; Meltzer 1988; Reid 1990), but the three children I have described had not achieved a proper balance between their own place *vis-à-vis* the mother, and whatever precious internal relationships of her own that her behaviour was felt to reflect. They oscillated between feeling that what they encountered in the mother's eyes was nothing to do with them, but merely the manifestation of her own preoccupations and relationships (Meltzer 1988); and feeling on the other hand that they completely displaced anybody else, so that they could find only echoes of themselves in a hall of mirrors, or even vengeful presences in what they perceived as a scene of empty devastation for which they felt entirely responsible.

These three children's material illustrates in different ways the importance of an enduring emotional setting, properly balanced between firmness and receptivity. Within this, new capacities can develop. Without an enduring, balanced setting, different aspects of the self may not be properly integrated (Bion 1950), and may be experienced as conflicting with one another (Bion 1950; E. Rhode 1994: chs 5, 6).

The three children's material shows how the repetition of words can imply many different nuances of emotional relationship. The spectrum extends from simple assertion of identity with another ('say good-bye to Mrs Rhode') through the 'double-you' voice of 'let's go to the room' and relating by matching ('gimme five') to the adoption of a third person's voice talking to the therapist about the child ('don't hold him on the stairs'). This culminates in the genuine internalisation of an emotional experience ('Anthony and Mrs Rhode') which can then be generalised ('red for clinic, green for holiday'). The stages of internalisation parallel Daniel's move from swallowing torn-off scraps of paper to sucking water without damaging the sponge. Instead of getting stuck in conflicts about taking over another person's voice, the children were able to move towards taking it in.

Acknowledgement

I wish to thank Anne Alvarez and Susan Reid for editorial suggestions.

7 Autism and trauma

Autistic Post-Traumatic Developmental Disorder

Susan Reid

The emphasis in this book is on the importance of recognising that each person with autism is a distinct and unique personality. It has become increasingly striking, however, that our patients fall into natural sub-groupings, with shared characteristics. The similarities within sub-groups and the differences between them is of considerable interest: there is of course some overlap. Our clinical attempts to reach these inaccessible children has led to conceptualising sub-groupings, not only on the basis of symptoms, but also including meta-psychological factors based on our experience of the way the children present: these include differences in the emotional responses they evoke in others, and in types of inaccessibility (see Chapter 1). This work on sub-groupings began some ten years ago, and it has been encouraging to discover that others, working within a different conceptual framework, have also been impressed by the existence of sub-groupings (Wing and Attwood 1987; O'Brien 1996). This chapter proposes a sub-group on an axis different from that of Wing's groupings – the sub-group Autistic Post-Traumatic Developmental Disorder. This sub-grouping has emerged from an initial exploration of a similarity in symptoms and presentation which subsequently suggested the possibility of a precipitating factor in the aetiology of autism in this sub-group.

I wish to draw attention to a remarkable similarity between the nature of the symptomatology in a small sub-group of children with autism and the symptomatology of Post-Traumatic Stress Disorder in children who are not autistic. I am hypothesising that an experience of trauma in the first two years of life may be a precipitating factor in the development of autism in this sub-group. Clinical experience seems to suggest that this factor may have combined with a biological or genetic predisposition in the infant which the traumatising event has then served to activate. It is clear that many other children who suffer apparently similar traumatic experiences do not develop autism, although there may be other pathological sequelae. Furthermore, other children who are diagnosed as having autism will not have experienced trauma, and children with autism may have their autistic condition exacerbated by subsequent trauma.

Because the traumas I describe in this sub-group occur within the first two years of life, their impact on all subsequent development is much more pervasive than is the case with traumas sustained later in childhood, adolescence or adulthood (see for example Gaensbauer 1993; B. Perry *et al.* 1995; Schore 1996). Developmental delay is a feature of all the children we have seen in this sub-group, although during assessment some reveal small 'pockets' of continuing cognitive and/or emotional development upon which progress can be built.

Because I am suggesting that it is the *impact of trauma in infancy* which precipitates an autistic withdrawal, leading to developmental delay, I am proposing the term Autistic Post-Traumatic Developmental Disorder (APTDD) to describe the condition. The primary evidential base for this hypothesis derives from the detailed case histories and process recordings from psychotherapy sessions gathered over nearly thirty years of my own clinical work, together with other cases I have supervised, and the collated clinical data from a large number of psychoanalytic clinicians who have presented their work to the Tavistock Autism Research Workshop since its inception in 1986. Whilst it is recognised that children with autism outside this sub-group may reveal evidence of some traumatisation, it is not considered a major contributory factor to their autism, nor is it considered central to their mode of presentation. I shall point to certain similarities between Post-Traumatic Stress Disorder (PTSD) and this proposed variant of autism, and identify categories of precipitating traumatising events leading to APTDD. Links are made to the work of neurobiologists such as Fox *et al.* (1994), Grigsby and Schneiders (1991), Pynoos (1996) and Schore (1996). Some clinical vignettes are given as illustrations, and a more detailed case study of one patient, Catherine, is presented in Chapter 8.

Post-Traumatic Stress Disorder

Before pointing to the similarities between APTDD and PTSD, I shall start by describing the currently accepted condition of PTSD. It is well recognised that traumatic events can have a lasting impact on the physiological, emotional, cognitive and behavioural functions of individuals (Fox *et al.* 1994; B. Perry *et al.* 1995). There are numerous accounts recording traumatic responses, particularly to natural disasters and the experiences of war (for example Kardiner 1941; Rado 1942). Since 1980 a distinct trauma-related syndrome, Post-Traumatic Stress Disorder, has been recognised. The diagnostic specification of PTSD first appeared in the American Psychiatric Association's third edition of the *Diagnostic and Statistical Manual of Mental Disorders* (DSM-III).[1]

Since 1980 the criteria for the diagnosis of PTSD has undergone two revisions (see Table 7.1, columns 2 and 3). These revisions are of particular interest in relation to an hypothesis of APTDD. By 1987 in DSM-III-R (Table 7.1, column 2), whilst the clusters of symptoms continued to be grouped under three sections, section C now included the *avoidance* of stimuli associated with the trauma as well as the *numbing* of responsiveness. Section D, which had been a miscellaneous grouping in DSM-III, now included *hypervigilance* (D4) and *physiologic reactivity* (D6) and is now more clearly defined as symptoms of increased arousal. The 1987 revised criteria are also noteworthy for the specific inclusion of *children* – 'in young children repetitive play in which themes or aspects of the trauma are expressed' (B1) and 'in young children, loss of recently acquired developmental skills such as toilet training or language skills' (C4) – and in doing so takes account of 'new knowledge' generated by the increase in studies of PTSD in children.

Further revisions appear in DSM-IV (APA 1994: Table 7.1, column 3) but of particular relevance to the ideas outlined in this chapter is the introduction of the notion of a *subjective* response to a traumatic event (A2): 'The person's response involved fear, helplessness or horror – in children this may be expressed instead by disorganised or agitated behaviour'. The inclusion of the affective response to the event denotes an important theoretical shift. There is now a recognition of the importance of the variations in individuals which transcends purely behavioural symptomatology. Whilst some events may be so overwhelming that most people would develop PTSD (i.e. a normal reaction), some do not: individual experiences of the same event are idiosyncratic.

The symptoms of PTSD

The symptoms of PTSD fall into three clusters which are defined in categories B(2), C and D (see Table 7.1, columns 1, 2, 3):

Category B	Persistent re-experiencing of the event
Category C	Persistent avoidance of stimuli associated with the trauma and numbing of general responsiveness
Category D	Persistent symptoms of increased arousal

Persistent re-experience of the event

Clinical work with children who are suffering from PTSD confirms that recurring and intrusive experience of traumatic events can be revealed in their repetitive play. In autistic children, however, rather than repetitive play, we see repetitive speech, behaviours or rituals, which are of course recognised as diagnostic (for example Joe, in this chapter). I am suggesting that these repetitive behaviours may derive from the same source – i.e. recurring and intrusive experiences of traumatisation which have occurred *in infancy*. It is the unchanging, repetitive and even compulsive nature of these activities which is so striking and may be indicative of early trauma which has interrupted the acquisition of the normal developmental capacity to find ways of digesting, representing and *symbolising* current and past experiences. The rituals seem to represent something undigested, or, perhaps more accurately, indigestible, unmetabolisable. Catherine, whose therapy is described in Chapter 8, compulsively flicked a button on a string, and Colin, whom I discuss later in this chapter, repeatedly tapped stones. Repetitive behaviours in children with autism are likely to be pre-symbolic if the trauma was experienced early in infancy but, sometimes in the course of psychotherapy, these previously meaningless repetitive acts do become open to meaning: when this happens the activity usually decreases or may even cease. When, in her third year of therapy, Catherine came to understand the meaning of her button flicking, she stopped carrying it around with her. There is of course evidence within the literature that stereotypic behaviours do change over time and decrease with age. However, with the benefit of both video and process recordings, it is possible to demonstrate that the cessation of such stereotypic behaviours is more likely a function of the therapeutic process and not simply of maturation.

Persistent avoidance of stimuli associated with the trauma and numbing of general responsiveness

Column 2, C4 of Table 7.1 (at end of this chapter) refers specifically to the 'loss of recently acquired developmental skills such as toilet training or language skills', and it is well recognised that many parents note the loss of recently acquired language in children with autism. However, where the impact of trauma occurs very early in infancy we would need to recognise that rather than a *loss* of major developmental skills, in APTDD, there is a possibility of a failure to reach these developmental milestones at all. Precursors of autistic development in babies may be indicated by a lack of 'pointing' or 'shared gaze' or 'babbling'. Children with APTDD may therefore present differing clinical pictures depending upon the age of onset of the trauma. Very early trauma may, because of the impact on the developing structure of the brain, be difficult to distinguish from genetically induced impairment. Similarly, the clinical picture, where genetic factors are involved, may be very similar in the two situations. Much more research is needed on these issues.

Clinicians observing children with PTSD who had witnessed catastrophes, saw the children as 'numb, robotic, non-reactive, daydreaming and staring off into space with a glazed look' (Terr 1988). When interviewed, a number of these children described themselves as 'going to a different place' or 'assuming the persona of heroes or animals', whilst others described themselves as 'just floating' (B. Perry *et al.* 1995). Autistic children cannot 'go to a different place' in fantasy but they can withdraw to an earlier 'plane' of existence, dominated by physical sensations. These descriptions will probably be familiar to those readers who work, or live with, a child with autism. My point is that ordinary children who are traumatised present, at the time of traumatisation, in some ways that are comparable with children who are diagnosed with autism.

With those children who fall into the APTDD classification, where trauma seems to have activated an autistic response in a possibly genetically/biologically vulnerable child, the course of therapeutic work can reveal the essential and idiosyncratic nature of the trauma which is particular to each child. Tustin (1981a) drew attention to the possibility of a premature psychological birth in children whom she describes as 'encapsulated' (they share much in common with this sub-group). She recognised that for some vulnerable children, the discovery that they were separate from their mothers, before they had the psychological equipment to deal with this knowledge, could bring about a 'psychogenic autism'. Interestingly, Evans-Jones and Rosenbloom (1978) and Hill and Rosenbloom (1986) in their study of young children with disintegrative psychosis and autistic behavioural features, found a high incidence of associated life-stress triggering factors.

Persistent symptoms of increased arousal

The third cluster of symptoms of PTSD is a feature observed in many of the children with autism whom we have seen. The physiological over-arousal described in PTSD is observable in their agitated hand-flapping, pacing up and down and finger-flapping – particularly following upon brief engagement with another person. Whilst outwardly apparently unresponsive, switched off, and in a world of their own, it is only close observation which reveals that, paradoxically, they can be simultaneously highly attuned to aspects of events going on around them that they might experience as a threat. Autistic children rarely engage in direct eye contact, contributing to their parents' sense that their children are unresponsive. Emotional hypervigilance is often revealed in their unfocused gaze which allows for greater peripheral vision (e.g. Sally in Chapter 2) – something that we all apparently employ in crowd situations, where our autonomy or personal boundaries might be threatened. The combination of extreme sensitivity on the one hand and the extraordinary, blunted reactions on the other, may be understood to have their origins in originally meaningful, life-protecting reactions.

Neurological evidence indicates that trauma can change the actual developing brain structure in the infant and literally inhibit the infant's capacity to perceive the world and events (Fox *et al.* 1994; Perry 1995; Schore 1996). Neurobiologists have demonstrated that children exposed to chronic traumatic experiences develop more neurological connections in areas of the brain that respond to perceived life threats. Over time, these hyperreactive parts of the brain can cause an extreme reaction to even very minor external stimulus (Schore 1994; Van der Kolk and Greenberg 1987). In clinical work it is a major task to introduce such children to the middle range of emotional experiences. Catherine, in Chapter 8, became able, only after some years of therapy, to discriminate between what she called 'BIG Memories' (that is, memories of her traumatic experiences) from 'Small Memories' (that is, memories of events which did not make her 'hyper' [her word] but became valued for their ordinary developmental significance). 'Small Memories' provide Catherine with a bank of useful, usable experiences – those which reveal the world to be interesting, rather than overwhelming, and where she is a participant and not a victim – where she feels potent and not impotent. At the beginning of her treatment she could only experience states of either hyper-arousal or of shut-down – what she called 'blobbying'. In therapy it is sometimes possible to discriminate states of over-arousal from those situations where the patient is attempting to block incoming arousing stimuli in order to self-regulate downwards to a less aroused state. It is extremely important as a stage on the road to either the recovery, or the discovery, of a sense of self, to recognise the precursors of a sense of agency or potency in this attempt to self-regulate. They carry strikingly different emotional valences for the individual. Colin, a patient of mine, when in a state of hyper-arousal, made it very clear to me that he felt the victim of bombardment by unbearable physical stimuli which he experienced as originating outside him. On entering puberty he became very disturbed by his increased sexual arousal; in sessions, when he was clearly experiencing an erection, he would sometimes moan, cover his head, lie on his stomach on the couch and use the cushion like a shield. He could not discriminate his own physiological states from attacks from outside and therefore felt very much the victim. At other times, when he had managed to engage in some work with me, he could make it clear that he needed a rest; at such times he would turn his back to me to tap with his stones on a hard surface and then flap his hands. These moments were felt very much to be of his volition, and it was important in my comments to recognise and value this. When I felt that he was a victim of over-arousal, I would use a quiet, sympathetic tone of voice and speak slowly in an attempt to calm him – sometimes this worked and he could hear me and not feel alone and under attack, and could then come out of his over-aroused state. On the other hand, when *he* withdrew from me, even though the tapping could be quite frenetic, I employed a much stronger, more masculine and emphatic voice, speaking *for him* – I would say something like 'Go away, I've had enough for now, stop talking to me, I am having a rest with my stones, I'll be back with you later'. There is debate within the literature in relation to the extent to which stereotypic behaviours should be 'allowed', and perhaps it would be useful to emphasise that there can be a way in which some stereotypic behaviours may be viewed as functional rather than mindless.

The impact of trauma in infancy

For the infant, a traumatic event is not an 'event' (as it can be for an older child). It is not a single experience of failure to protect, or be protected, viewed against a backdrop of other protective and life-sustaining experiences. The experience of a traumatic event is influenced by the developmental age of the individual at the time of that event. From the beginning of life through to adulthood, there is, in normal development, a natural progression in the evolution of a sense of self. Alongside this goes a developing awareness, first of a sense of 'another', and then of 'others', with a consequent ability to differentiate self from others. This capacity supports the development of healthy attachments, together with increasing self-reliance, while fostering the capacity to discriminate. In traumatised infants it is clear that the process of normal individuation will have only just begun. The infant is entirely dependent on important caregivers to discover that she 'is', and this is achieved through repeated experiences of her impact on others, a sense of agency (Alvarez and Furgiuele 1997), which in turn brings about a healthy sense of potency (Alvarez 1992a). Traumatic experiences sustained in infancy are overwhelming because there is little or nothing to counterbalance them and they are therefore liable to colour, influence and even distort the infant's entire world-view. But trauma does more than just emotionally 'colour' the infant's world-view. In infancy the brain develops very rapidly and in response to arousal of stimuli; if the parts of the brain connected with survival become over-used then smaller and smaller stimuli trigger the same survival responses. If only certain parts of the brain are activated, then other parts will not develop. Perry describes the brain as 'use-dependent' (B. Perry *et al.* 1995). It is clear then that patients present different clinical pictures depending upon how early the trauma occurred. The consequences of very early trauma are difficult to distinguish from constitutional neurological damage.

All human adults have a potential range of emotional/neurological responses to the perception of danger which develops from infancy. These include the 'freeze' and the 'fight-flight' responses (Cannon 1914; Selye 1936; Mason 1971; Goldstein 1995; B. Perry *et al.* 1995). An infant is unable to 'fight' or 'flee' the perceived threat or danger and therefore the more primitive or extreme survival mechanism of freezing will be triggered. It is clear that the degree of maturity and individuation reached by any infant at the time of the trauma will have particular importance. In addition to the importance of the relative neurological and physical immaturity of an infant, other factors will affect the impact of trauma on subsequent development: the severity or chronicity of the trauma, the child's temperament, as well as the availability of emotionally responsive and protective adults or siblings.

Dissociative states

In the 'frozen' state the child is apparently unresponsive to external stimuli (B. Perry *et al.* 1995). Children with autism are frequently suspected of being deaf, although testing usually reveals this not to be the case. There is similarly often a lack of an appropriate response to pain (Kanner 1943). An example of this was vividly provided by one autistic boy who, at around eighteen months of age, had to have a cut on his eye stitched. This was done without benefit of anaesthesia, and he reportedly did not even flinch. Hospital staff called him a 'model patient' but, for his experienced foster mother, it was one more indication that this little boy's development was not proceeding normally. Although this is a rather dramatic example, many parents and teachers note that these children tend not to react when they fall or hurt themselves and do not seek comfort in an ordinary way. Similarly, they seem unaware when they cause pain to others.

In these dissociative states there is a disengagement from stimuli in the external world which, in autism, can be replaced by an all-engaging preoccupation with self-induced body stimulation (Meltzer *et al.* 1975; Frith 1989; Tustin 1981a, 1986, 1990; Alvarez 1992a). Where trauma has occurred in infancy, before there is adequate differentiation of self from other, and before the development of the capacity to symbolise, the child cannot withdraw into daydreaming and fantasy, which has been noted in adults and children suffering from post-traumatic stress disorders. In PTSD, feelings of helplessness have been recognised as central to the trauma. Central to a person's capacity for recovery is the introduction of potency into a situation where their actual experience was one of complete helplessness (Pynoos 1996). This can be achieved in the course of various types of therapies (for example Milgram 1986; Galante and Foa 1986) where the original traumatic situation can be 'rewritten' and sometimes even revenge scenarios fantasised. In psychoanalytic psychotherapy, via the transference relationship, the therapist may be temporarily placed in the position of victim to allow the patient some relief or new perspective or exploration of their own helplessness and evoked aggression. But in adults, the very fact that traumatic experiences have usually occurred against a backdrop of other life experiences is also influential in promoting recovery. For very young infants, however, fantasising a different outcome to traumatic events, or 'rewriting' of personal history, is a developmental achievement which is unavailable to them. But the infant and young child can withdraw to a world of auto-generated sensations where they can control the intensity, duration, frequency and type of sensation, thereby introducing some degree of self-will or potency. When understood in this way, some autistic people's dependence on bodily sensations, and on particular objects which can induce them, seems less 'pathological' and rigidly fixed, and more understandable and potentially open to amelioration. Indeed, when understood as, partly at least, a survival response, then some children's determination to survive in what initially seems a very alien way can seem positively heroic. I describe in Chapter 8 the bodily sensations and mental repetitions that Catherine induced in order to survive in a world she perceived as full of threat. What is more problematic is that these originally defensive mechanisms can become addictive and in some cases even perverse, and the older a child is, the more 'addicted' to these rituals she or he may become. This has profound implications for the importance of early treatment interventions.

Trauma and developmental disorder

The ongoing preoccupation with threat or 'not me,' as Tustin (1981a) described it, has enormous implications for cognitive development (B. Perry *et al.* 1995; Shore 1996) as well as for the development of emotional intelligence (Mayer 1993; Mayer and Salovey 1995, Mayer and Geher 1996). As all the child's awareness is directed towards life-preserving and not life-discovering processes, a world perceived as threatening is shut out by the generating of all-enveloping sensations which push out thoughts, ideas and emotions. Thus traumas sustained in infancy may distort all future development in vulnerable babies, since any ongoing intercourse with the outside world is severely curtailed.

I have been interested to note, clinically, that in spite of extreme dissociation there are, in some cases, signs of some continued cognitive and emotional development. These, however, only appear as isolated islands of development, not linked to one another. The neurobiological literature on trauma explains it thus: 'dissociation allows one to maintain or even diminish internal states of physiological hyper-arousal, thereby allowing cognitive activity and problem-solving at a higher level of capability than would be possible in a state of absolute terror' (B. Perry *et al.* 1995).

When we look at certain children with autism from a perspective of trauma-induced shut-down, then symptoms of the avoidance of external stimuli and of other human beings, the dependence upon sensations generated within their own bodies and the use of autistic objects (Tustin 1981a) begin to seem more reasonable. It may be that many of the children Tustin described as 'encapsulated' and suffering from 'black hole catastrophes', were indeed the vulnerable victims of trauma. In states of hyper-arousal, an alarm reaction is initiated which is characterised by increased activity in the sympathetic nervous system, resulting in 'increased heart rate, blood pressure, respiration, release of stored sugar and increased muscle tone' – all of which can be observed in children with autism (Dawson *et al.* 1989; B. Perry *et al.* 1995). In this state there is a tuning-out of all non-critical information: these activities prepare the body for defence. When employed by a child with autism, it has the same sequelae as in an adult with PTSD. The child is easily moved from being mildly anxious to feeling threatened and then overwhelmed.

Categories of traumatic events

Traumatic events which may contribute to the development of APTDD may be either acute or chronic: clinical experience, so far, suggests four categories of traumatising events:

1 An actual event in the physical environment which would be recognised objectively as traumatising.
2 An actual event in interpersonal relationships which would be recognised as traumatising to any infant.
3 A traumatic response to events which are generally recognised as only temporarily traumatising or disturbing.
4 Traumas which originate in parents' experiences or even in those of the grandparents' generation.

An actual event in the physical environment which would be recognised objectively as traumatising

Examples of these would be:

(a) severe physical abuse;
(b) sexual abuse;

(c) violence to the self and/or important others, for example in war-torn countries;

(d) severe medical conditions resulting in long hospitalisations and/or surgery (see Catherine below in this chapter);

(e) extreme prematurity necessitating invasive procedures to keep the infant alive.

A clinical example

In 1972 I began working with the mother of an autistic boy, one of twins. Both twins were born prematurely – but one twin seemed significantly more affected by being in an incubator, and he subsequently developed autism while his brother developed normally. The mother described Joe as 'stiff as a board' when she tried to feed him: he would only feed if his mother stood up and held him against her chest with Joe facing outwards to suck on his bottle. We agreed that he sounded as if he were in shock.

Joe's mother remembered how different the twins were from birth. Joe, she remembered vividly as 'coming out with his eyes open'. In our work together, it became apparent that he could not shut off – escape into sleep as his healthier twin had been able to do – and so everything impinged upon him, making him much more vulnerable to traumatisation. What emerged in the course of our work together, and in the course of Joe's therapy, was a picture of a hypersensitive baby who had felt torn away from both his mother and his twin. With an easier start to life, he might just have been a bright, sensitive boy who always needed careful handling, but for him, the combination of prematurity, loss of both mother and twin, the period in intensive care and his own over-alertness made this experience too much for him. His therapy suggests that the incubator might have felt particularly hostile and alien. Not only had he been wrenched from inside the warm, responsive environment of his mother's body, but separation from his twin, his other half, also seemed to have left a wound. Sandra Piontelli's work illustrates twins' sensitivity to one another's existence, even *in utero* (Piontelli 1989).

When his speech began to develop it was echolalic. He had a repetitive question which he addressed to everyone – family, friends and total strangers alike – 'You won't leak down, will you?' Apparently no answer ever satisfied him. He repeated his question over and over again. His mother and I came to understand this as relating to his experiences in the incubator. She described this time vividly: 'Tubes going into him, tubes coming out of him'. The question he asked everyone seemed to encapsulate his experience as an infant when it would seem he had felt as if he were leaking away, down the very tubes which were intended to be life-preserving. Moreover, not having had an opportunity to develop a separate identity at the time of his trauma, he seemed to assume that his experience was everyone's experience. His elemental terror was then exacerbated by the fear that everyone else would 'leak down', too.

Joe made good use of a period of psychotherapy as a young child and then, in adolescence, requested further help. An account of his therapy in adolescence is included in Chapter 15 of this volume.

Actual events in interpersonal relationships which would be recognised as traumatising to any infant

Examples of these would be

(a) the institutionalised babies whom Spitz observed as long ago as 1946. He described the dramatic withdrawal of affective engagement with their world without the presence of demonstrable organic disease. The important point that Spitz made was that it was the quality of care which induced this withdrawal, rather than the fact of institutionalisation *per se* (Spitz 1946);

(b) infants observed in orphanages in countries undergoing major social upheaval or war, where there is the presence of severe emotional neglect (China, the former Yugoslavia, Rwanda). Rutter and his colleagues, exploring the extent of developmental deficit and catch-up following adoption after severe global early privation, concluded that 'the remaining cognitive deficit was likely to be a consequence of gross early privation, with psychological privation probably more important than nutritional privation' (Rutter *et al.* 1998: 465). Tronick and Weinberg maintain that it is not just the body that is affected by caretaker behaviour, but the brain as well. Their research indicates that the quality of care-taking affects the function, structure and neurochemical architecture of the brain (Tronick and Weinberg 1996);

(c) severe emotional bombardment by parents who are mentally disturbed (Murray 1988, 1991b; Reid 1997b). Elsewhere I have given an account of the treatment of a little boy in this category (Reid 1990).

A traumatic response to events which are generally recognised as only temporarily traumatising or disturbing

These events are often viewed as part of the normal life cycle and would include, for example

(a) the birth of a new baby in a family: most families recognise that the birth of a sibling can generate considerable ambivalence in any young child, resulting in some temporary regression, but it is noteworthy that in many case histories in the literature, parents relate the timing of the onset of autism to the birth of a younger sibling;

(b) an accident such as a severe scalding from a teapot or kettle, or being thrown violently from a pram when it tipped over;

(c) repeated infections in the first two years of life, particularly ear infections: it seems that the loss of hearing in an already vulnerable child can push them further along the pathway of withdrawal from friendly interaction with others (where there are repeated illnesses in the first two years they have overshadowed family life and are remembered as traumatic);

(d) a severe reaction to immunisation: in some of the children we have seen, immunisation seems to have caused a severe setback from which the children did not spontaneously recover.

Our case histories frequently reveal the presence of more than one of these ordinary life situations coinciding at a particular point in time, and it is the coincidence of these situations which seems to be more than some vulnerable or particularly sensitive infants can process. It is the element of chance which is significant here. Intense or repeated traumatic experiences interfere with the resolution of developmental tasks; moreover, the trauma seems to distort the child's subsequent experiences of life events. The point is that in all of these examples, 'life's traumas' are experienced by them as 'TRAUMATIC'.

Traumas which originate in parents' experiences or even in those of the grandparents' generation

Life experiences which were too overwhelming to be processed can result in an intergenerational transfer of unprocessed trauma. This has been well documented in relation to Holocaust victims and their children (Barocas and Barocas 1973; Bergmann and Jucovy 1982; Auehahn and Prelinge 1983; Pines 1993; Karpf 1996; Yehuda 1996) and more recently in work with refugees. The attachment theorists, Main and Hesse (1990: 163) hypothesise that 'the traumatised adults' continuing state of fear together with its interactional/behavioural concomitants (frightened and/or frightening behaviour) is the mechanism linking unresolved trauma to the infant's display of disorganised/disoriented behaviours'.

These are dramatic, traumatic experiences, unusual in some way, but there are other events which, because they are not apparently momentous, can go unrecognised as traumatic experiences for the individuals involved. Because they are not particularly unusual events, it seems that those whom they affect may also feel that their experiences do not deserve attention. In this case I would place as examples: still births; repeated miscarriages; the unhappy coincidence of events which may form part of the life cycle, for example, the death of a parent's parents at or around the time of the birth of their own child; the birth of a child coinciding with the severe illness of another sibling (Sally in my chapter on assessment, Chapter 2 of this volume); and the birth of a child coinciding with one parent departing or being made redundant.

A clinical example

Mike was remembered by his parents as a very good baby who could occupy himself for hours at a time in his baby bouncer and who was, therefore, the envy of their friends. As he moved into toddlerhood however, his parents became increasingly worried about him. Everyone tried to persuade them that Mike would 'grow out of it' and they really had to persevere in seeking a referral for an assessment with us. Mike's parents remembered that although he could spend hours in his baby bouncer, Mike never sought anyone else's company and did not even look up when other people passed by. This, in retrospect, could be understood not as a healthy capacity to occupy himself for a little while, having first enjoyed his mother or father's company, but rather this all-engaging physical activity seems to have involved a withdrawal of interest in the company of others, and in the world around him. As a toddler he had insisted on long walks and, because he had made so few demands as a baby, these demands were acceded to, although they caused his parents some disquiet. Mike refused to sit in his pushchair but insisted that he push it. His parents subsequently realised that, as the frame of the pushchair was at eye level it functioned as a shield, protecting his eyes from any impingements from the world around him. He insisted they always follow the same route, never stopping to talk to anyone or look at anything. Any deviations provoked temper tantrums and collapse. Thus as a toddler he walked, or rather marched, like a boy with a blindfold behind a huge shield. These walks, we realised, had simply become an empty ritual, which fed into his all-too-private and lonely omnipotence.

Mike's parents' first child was stillborn and they were advised to try immediately for another baby. Mike was due on the anniversary of the first baby's death and his parents, already anxious enough about whether this pregnancy would go to term, insisted that the birth be induced so that he was not born on the same day as the anniversary of the death. Neither mother nor father had had adequate time to grieve the stillbirth. The birth of a healthy child mobilised pleasure and relief, but naturally also a mourning for her first loss. Mike, a hypersensitive child, seems to have withdrawn from his mother's sadness. It is striking that he did this in spite of the presence of his nanny, whom his parents considered a lively person with no reason to feel sad or preoccupied. Mike, however, withdrew affective contact from everyone. Mike's mother recalled that she really allowed herself to become concerned when Mike was about fifteen months old and there was no speech developing. She explained that she usually slipped away when she left for work, not acknowledging that she was going, as she feared upsetting him. At the time when she became more consciously aware of her concerns, she also became aware of her own denial of the importance of separations between them: the separation, by death, from her first child had temporarily infused all separations with the same intense anxiety – she was temporarily traumatised by the stillbirth of her first baby. She then decided to change her usual practice and so told Mike when she left for work, 'It's all right to get upset when Mummy goes'. Mike promptly burst into tears and sobbed in his nanny's arms. On his mother's return, he spoke his first words: 'Gone to work – Mummy come back again!' This seemingly miraculous development coincided with the mother's pre-conscious link that it was all right to get upset and that the advice to become pregnant so quickly had not been helpful, since it denied her the right to mourn the loss of the baby she had carried for nine months. Indeed, it is clear that it is essential to a healthy emotional life to be allowed to respond appropriately to distressing events. What is particularly noteworthy about this example is that although there were other people available to Mike, and his mother was by no means always preoccupied with her sadness and sense of loss for her first child, he was extremely sensitive, highly intelligent, but also intolerant of anything less than perfection in people. These qualities seemed to have made him particularly vulnerable to a very painful, but sadly not so unusual, life experience.

Case histories obtained from parents, together with the opportunity to observe a child over several months in the assessment phase of the psychotherapeutic work, indicate that many of the children in this sub-group, especially in those cases where the traumatising event was primarily psychological, seemed to have been particularly thin-skinned, hypersensitive from infancy, and therefore especially vulnerable to the emotional atmospheres of their environments. Along with their extreme sensitivity goes a profound intolerance of any frustration of their wishes or needs. They seem to require perfect conditions in their environment if they are to thrive, and have little or no resilience: they are the 'hothouse orchids' of the infant population.

Because I am describing trauma sustained in infancy, the emotional resources of the parents at that time also have particular significance (Murray 1988). The capacity of a parent to provide a protective shield for their infant, and to contain catastrophic anxieties, varies from parent to parent and for any parent will vary according to their own current resources. For any adult, certain situations may prove more stressful than others, and these are partly dependent on our own childhood experiences and exposure to unusual stresses or traumas in infancy and childhood and to the quality of support available at the time. Sometimes there is an unfortunate conjunction between a trauma experienced by an infant and that experienced by their mother or father, either in their own childhood or in adulthood. It is clear that any mother will be extremely anxious about the survival of a severely premature infant. However, if the mother also had a sibling who died in infancy or an earlier pregnancy resulting in stillbirth, or several miscarriages (and mourning has not proved possible) then the chances may be increased that the mother's own fears may overwhelm her and inhibit her capacity to provide this protective shield for her especially sensitive infant.

The number of variables at play, internal and external, in parent and infant, are enormous and this helps us to understand why one infant may develop APTDD, whilst another in similar conditions does not. Sharing this understanding with parents can help them to move on from a preoccupation with responsibility and guilt. But a recognition of those situations which render infants more vulnerable to psychological withdrawal, combined with early detection by health professionals of those infants who display early signs of withdrawal from affective contact with others, would allow for early treatment interventions (Fenske *et al.* 1985; McEachin *et al.* 1993; B. Perry *et al.* 1995;

Baron-Cohen *et al.* 1996). Our clinical interventions with these children indicate that the earlier treatment is offered, the greater our hopes of success, as the earlier the age at which trauma is sustained, the more pervasive it is likely to be. The younger the child is on beginning treatment, the less entrenched certain behaviours will be; the more plastic their responses, the less addicted they may be to rituals, and the less abandoned to despair and hopelessness.

False reassurance from health professionals that a child will 'grow out of it' or that they are 'just a late developer', although well intentioned, is therefore in these cases positively harmful. Many of the babies within this autistic sub-group have also been described as 'good babies' who, because they made few demands on their parents, and because also of the variously difficult situations with which their parents were struggling at the time, seemed able to be left to occupy themselves. It is, however, important to remember that parenting is a two-way process and that, as parents, we are partly dependent on our babies' capacity to indicate their wish for company. Most parents, if honest, would admit that they would be grateful for a 'good baby'. We probably need to be experienced parents, and in good shape ourselves at the time of our babies' births, in order to question their willingness to occupy themselves for hours at a time. Parents in our clinical sample often recall feeling grateful at the time to have had such good babies who, subsequently, as toddlers also made little demand on adult attention, often content to watch videos. Because these children make so few demands, the demands they do make seem largely to be acceded to, and their idiosyncratic nature therefore goes unchallenged for some time. Unusual likes and dislikes can be accommodated into a family until inexorably and covertly they can come to dominate a family's life.

The child's personality: its contribution to the autistic withdrawal and its impact on parenting

In treatment many of these children reveal a considerable intolerance to anything less than perfection in important adults, including the therapist. This I now believe to be central to their character structure and a contributing factor, from the child, to the withdrawal from contact with the world. It is the combination of extreme sensitivity on the one hand and an extreme intolerance of frustration on the other: either one of these on its own does not appear to lead to such extreme emotional withdrawal. These children, however, simply cannot bear to be thwarted; they feel the need for something so intensely that its absence, or less than perfect fulfilment, evokes either hot rage or icy aloofness. This issue usually only emerges clearly in the course of psychoanalytic psychotherapy (Carmen, Chapter 12, and Edward, Chapter 10 of this volume). They are often quite lordly or queenly in temperament when they emerge from their autism, and the therapist then experiences at first hand the penalties for thwarting these little rajahs! These are children who find it hard to forgive and are, in temperament, the very opposite of those truly easy-going babies who seem able to make the best of everything. Experience of numbers of children like this in psychoanalytic psychotherapy leads me to hypothesise that, born into circumstances as close to ideal as any family ever manages, these children would still have had difficult temperaments. Mike, for example, when he emerged from his autism (and he managed a normal school environment) could still be a very controlling little boy who found it hard to need to learn from others. He wanted to know it all already. It was as if his need to learn was experienced by him as evidence of his own imperfections, and was therefore deeply humiliating. Although Mike turned out to be a very bright and in many ways gifted boy, who gave his parents considerable pleasure, he was certainly not always easy to live with. He often made his parents feel they did not measure up, and their actual good parenting was not often confirmed by him. This, happily, was counterbalanced by their pleasure in his joining the 'normal' world, the evidence of his intelligence and many gifts, their own lively, flexible temperaments, and the confirmation they did receive from his brother, who was a much more ordinarily robust little boy, that they were good, appreciated parents!

A clinical example

Many parents tell us that they have very different experiences with siblings; as Barry's mother put it, 'James would not have let us get away with it'. She recalled the time when Barry was around one year old, when she had felt depressed and overwhelmed by a combination of distressing family events, 'I would sit behind my newspaper with a cup of coffee whilst Barry did his own thing'. James, his brother, in contrast, would nag and pull at her, and even shout until he got his mother's attention. 'You just couldn't ignore James', she said. Barry developed severe autism. It helped his mother to understand that she had not done something terrible to Barry, but that he was highly attuned to her state of mind and also extremely intolerant of any frustration of his needs. At the beginning of his assessment, Barry's parents were burdened with guilt. They felt they must have done something terrible to their son and felt helpless and hopeless. In the course of the long assessment it became more possible for them to stand back a little from the situation, and to use the sessions with me to watch their son's responses to the situation in which he now found himself. For the first time it became possible for them to acknowledge that Barry was not an easy little boy. It became clearer to them how quickly he would switch off rather than be open to anyone he experienced as being less than perfectly attuned to him; and being perfectly attuned meant not only understanding his wishes but also agreeing to them. He could not tolerate two people talking together for even a few seconds; he made it clear that he had to be the centre of the world all the time or he could not bear to be part of it at all. His assessment also helped his parents to understand that, after all, distressing circumstances are not uncommon in family life, and many parents go through periods of depression without their children becoming autistic

It seems to have become enshrined in mythology that psychoanalysts blame the mothers of autistic children for their condition. On the contrary, we find that many of the parents we see, like Barry's parents, blame themselves, and it helps parents to realise that we are not about to apportion blame but rather that we see it as part of our task to free them from a paralysing sense of guilt. Listening to the stories of many families with a child with autism, one is left with the recognition that there, but for the grace of God, go I.

Conclusion

What is observed in APTDD is a set of emotional, behavioural and cognitive features which, though rooted in an original adaptive response to trauma, have become maladaptive. As Catherine's mother said, when reflecting upon Catherine's apparent emotional indifference to her intrusive hospitalisations in infancy and early childhood, 'Maybe it was just as well, or we would never have got through it'. The very fact that these children's responses were originally healthy and adaptive may be the reason why they tend to have a good outcome in psychotherapy.

Acknowledgements

I am grateful to Mary Sue Moore for bringing the attention of the Autism Research Workshop to recent neurological research, and for her helpful comments on this chapter; and to Dr Anthony Lee for his careful reading and many helpful comments.

Note

1 For reference, the criteria for PTSD, as outlined in DSM-III, and the subsequent revisions in DSM-IIIR and DSM-IV are shown in Table 7.1 (see p. 110).

Table 7.1 Criteria for PTSD and subsequent revisions

Column 1	Column 2	Column 3
DSM-III criteria for PTSD	*DSM-III-R criteria for PTSD*	*DSM-IV criteria for PTSD*
1 The existence of a recognisable stressor that would evoke significant symptoms of distress in almost anyone	A The person has experienced an event that is outside the range of usual human experience and that would be markedly distressing to almost anyone, e.g., serious threat to one's life or physical integrity; serious threat or harm to one's children, spouse or other close relatives and friends; sudden destruction of one's home or community; or seeing another person who has recently been, or is being, seriously injured or killed as the result of an accident or physical violence.	A The person has been exposed to a traumatic event in which both the following were present: 1 the person experienced, witnessed, or was confronted with an event or events that involved actual or threatened death or serious injury, or a threat to the physical integrity of self or others 2 *the person's response involved fear, helplessness, or horror. Note: in CHILDREN, this may be expressed instead by disorganised or agitated behaviour.*
2 Re-experiencing of the trauma as evidenced by at least one of the following: (a) recurrent and intrusive recollections of the event (b) recurrent dreams of the event (c) sudden acting or feeling as if the traumatic event were recurring, because of an association with an environmental or ideational stimulus	B The traumatic event is persistently re-experienced in at least one of the following ways: 1 recurrent and intrusive distressing recollections of the event (*in young CHILDREN, repetitive play in which themes or aspects of the trauma are expressed*) 2 recurrent distressing dreams of the event 3 sudden acting or feeling as if the traumatic event were recurring (includes a sense of reliving the experience, illusions, hallucination and dissociative (flashback) episodes, even those that occur upon awakening or when intoxicated) 4 intense psychological distress or exposure to events that symbolise or resemble an aspect of the traumatic event, including anniversaries of the trauma	B The traumatic event is persistently re-experienced in at least one of the following ways: 1 recurrent and intrusive distressing recollections of the event, including images, thoughts, or perceptions. Note: *in young CHILDREN, repetitive play in which themes or aspects of the trauma are expressed*) 2 recurrent distressing dreams of the event. Note: in CHILDREN, there may be frightening dreams without recognisable content. 3 acting or feeling as if the traumatic event were recurring (includes a sense of reliving the experience, illusions, hallucination and dissociative flashback episodes, including those that occur upon awakening or when intoxicated). Note: in young CHILDREN, trauma-specific re-enactment may occur. 4 intense psychological distress at exposure to internal or external cues that symbolise or resemble an aspect of the traumatic event 5 physiological reactivity on exposure to internal or external cues that symbolise or resemble an aspect of the traumatic event

3 Numbing of responsiveness to or reduced involvement with the external world, beginning some time after the trauma, as shown by at least one of the following:

(a) markedly diminished interest in one or more significant activities

(b) feeling of detachment or estrangement from others

(c) constricted affect

4 At least two of the following symptoms that were not present before the trauma:

(a) hyperalertness or exaggerated startle response

(b) sleep disturbance

(c) guilt about surviving when others have not, or about behaviour required for survival

(d) memory impairment or trouble concentrating

(e) avoidance of activities that arouse recollection of the traumatic event

(f) intensification of symptoms by exposure to events that symbolise or resemble the traumatic event

C. Persistent *avoidance of stimuli associated with the trauma* or numbing of responsiveness (not present before the trauma), as indicated by at least three of the following:

1 *efforts to avoid thoughts or feelings associated with the trauma*

2 *efforts to avoid activities or situations that arouse recollections of the trauma*

3 inability to recall an important aspect of the trauma (psychogenic amnesia)

4 markedly diminished interest in significant activities *(in young CHILDREN, loss of recently acquired developmental skills such as toilet training or language skills)*

5 feeling of detachment or estrangement from others

6 restricted range of affect, e.g. CHILD does not expect to have a career, marriage, children, or a long life

D Persistent symptoms of increased arousal (not present before the trauma), as indicated by at least two of the following:

1 difficulty falling or staying asleep

2 irritability or outbursts of anger

3 difficulty concentrating

4 hypervigiliance

5 exaggerated startle response

6 physiologic reactivity at exposure to events that symbolise or resemble an aspect of the traumatic event (e.g. a woman who was raped in an elevator breaks out in a sweat when entering any elevator)

C Persistent *avoidance of stimuli associated with the trauma* or numbing of responsiveness (not present before the trauma), as indicated by three (or more) of the following:

1 *efforts to avoid thought, feelings or conversations associated with the trauma*

2 *efforts to avoid activities, places or people that arouse recollections of the trauma*

3 inability to recall an important aspect of the trauma

4 markedly diminished interest in significant activities

5 feeling of detachment or estrangement from others

6 restricted range of affect, (e.g. unable to have loving feelings)

7 sense of foreshortened future (e.g. does not expect to have a career, marriage, children, or a normal life span)

D Persistent *symptoms of increased arousal* (not present before the trauma), as indicated by two or more of the following:

1 difficulty falling or staying asleep

2 irritability or outbursts of anger

3 difficulty concentrating

4 *hypervigilance*

5 exaggerated startle response

Table 7.1 (Continued)

DSM-III criteria for PTSD	DSM-III-R criteria for PTSD	DSM-IV criteria for PTSD
	E Duration of the disturbance (symptoms in B, C and D) of at least one month.	E Duration of the disturbance (symptoms in B, C, and D) is more than 1 month
		F The disturbance causes clinically significant distress or impairment in social, occupational or other important areas of functioning.

Note: Author's italics and capitalising throughout

Part II
Case studies

8　Catherine

The wind beneath my wings: the importance of hope in recovery from trauma

Susan Reid

The discovery on Christmas Eve that eight week-old Catherine was blind was devastating for her parents, but this was only the beginning of their sorrows. Eleven years later, when meeting me for the first time, Mother could recall 'as if it were only yesterday', the bitter cold weather and the matter-of-fact way this bleak diagnosis was first delivered, before Mother, Father and baby were 'turfed out of the hospital to have a Christmas'.

The early years: a traumatic history

Catherine's early history can be summarised as traumatic event upon traumatic event, any single one of which would cause distress for any ordinary family. Catherine's was a difficult birth resulting in a forceps delivery. At five months Catherine's total blindness was confirmed and in her first year of life she had both sleeping and feeding difficulties. Her parents separated in her second year, and since that time there has been no further contact with Father. By two years of age, she showed considerable separation problems, had withdrawn from all social contact and was diagnosed as autistic by a specialist centre. At two and a half some speech began, but only in imitation of the nursery tapes her mother played to her: speech developed over the following years but it was always echolalic. At just after two and a half, hearing difficulties were diagnosed and she was hospitalised and had surgery. At this time she began what her mother described as 'episodic attacks'. During these attacks Catherine would appear well during the day but at night she became feverish with irregular breathing and severe vomiting, leaving her weak for several days. At four years of age, after a few days of sickness and diarrhoea, she became sleepy, grey and hypoglycaemic, resulting in yet another hospitalisation when she was put on a drip, force-fed and given a lumbar puncture. At four and a half, further tests indicated growth problems and she began three-times weekly injections of growth hormones, first administered by a nurse and then by her mother. At six years her cortisol levels were found to be deficient and she was put on hydrocortisone. Later, she was hospitalised for a brain scan which seems to have been a particularly nightmarish experience.

As I listened to Catherine's mother's account of her daughter's early years, initially I could stay emotionally in touch. I could feel the shock of the diagnosis of blindness and imagine what life must have been like trying to keep going with a blind baby who was also not eating nor sleeping well. My sympathy stayed alive as I listened to the distress they had felt when speech did not develop in an ordinary way; I could feel the devastation produced by the crowning blow of discovering that Catherine was not only blind but was also autistic. But this was not really the crowning blow at all – the catalogue of disasters continued, and at some point, whilst my mind continued to record the details, I also noticed that I felt frozen – in a state of numb disbelief. How could so many terrible things happen to one child and her mother? How could anyone survive? My counter-transference response of numbness, an emotional incapacity to keep responding, helped me to empathise with Catherine's own emotional withdrawal and to respect her mother's extraordinary capacity to keep hope alive.

The importance of hope

When she was eleven years old Catherine was referred to me in the hope that I might be able to help. Who held this hope? Catherine's educational psychologist, who instituted the referral, had been with her for several years and her belief in Catherine was infectious. In Catherine's mother, hope burned brightly, not for a cure but for someone to reach Catherine. Most importantly, in Catherine herself the candle burned quietly and in secret. In our first meeting Catherine surprised her mother and me by suddenly revealing that she had aspirations for herself. I asked Catherine what she would like my help with. – 'Braining', she responded. Her mother reasonably assumed that she had meant 'brailing' and therefore corrected her. Catherine repeated 'Braining!'. Mother, looking puzzled, asked, 'What is it?' Catherine responded, 'It is a brain in your head that helps you think'. I commented that Catherine was quite clear that she hoped that I would be able to help her to think better. She answered seriously, 'Yes'.

From our first meeting Catherine's mother seemed particularly attuned to the fact that whilst, in the past, the unusual closeness between herself and her daughter had been necessary and even essential to Catherine's survival, it could become an obstacle to her future development. What had been life-preserving had become life-limiting for each of them. She was aware that she had done what she could for her daughter, but now she hoped that a psychotherapist might get through to what she believed was trapped in Catherine's mind. In parallel, however, with a hope that Catherine could be helped to open up to the world around her, was her concern about Catherine's extreme passivity – Catherine would sit in the bath until the water ran cold and not think of getting out; she never even asked to use the toilet. Another overriding concern was Catherine's approaching puberty; Mother sensed that Catherine was becoming more preoccupied with sexuality and yet had so little sense of self she did not 'know her top from her bottom, her back from her front and won't know what hits her when her periods finally start'. She felt that this made Catherine very vulnerable.

The assessment

When I went to meet Catherine for the first time she was sitting in the waiting room next to her mother, dressed prettily in a pale yellow dress, with shoulder-length brown hair. She looked rather like her mother. When Catherine's mother asked 'Would you like to sit on a chair by yourself or on the settee with me?', Catherine simply repeated 'Settee with me'.

I was quickly fascinated by the way in which she spoke and the extraordinary way in which, although she could not respond to me directly, she could find a story which ran in parallel to a question I had asked or a comment I had made. Her stories were always confused and 'unravelled' but they had a certain magnetic impact on me. When I asked Catherine why she thought Mummy had brought her to meet me, she replied 'If she says do you want to sit on a chair by yourself or do you want to sit with me, I say yes', and then launched into an entangled story about her 'best boy-friend' which revealed that in her friend's family there were brothers and sisters, a mummy and a daddy, and that the children slept in their own beds and the mummy and daddy together. I commented, simply, that she was interested in different kinds of families; Catherine responded, 'When I was a baby, I had a mummy and a daddy...'. She then began to tell me a story about going to have a brain scan. She told it as if she were currently living it. But also, during the course of the telling, she lived both the parts when she was awake and the parts when she was under anaesthesia; she also lived and inhabited the experiences of her mother, the nurse, the doctor and so on. Her story had a terrible, nightmarish quality to it, as she managed to convey the sense in which the experience of having a brain scan had seared into her mind and never really left her, but carried on having a constant life inside that could easily be activated. In her account, when she awoke from the anaesthesia, there was only Mummy there; the nurse told Mummy 'You will have to carry her then', and Mummy had to struggle with a heavy Catherine in her arms, down in the lift – 'and then we went home and listened to my baby tapes. And then we went to bed'. In order to clarify my own sense that Father had disappeared from the picture, I asked 'Who is we?' Her reply was: 'You and me'. I told her I had listened carefully to her story; at the beginning, her Daddy was there, but by the end there was only herself and Mummy, so I thought she was telling me that *she felt* she had a Daddy until she had a brain scan, and that her Daddy had then got frightened and left them, leaving Mummy to do all the carrying and looking after Catherine, and that sometimes this was too much for Mummy on her own. She seemed thoughtful. Catherine had brought a button on a piece of string, something she carried with her constantly, and on and off throughout the assessment sessions her button was shaken, sometimes in her lap, sometimes up by her ears, and sometimes in front of her face. It was not until Catherine had been in therapy for some time that we came to understanding the meaning the 'button on a string' carried for her.

Later, in the first assessment session, I wondered if she might manage some time on her own with me. In a quavering voice Catherine answered 'No', tucking herself into her mother's body – she clearly wanted to cry. I said that we were not going to do anything here that she did not want to do, but that I thought that perhaps coming to the Tavistock had reminded her of hospitals, and she had told me a story about a brain scan because she had been worried that I too was going to do something like that to her. 'Yes', she answered, tremulously. I explained that my way of working was talking and playing and that I was not going to put anything on her head or give her injections or put her to sleep. Her response was immediate – 'I'll let my mum go and have a cup of tea then'. I was deeply moved by her courage and by her capacity to use some understanding of her unconscious fears.

At the beginning of the second assessment session, Catherine opted to sit on a chair on her own, surprising and pleasing her mother. She recounted their stressful journey to the Tavistock: I said that I thought that one of the things that worried her during this journey was that she thought her Mum was worried. She agreed and immediately indicated that she wanted to sit next to her, which Mum allowed. Catherine then turned to her mother, fiddling with Mum's hair, and sniffing up its smell. I made a link to our previous meeting, suggesting that when Catherine was worried she seemed to need to feel very close indeed to Mum, 'As if she is breathing the same bit of air as you', I said. 'Well we do', her mother replied. I added that Catherine always seemed preoccupied with how Mum was feeling and before I could finish, Mum added 'And I am always concerned about how Catherine is, and that is the nature of it'. Catherine immediately launched into an unpunctuated tale – she had had a tummy bug and diarrhoea and when she got into bed Mum had said to her 'What's that smell?' and then she had had to clean out her bed, and then Catherine went into her bedroom, bedroom number two, and she was sick and then Mum had to clear that up too, and she had started shaking, she was upset and very unhappy – 'What can I do about her shaking?'. Catherine had to make several attempts at this last sentence, struggling to make it clear that it was her mother who was speaking these words. Catherine was right inside the story as she told it, and what became very clear as she talked was that she was both herself, and her mother, and this left her enormously burdened. The story continued with her being taken to hospital. I was told about the telephone operator, the ambulance man, the nurse, the doctor, but Catherine *was* the nurse, she was the doctor, she was the ambulance man. It was distressing and relentless to listen to. I could feel how absolutely exhausting this was for Catherine. Not only was her anxiety not contained but she was invaded by everybody else's distress. There was no respite for her at all.

Towards the end of the second session, Mrs A and I had discussed the viability of Catherine coming to the Tavistock regularly for psychotherapy. The length of the journey made her mother feel that it would be better if something could be found closer to home. Returning to this discussion with Catherine in the third assessment session, she went quiet but then volunteered 'I am thinking something *in my head* taking something at home I take hydrocortisone which is an unpleasant medicine'. She then went on to list all the other medicines she took, and her injections. She told me about the medical bracelet which she wears on her wrist, with all the medical directions on it, all of which she reported apparently accurately, including long medical names. Although she could recite this information she was quite unable to say how she felt about any of it. Then she added, 'I need a bit more medicine and a bit more injections'. As she spoke I was overwhelmed with sadness at the prospect of not continuing the work with her. I felt she was telling me that she wanted more time with me. I told Catherine that I had noticed that today she could allow a pause before she spoke and that she seemed to feel now she had a space called 'in my head', where she could find her thoughts – but she felt that she needed more time with me.

After my assessment with Catherine, I could not get her out of my mind: I was struck by the traumatic events in Catherine's short life, events which together seemed to have robbed her of a meaningful future. But she had inspired in me the same feelings she had inspired in her educational psychologist – I too felt full of hope for her and determined to ensure that she got the help she needed. However, local resources could not be found for psychotherapy and it took exactly another year before all the arrangements could be made for Catherine to begin once-weekly therapy with me at the Tavistock – all that was viable in view of their long journey. Catherine, to my amazement, retained a memory of her assessment with me and was able, from the beginning, to stay the full fifty minutes, leaving her mother in the waiting room.

The beginning of psychotherapy: technical difficulties

Trauma comes from the Greek meaning 'to pierce'. What seemed in Catherine to have been ruptured by the many invasive hospital procedures was a psychic 'membrane' around herself so that her contents were felt to have spilled out and dispersed and she experienced herself as both everywhere and nowhere. She had no reliable 'form' or sense of self; everything felt a part of her and she inhabited everything and everyone. In the early months of therapy the waiting room was a source of absolute terror to her: she was frequently unable to tolerate being in there and had to be removed to the corridor where I would find her slumped against the wall, conveying a sense of having left her mind. When she began to be able to speak to me about the waiting room experience she was able to tell me that the waiting room felt full of hostile sounds. She felt that everything that was said was to her, or about her; the words could pierce her skin like arrows; words were solid objects which went down her ear canal, and hence inside her, remaining there as foreign bodies – intruders. It was some considerable time before she could make any distinction between the different voices – children's or adults', friendly, sad or angry voices, and only after that to distinguish who was speaking to whom. To Catherine initially it was just a threatening cacophony which left her shuddering. When taking her from the waiting room to my consulting room, I felt I was guiding something so fragile through the vicissitudes of the waiting room and corridor that it was as if we were negotiating a minefield, a war zone. And yet when I took her hand in mine it was lumpen, flabby, utterly unresponsive to my hand; it did not grasp, register my hand or make an adjustment to it. She walked with her hands hanging limply by her sides – she would not take a step on her own. It is hard to describe the juxtaposition in Catherine of something formless, blobby, inert and unresponsive, revealed in her heavy, ponderous way of walking and in her sometimes slow, hesitant speech – alongside something so skinless, fragile, vulnerable, so oversensitive, which emerged at other moments in her rapid breathing and the way in which her lumpen body could shake like jelly.

Catherine always waited for me to speak first but she could then talk for fifty minutes without pause. My head felt that it would burst with the very effort of concentration as she filled it with an unpunctuated stream of talk which had little or no recognisable structure and endless, endless repetitions. The analogy that most frequently came to my mind was that of being faced with a bowl of spaghetti. I would catch a line of thought only to have it unravel or drag on to an adjacent thought, snaring it as she went on talking so that I ended up with my head bursting, containing a spaghetti bowl of ideas, thoughts, fragments all entangled. I would often find myself with a hand on either side of my head, in the very effort to keep her thoughts in my mind – as if for me, too, her words had become 'things'. Pronouns constantly changed, adding to my confusion, and words that sounded similar could be sucked up, causing her to suddenly veer off on another tack. Occasionally, I had a tantalising impression of something meaningful taking shape, analogous to the relief one would feel on seeing a friendly figure emerge from a thick fog, but soon any shape was lost again in a swirling mass of fragments. The impact upon me was enormous – sometimes an idea about her, which glowed brightly in my mind only minutes before, would be extinguished, never to be recalled, and I would feel a growing sense of panic. An undertow of anxiety pulled her relentlessly under so that she began to drown in the very experience which she seemed to want to recount. I never knew when, or whether to intervene: I felt in a terrible dilemma. When I spoke I interrupted her flow; as soon as I finished speaking Catherine would quickly follow on the end of my words, usually with a conjunction: '*and…*'. Sometimes my counter-transference suggested that indeed the rupture caused by my interruption had been speedily repaired by the insertion of her 'and', as though some amoeba had treated my words as foreign bodies to be swiftly ingested. At other times her 'and' seemed more inclusive, and served, it would seem, to sew my words to her words so that any gaps between us, any breaks in our combined skin, were swiftly sewn together so that we became a single person 'breathing the same air'.

By the time I spoke I was often left feeling that even if I had said the right thing, it had been at the wrong time. However, if I did not interrupt her, how would she ever discover my separate existence? By the time I came to speak I had another dilemma: should I try to synthesise what she had said, or go for one of the ideas that had begun to take a shape, or simply base my interpretation on the last thing she had talked about? I had to wait long enough for shapes to grow in my mind, but not so long that I became as confused and entangled in this mass of words as she was herself.

In the early weeks and months of her sessions, she had little sense of me as an 'other' and therefore could not judge her impact on me. This difficulty was undoubtedly compounded by the combination of her blindness and her autism. Catherine could not see my responses to what she said, she could not see when I might want to speak or when I could no longer attend, or, more recently, when I became bored and even impatient. Very importantly for Catherine, she could not see whether my responses were friendly or not.

With Catherine, my only way into her world was to notice everything about her, mental and physical: when my interpretations flowed from a deep connect-edness at many sensory levels, then sometimes I succeeded in creating a flow of words which followed the contours of her mind as the skin follows the contours of the body. When I could sustain an empathic responsiveness, then Catherine experienced me as containing her psyche as the skin contains the body (Bick 1986). Then the flow of my words was allowed to replace her unpunctuated stream of talk. When contained in this way she seemed to feel the boundaries drawn around her, and she could then experience *herself*. Potentially, because interpretations change to fit the situation, the therapist's words can then be as elastic as the skin itself, growing, changing imperceptibly, to fit the body; after all, no-one ever notices their skin grow – my 'interpretive fit' was not up to this standard! Initially the breakdown in 'perfect' containment produced frustration and a turning away from me, and I felt reproached at the deepest level and had to struggle with some mad notion that I could, or should, be perfect.

For Catherine it had become necessary to keep whole areas of experience thoroughly sequestered, unavailable for thinking and feeling to come together. They survived intact, ready, it seemed, for some union of mind and experience. Thus I had to see for her what something would be like, feel it for her, think about it before she could take any measure of it back. As I listened to her, someone painted pictures in my mind; vivid, pictorial images, strong metaphors, lively representations. I therefore began to tell her that as I listened to her I had begun to have a picture in my mind. If she seemed to pause at all I would then begin to describe it. My intention was to try to provide a tolerable conjunction between her experience and mine, where the meaning could be experienced first of all by me, and then by Catherine, and then even give some pleasure. It gave me enormous hope that Catherine, potentially, was a person of some creativity.

The wind beneath my wings

Whatever else I felt in the first year, I was never bored. There was something about this strange child that engaged me from the beginning, and whenever we made a contact my heart soared and my mind cleared. It became evident, too, that Catherine enjoyed being understood. Catherine, as I recorded even at the time of her assessment, has always been capable of giving me heart-stopping surprises. As I have tried to describe, much of the time her speech was laboured, as if each phrase could carry her over the edge of a precipice. But when she sang she soared and took flight.

In the second week of her therapy, as she sat on the couch, I noticed her fingers moving delicately, almost secretly, suggestive of someone playing a piano. Feeling slightly foolish, I said that I had noticed her fingers moving as if she might be playing the piano. 'Yes', she said very matter-of-factly – her movements then became bolder, which encouraged me to ask if there was a tune she was playing in her mind. 'Yes', she said, ' "The Wind Beneath My Wings" '. I told her I did not know this song, and asked her to tell me about it. Catherine erupted into song – a strong, vibrant voice, full of emotion, which made me shiver. The song expresses the bird's need for the wind, for without it it cannot fly. Via the song, Catherine introduced her recognition, somewhere, that she needed support or she too could not fly – could not reach her hopes and dreams, achieve her aspirations. I was both shocked and thrilled to hear this powerful voice; although the singing was 'on loan', since she was clearly imitating the voice of the original singer. The song, she thought, came from a film, *Beauty and the Beast*.

Over the following weeks, one of the ideas which resurfaced in a tangle of other ideas, was that of metamorphosis, of things not always being what they seemed, and of the power of love to unlock an imprisoned soul as Beauty does with her love for the Beast. Later on, in the first term of work, as I tried to observe her smallest movements, she again suddenly launched into song. This time the song was 'Put Your Body to the Test'. I thought this was a most eloquent way for her to convey the way in which she did indeed put my body to the test, since I had to use every one of my senses to find my way into her world. But she also made me laugh, as there was a certain cheekiness in her choice of song; and from then on humour also became a feature of our work.

Later in the same session, when I had seemingly passed another test she had unconsciously set me, she again launched into song, singing ' "Bitter, sweet and strange, finding you can change" '. As she sang, again a shiver went through me; I was profoundly moved by her strange but evocative mode of communication. Sometimes I would stop to reflect upon what it was in Catherine that had inspired my wish to help her from the beginning. Sometimes my pleasure felt foolish and disproportionate to some small piece of understanding that would be taken so much for granted by most human infants and their mothers.

A voice of my own

Initially Catherine had to borrow someone else's voice to let me know about something which was 'on her brain' but not yet 'in her mind'. I had to provide the mind whilst someone else, not yet Catherine, provided the words. Through Catherine I came to understand that traumatic memories could continue to exist inside an individual untouched, and in non-verbal form, but accessible to verbalisation once language develops. It was as if a particular story or song somehow resonated in the very core of Catherine's being, but she could not think about its meaning – that was my task.

Catherine, in her third week of therapy, suddenly said 'It came into my head too, a funny little story'. She then began to recite without pause, 'My Naughty Little Sister and the Big Girl's Bed' (a well known children's story by Dorothy Edwards). The story was told not to me, but rather I was allowed to listen – just like a tape recording, she made no pauses for my response. As I listened to this story, told clearly in the voice of the original storyteller, including the original storyteller's inflections, I was entranced, as entranced as I felt she was when she listened to the tape. In the story, the naughty little sister is always naughty until one day the time comes for her to move from a cot to a bed of her own. This time it is her own bed she is to have and she is going to have a brand-new counterpane. Everything else she has ever had has been a hand-me-down from her big sister. I interpreted Catherine's wish to have something that was her own, not something secondhand. I linked this to the way she had told me the story: I told her I had noticed that she was using a voice which I thought must be the voice of the lady on the story tape. She replied 'It is'. I added that I thought she wanted me to know that she, like the naughty little sister, would like to have something that was her very own and that what she wanted to have of her own was her own voice. Catherine agreed with this. Her wish for her own voice and her hope that I would help her to discover it has proved a cornerstone of our work.

The first holiday break approached and I was worried as to how she would manage.

The first holiday break and real communication: autistic sounds

Catherine returned after the first Christmas break ready for work; unusually, she did not wait for me to speak first, but began to tell me about her Christmas presents. 'I had a really interesting tape with space for someone to sing along on it, and a Cinderella tape'. Linked to her tolerance of us as separate people, she revealed a new idea – a space for someone to join in; the possibility of real conversation. She also received 'a frightening present – three tins of talcum powder'. She explained that she hated the noise the talcum powder made as it came out: 'swoosh, swoosh, swoosh' – she managed to convey the intimidating sound which an innocent box of talcum powder made, adding that it used to frighten her when she was a little baby. I told her that she had made it possible for me to understand why. I talked about how, as she could not see, she could not know what this stuff was, she just heard this menacing sound. I linked her capacity to tell me about the things that frightened her with the song of hope, 'The Wind Beneath My Wings' and the story of Cinderella, indicating the possibility of change. I spoke about her hopes for the future. But I had timed it wrongly: she began to speak over me – 'I had a Blobby tape [a reference to a TV character] and Mr Blobby says, "Blobby, blobby, blobby", and when Mr

Blobby says, "Blobby, blobby" I laugh'. This made it possible for us to differen-tiate a Catherine who liked to think, from a Catherine who liked to 'blob out'. Later in the session she told me 'It's my Mum's turn to be poorly'. She told me the story of her mother's illness at Christmas and did not at any point get confused with her. Catherine told me how she had called for help and I acknowledged that she was getting stronger. I also drew her attention to the fact that she was not playing with her button. Her response to this was 'For an emergency we ring 999'. I suggested that she might be wondering what she should do if she really needed me. Her response took me by surprise: she said, 'I think when I need you I think that I will be all clear if I needed you and honourable, well if people are honourable and intelligent, the fact is that these people are very special people and I sometimes feel special too'. She told me about a little girl who couldn't play much, who played with a Fisher-Price tele-phone which is pretend, and plays Mr Blobby. I suggested that a frightened little girl in her had needed to use her sounds to blob out frightening things but there was also now, alongside, a more grown-up self who could think. I asked Catherine if she could tell me what she had meant when she said that she would be clearer if she needed me. She repeated 'I think I need you is the best fright-ening thing to happen because when I feel frightened and when I have been stung by a wasp. I say no go away wasp and so I say that when everything gets in my way and me being cross and worried and displeased and very upset. And when something frightens me *I worry out of my mind*'. I interpreted that some-times, in the past, things were so frightening that she literally had to leave her mind and go outside of it in the way she had shown me in the assessment, but that she was finding it possible to be more and more in her mind. She told me about Charlie who says funny things. She then said, in a quieter voice, the words squeezed together, 'Lynnearooee' (Lynn is her Mother's name). When I said that I thought I knew what this meant she smiled quickly but then flicked her button near her ear. I interpreted the words as meaning her wish to be close to Mummy (Lynn-near-you); her recognition that she needed other people and knew that she did not really want to live 'out of her mind'. She then volun-teered, 'My other funny word is "Clisha-clasha, oo-ee oo-ee oo-ee"'. This, after some time, I understood was a code for the tune of 'Chopsticks'. It emerged that when she was little she had heard her uncle playing the piano and had encoded the sounds in her mind so that she could play back the tune whenever she switched on 'her mind tape'. (She subsequently taught herself to play the piano.) Later in the same session she told me about someone at school she called 'my own boy' who, as she told me in a singsong voice, said 'Holes in your pages, wibbly wobbly woo'. She ended by telling me 'Blobby is a sound when your voice pretends to be even more spooky like a dungeon, horrible place in my mind'. She then rattled her button.

The sounds that Catherine had allowed me to know about kept us busy for many weeks to come. Through many encounters in different sessions I began to understand the significance of the different sounds and their different functions in her world. Hearing the world through her ears I could feel the fascination of

'Holes in your pages, wibbly wobbly woo' and the intoxicatingly mind-numbing effect it had whilst its jolly upbeat rhythm provided a counterpoint to the terrifying, hostile sounds from outside. 'Clisha-clasha' kept both a friendly link to her beloved uncle, but with its hard consonants it made a horrible warning sound – like a snake's hiss with which she threatened her enemies.

The emergence of friendliness

A few months later, laughing, Catherine said, 'When I was in primary a big boy who was called Eleven Years Old...' She began to unravel and started again; 'He is called Johnny and shouted out "Hello, is there anybody there?", and then he burped and I laughed even more'. I talked about Johnny feeling lonely and not very hopeful that there was anybody there, only his own burp. Catherine added 'And he shouted out again, "is there anybody there?" and he didn't get an answer from his burp and I thought "I am there"'.

Within the space of a few months Catherine had moved from feeling that she and I 'breathed the same air', to some recognition that she needed support if she were really to reach her potential – 'The Wind Beneath My Wings'. Her hope that she would find her own voice had found expression via the story 'My Naughty Little Sister'. The beginning of the individuation process had begun, but, in those brief moments when she could tolerate an experience of being separate, she experienced loneliness – probably for the first time. But even this contained the seeds of hope since someone, called 'Johnny' in Catherine's account, could at least call out in some hope that there might be somebody there who would respond.

A few sessions later Catherine began another *My Naughty Little Sister* story; in this story the family babysits another family's baby boy. At first the naughty little sister is only jealous, but gradually she becomes curious until the story ends with how the naughty little sister can do things for the baby that her big sister did for her. In this way it became possible to talk about her understanding that, although she was dependent on me in the session to do all the thinking for her in the first instance, the time would come when she would be able to do it for herself. This led into a third *My Naughty Little Sister* story; this one about 'helping the cleaner with the housework' in which the naughty little sister enjoys helping the lady next door and even has her own little brush to do the housework with. Via this story, Catherine showed a recognition that first you have to tolerate and even enjoy being little (she had much emphasised her own *little* brush) and then you can help Mummy, and learn from experience what a mummy-cleaner does, not by taking over or stealing Mother's qualities, breathing in her air, but by working *with* Mother.

Becoming separate

On one occasion her capacity for incorporation left me breathless – literally. I noticed my difficulty in breathing as I began to breathe more and more quickly:

when I reflected on my counter-transference feeling, somatised at this point in time, I felt suffocated and short of air. I described to Catherine her way of sticking her words so tightly onto the end of my own that it was almost as if she had swallowed my words up. Catherine's response was shockingly straightforward. She told me in a very matter-of-fact way that, as I spoke, she sucked my words up her nose, swallowed them down and then spoke them out of her mouth. A concrete description of a process that should be at a mental level and had been somatised. The usual mental taking in of experience, of absorbing something into one's own mind to then allow it to interact with other experiences, subsequently to be reproduced as something of one's own, had in Catherine become breathed up and absorbed into her very bloodstream. I told her that it reminded me of how, when she had first come to see me, she and Mother seemed to breathe the same air. Catherine nodded 'Yes', and turned her head towards me, showing that she was interested. I said that we could now see something slightly different happening. It was indeed as if we shared the same air but the difficulty was that she seemed to feel that if we became separate only one of us would live. When she breathed up my words I was literally having my life's breath drawn from me. For Catherine the death of either of us was equally terrifying. My interpretation seemed to make it possible for her to take back the experience, and she then began to notice her own difficulty in breathing and swallowing; she could tell me that she had difficulty with 'the liquid in my throat that will not go down'. It was possible to name it 'being anxious', and once understood by her, this experience could be banked, enriching her inner world and ready to be drawn upon in similar situations. Experiences such as this gradually gave Catherine the resources she needed to become increasingly emotionally literate.

As always, Catherine's first response to being understood was to smile, but it was swiftly followed by a sharp shaking of her button. This led us to a discussion of her button; she managed to convey that the sound filled her ears and stopped unpleasant sounds, sounds from outside, getting in. Many sessions were spent in unpacking the meaning and function of her 'button on a string'. The button was firm, hard and strong, and when holding it she felt she incorporated these hard qualities into herself. It was also on a string and this sustained the illusion that she was still joined-up (Lynnearooee) to an omnipresent mother. As she gained her own strength, she used the button less and less until finally it disappeared, never to return.

As may become apparent from this, Catherine's initial wish for help with 'braining' seemed to indicate some very real intuition that whilst she had a brain, she did not yet have a mind. She did not really know what it was to think, to reflect, to pause, to select a word, and so on. Once I had understood this, I decided to be most careful to ensure that my communications to her included a description of what I was trying to do, and how I was trying to do it. Thus I had to wear my mind on the outside, so to speak. For example, I might say 'I'm searching for the right word' or 'No, that's not what I wanted to say' or 'I'm going to try that again, I don't think I made sense'. Catherine became interested in this process and began to experiment with it herself. Catherine did what all toddlers do. In the early stages of experimenting with speaking and thinking she would adopt my ways of talking, speaking and thinking. But it became apparent that there was a real difference between those times when she metaphorically wore my shoes and became me, and when she was trying, as every child does, mother's shoes on for size.

In the second half of her first year of therapy she told me that her session was the most important thing in her week.

The possibility of feeling anger

In the last session before a holiday break in the following year, a new theme emerged called 'The Whole World'. She told me that she wanted to 'niff' the whole world up her nose and irritably insisted that she could do so. She was quite amused by my interpretation that she wanted to be the queen of my whole world. Gradually she came more in contact with the fact that *she* was cross with *me* and that perhaps I was *not* cross with her. For the first time she had a sense that we might have different kinds of feelings. To her surprise her voice became stronger as she became crosser, and this made it possible to show her that being in touch with her crossness might actually make her stronger, not weaker. At the end of the session she walked the whole way with her arms out, her hands feeling the wall and exploring the doors before she opened them. She also pressed the buttons in the lift for herself. Feeling anger signals the beginning of recovery from PTSD, where the feelings of helplessness engendered in victims has been recognised as central to the trauma (Pynoos 1996). Whilst anger tends to be viewed primarily as a negative emotion, a destructive force, work with patients such as Catherine vividly illustrates our vulnerability when the recognition and expression of anger are inhibited.

Two years after her therapy began, in our termly review, Catherine's mother said there were times when she found it hard to remember how autistic Catherine really had been: the balance had shifted now towards Catherine living more in the real world rather than withdrawing to her own. Mother then said 'You were quite right, when we first came to you, you said it was like we breathed the same air, shared the same anxieties, but we are definitely two separate people now'. (School too had noticed an improvement.) Catherine was also continuing to grow physically even though she had been taken off growth hormones. 'She turns everyone's expectations upside down – I wonder what the consultant will make of this?' her mother said.

Her mother reported another important development. Catherine had demonstrated a very ordinary response to a recent hospital visit. She asked her mother, of an impending blood test, 'Will it hurt?'. She had allowed her blood to be taken and then commented, when it was over, that she had been a bit frightened *before*.

Early in the third year of therapy, in an extraordinary session which left me reeling, Catherine set out to delineate what she called 'three dark areas of my mind'. The first she described as 'the dark, cold dungeon with the locked doors where the feelings inside are lonely'. The second was 'a slimy dark cellar' and the third 'a dungeon without walls or doors that is suffocating'. Later she differentiated a cellar from a basement, the cellar being the place where valuable things such as precious wines were stored. Towards the end of that session, Catherine was able to tell me that I, as the therapist, had the key to unlock the door but that *she* would have to open it.

Six months later, just before the summer holiday, when struggling with one of her particularly gluey sessions, I had tried to describe her wish to struggle to stay with 'clear thinking'. However, my exhaustion by the end of the session, and struggle against the glueyness of her communications were revealed when I referred to 'thear clinking' (*sic.*). This caused her to giggle so much so that she was still chuckling when we left the room. She often returned to tease me with 'thear clinking' in subsequent sessions. Via this it became possible to think about her relief that my mind was not perfect, that I made mistakes and had to correct myself. But also, another part of her took pleasure in other people not being able to do things, and I had my first glimpse of some very ordinary adolescent contempt!

I'm not autistic but I am blind

By the middle of the third year Catherine had become increasingly interested in her blindness. She talked about 'little illnesses that get better, bigger illnesses that take longer to get better and some illnesses which never get better'. This made it possible to describe to her how her 'braining' had got much better but that her blindness was not something that could be cured. She told me how 'tears would need to pour down a person's cheek if they think about being blind'. I found to my embarrassment that tears were pouring down my cheek while she appeared perfectly calm. I therefore told her that she was telling me that I must hold all the sadness and pain about her being blind until such time as she could bear to think about it for herself.

The following year was a particularly difficult one – we seemed to make little progress and Catherine withdrew for long periods of time to her more autistic way of functioning. At other times Catherine, too, was frustrated that she 'could not stick to the point'. I felt despair, boredom and guilt – guilt that when she was not autistic, she knew, in a way that she had not really known before, that she was incurably blind. For several months Catherine refused to believe that I could not 'cure' her blindness: she reproached me, telling me that I had made her brain work so why couldn't I make her eyes see? Her mother confirmed that blindness had never been the main issue – the autism had dominated everything else and now she, too, was having to face the implications of Catherine's blindness, almost for the first time.

When I felt I was losing hope that we would ever move forward, Catherine suddenly told me that her mother was sad that Catherine was blind: she seemed to understand, however, that her mother was sad but not devastated – that

Mum would help her face this, just as she had helped her throughout her life. Three sessions of extraordinary intensity followed: first Catherine wanted to know what had made her blind – she had many theories about it, but she also asked her mother to explain it to her. This opened up her wish to know about her early years and to reclaim her lost childhood. Then she compared her blindness with other handicaps and reflected upon what real limitations blindness imposed.

The following year brought many changes: she began to wear her watch, to use her white stick, and became determinedly independent. Catherine achieved great personal success and managed to gain a much sought-after place in a special residential college for the blind.

In a recent session Catherine struggled to stay with *feeling* sad and *thinking* about the sadness, but it was too much. She said 'I'm getting a bit stuck with this, can you put it right for me – my big girl self knows how to explain easy things but the little girl in me keeps going back to too many unhappy sad memories'. I suggested that it was bringing together thinking and feeling which she was finding so difficult. Catherine responded by reviewing many of the traumatic memories from her early years. She then suddenly announced 'It's a case of *little* and *BIG Memories*!' I suggested that the BIG memories belonged, now, to the past, and tried to differentiate the frightened little autistic blind girl of the past, from the blind, non-autistic, more independent sixteen year-old young woman of the present. Catherine said 'Now I remember a *small memory*', and proceeded to recount an ordinary memory of a visit, as a little girl, to her uncle's house, where she had explored the house and garden on her own. This seemed to free her to begin to let go of her traumatic memories – to have permission to 'forget' and to have space in her mind for the more ordinary, everyday experiences which are a source of extraordinary pleasure to her.

With the impending separation from her mother, and an increasingly strong sense of personal identity, Catherine has become aware, for the first time, of her mother's qualities. A sense of deep love, appreciation and gratitude for her has emerged. Although there is still a long way to go, I believe that Catherine has confirmed her mother's hope and belief in her daughter. They have become two separate people.

Conclusion

Working with Catherine has been a privilege. Because she has language, she has allowed me a particularly vivid access into her world, and in doing so has given added richness to my understanding of autistic phenomena. Working with her has given me increased conviction when I work with more severely autistic children, and children with little or no language at their disposal. Exploring with Catherine her strange autistic world, we have discovered many extraordinary things. She has increased my passionate belief that the seemingly meaningless behaviour observed in autistic children can gradually yield meaning as we find a way into each of these children's unique worlds.

Our work together has been a struggle against enormous odds, a struggle which is ongoing. Yet now, all those close to Catherine, and Catherine herself, dare to hope that she has a future. I will let Catherine have the last words. 'When I am a grown-up lady, I want to have a house with a garden, with my own flowers in it, with my own pet to look after and one day I want to grow a baby in my own tummy and then look after it'.

9 Sean

From solitary invulnerability to the beginnings of reciprocity at very early infantile levels

Pamela Bartram

This little boy and his parents were assessed by colleagues over a period of several months. His parents had referred him when he was nearly two years old. Their particular causes for concern were his lack of social relations and communications skills, inability to play, sleeplessness, poor eating, and a repetitive action which, once begun, took him over and was interrupted only with great difficulty – termed 'rocking' by the family.

Sean's development had apparently been normal until he was around eighteen months old. His birth had gone well. His mother described him as an easy, but lively baby. He attained the normal milestones within the first year and had begun to use words in the second. He was sociable and interested in other people. However, he became less responsive and lost the words he had begun to use. The family dated his deterioration to a period when they had suffered a traumatic loss. At around this time the 'rocking' began.

During the assessment Sean was felt to be, notwithstanding his considerable difficulties, an endearing child in whose eyes could be glimpsed flashes of alertness and even mischief. He showed some response to attempts to discourage his autistic behaviours, and over the months of the assessment his parents reported improvement in his eye contact and sleeping patterns, and an increase in his vocalisations. There were indications that he might be reachable, although there were concerns about the way in which the strength of his will and determination might reinforce his tendency to avoid contact. Sean began three-times weekly individual psychotherapy sessions with me four months before he turned three.

On meeting Sean I was straight away struck by his physical presence. He was a good looking, slim, well coordinated little boy, who spent much of the time in ceaseless physical activity. His feet rarely touched the floor of the room, as he roved surefootedly from the arm of a chair to a tabletop, to the window sill, rarely stumbling or falling. If he did lose his footing, either his face would register nothing, as if there had been no bump or hurt, or a few minutes later he would cry and grasp the door handle as if to leave the room. It took some time before I began to see that this was, in fact, a delayed response to his injury, so separated in time had they become from each other.

When he undertook unfeasible manoeuvres, such as stepping from the tabletop onto the back of a chair which would have tipped over, I found myself stepping in to support him, to prevent him falling. He would then use me to balance on and to complete the manoeuvre, of which I had simply become a part. One day I registered that his calves were like those of a ballet dancer, the muscles bulging as a result of what must have been hours of 'practice'. His demeanour while he performed these feats was aloof and self-assured. Even when attempting to bridge two impossibly distant pieces of furniture, he betrayed no flicker of doubt that it could be done.

He jumped habitually and this too contributed to his musculature. Jumping seemed to have almost magical qualities and powers for him. When he wanted the door to open or the tap to go on, he would stare at it, eyes widened, jumping with an athlete's power, grinning and squealing, as though he really believed his jumps would open the door.

Like his climbing and jumping, his 'rocking' also had the effect of locking and isolating him within the world of his body. This was a movement in which he used both hands to clutch himself at the inside of his thighs or under the perineum whilst making a regular rhythmic pushing movement with his feet. He usually lay on his back, face upwards when doing this. It did not seem to be masturbatory in character, but involved Sean both in holding himself in, as if afraid that something would fall out from between his legs, and simultaneously pushing something away with his feet. Sometimes he spent the whole fifty-minute session 'rocking'. As a result I was able to learn something about the immense physical effort it took to repeat these movements over and over again. I would sometimes try to hold his hands away from his thighs in an attempt to interrupt the activity. For a moment he would allow his hands to be held, then like coils of metal they would spring back into place. Time and again I marvelled at the physical strength and tautness of this movement, and despaired at how far from me it had taken him. At such moments neither my words nor actions seemed capable of having an impact on him, and it brought forcibly to my mind how difficult it must be for his parents to deal with this in the course of his everyday life. McDougall has described this powerfully:

> The curtains on the mind's stage were tightly drawn, so to speak; no sound reached the outside ears, and yet a drama was being played out in this secret theatre that threatened the very life of the theatre owner himself.
>
> (McDougall 1989: 2)

The 'theatre of the body'

From all that I have described so far, it can be seen that I found myself preoccupied by the state of Sean's body. I came to think about this in terms of a mother's preoccupation with her baby's physical state, particularly in the early weeks of life during which babies' states of mind are intimately bound up with their bodily needs. Although Sean seemed not in the slightest degree exhausted by his exertions, I began to feel that I was with an overtired baby who could not allow himself to rest and to sleep, and indeed this accorded with his parents' account of his sleeplessness at night.

Thus it became important that I notice any small sign he gave of tiredness, and that I construed some of his exhaust*ing* behaviour as exhaust*ed* behaviour, and spoke to him about it, offering the pillow and blanket on the couch to rest on. With time and practice he developed a capacity to rest, and to recognise the word 'tired' when I used it. He began to take pleasure in resting and in the more intimate exchanges which became possible once he had stopped being constantly on the move.

The possibility of feeling tired was also explored when we began to play games together, such as ring-a-ring-a-roses. Sean wanted to repeat it many times over. I felt this was not simply an empty mindless repetition, but was more like the way in which a small child wants a nice thing over and over again. I struggled with myself over my own physical tiredness, wanting to allow him to find repeatedly the experience he sought, to give him an experience of 'there's plenty more where that came from'; I marvelled at how large was his appetite for it, but also I talked about my own tiredness and went to the couch for a rest between bouts of going round. My notebook records:

> Sean wanted to go round again and I said this would be the last time because I was tired. When it was finished I went over and sat on the couch saying, 'Oh, I'm tired out'. Sean looked over at me, then scooted over and got up beside me on the couch, sitting very close. He gave me a joyful look and snuggled up against me, and a rush of affection for him rose up in me. I said, 'That's so nice, we're having a rest together'. Sean got down, took my hands and led me to do the game again. Then straight after it finished, *he* led *me* back to the couch. Again I sat down. He snuggled up close to me and looked into my face, smiling. I said 'Another rest. That's right, we need it. So tired ... oh it's nice'.

Sean began to develop a capacity to rest, which involved both an awareness of his own tiredness, and also an ability to let go rather than driving himself on. By the third term of work he began to sleep for longer periods through the night.

As our work continued, the rocking diminished, although at times of stress it returned. His body was more relaxed and he climbed much less. When he did, he was more prone to losing his footing, possibly indicating a less certain sense of invulnerability. If he did slip, he would register the hurt and allow me to attend to it. Then he spent long periods sitting or lying on the couch, with me kneeling beside him, our faces eight or nine inches apart. It is at this distance that in the early weeks of life, the baby optimally focuses, (i.e. the distance between his own eyes and his mother's eyes when feeding (Stern 1977a: 44).

The theatre of the mouth

I came to learn that Sean's mouth seemed to function as an arena within which dramas were enacted but to which my access was, of necessity, very restricted. What he did in his mouth was not easily knowable. One of the more obvious examples was the way he 'plugged' his mouth with a suitable portable object, for example the head of a drumstick. He also inflated his cheeks as if finding yet another way of giving himself an experience of having a full mouth.

In an early session he touched the toy truck with his tongue as if to get to know it. It struck me how unshareable a way of knowing something this was, how different from us both looking together at the truck. His tongue experience of it could only be private. Of course, tongue exploration is part of normal development, but Sean seemed to have become stuck at that stage. Meltzer has written about the mouth as the theatre for the development of meaning and of the developmental shift which takes place when the play of the playroom of the mouth goes upwards to occupy the mind and outwards into the hands (Meltzer 1986: 178ff).

Sean also often picked up minute pieces of rubbish from the floor to pop quickly into his mouth, and picked his nose and put the contents into his mouth. These acts of scavenging and appropriation (which I stopped when I could), so much in contrast with his eating inhibitions, reminded me of another patient who described feeling that he 'recycles the contents of his own mind'. Sean felt he required no external feeder, no nutritious food. He had a way of burping and swallowing over and over again, as if bringing up something from far down inside himself and then sending it back down again. (Many of these children have strange feeding habits – a somewhat neglected area of study – but see Sybille Janert's research [1993]).

On one occasion, I had been singing to accompany his cymbal beats. He seemed intrigued by the singing, came over to me and tried to put his whole fist into my mouth, as if to find out what the singing was and where it had come from. He almost seemed to feel that he could concretely touch the singing with his hand.

Throughout the sessions Sean made various babbling sounds, including 'baba', 'mama' and 'dada', particularly when moving around the room, sometimes doing it in such a way as to leave me feeling out of touch with him. What seemed to be important to Sean was the feel, the shape of the words in his mouth, rather than a sense of their communicative potential. In normal development, both are important. One idiosyncratic sound which was prevalent was 'mmm ccho', which he began to make in the corridor on our way to the consulting room. This had the feeling of something taken in or held in the mouth (the 'mmm' sound) then coughed or spat out from down the throat (the 'ccho' sound). Some light was to be shed on this by the development of his water play, which I shall describe later.

A significant development arose when Sean's teeth came more into focus. At one point, Sean very much wanted to play with the water, and as this entailed much flooding and splashing I tried to insist that he wore the apron. However, he would resist this strongly and, rather than wear the apron, gladly forfeit the water. I struggled with him and puzzled over this until one day I saw him staring at the elasticated cuff as he tried to evade the apron, and simultaneously setting his jaw as if to bite it. It seemed to me that he thought there was a bite in the cuff, the part of the apron which grips, and this enabled me to talk to him about his fear, and to tell him that he was quite wrong, there was in fact no bite in the cuff: 'You *think* there's a bite there but no, the bite's in *there* [in his mouth] not *here* [the cuff]'. He began to be more willing to wear the apron.

There were other indications that Sean felt that wherever two things met, there would be something sharp, a bite or nip; for example the way in which he repeatedly ran his fingers along the space between the door and its frame, while starting to close the door, threatening to nip his fingers in the hinges. Games developed, for example 'eat you all up', in which I was to be the biting one who wanted to bite Sean up into little pieces. Sean very much liked these games. For my own part, every time we played it I was aware of the two opposite meanings of 'eat you all up'. The sense of sharp biting teeth devouring and destroying, and the sense of Sean being so delicious that a Mrs Bartram-person could not avoid wanting to bite and eat him all up. These games seemed to allow the exploration of his anxiety about biting, and allowed its positive connotation to counterbalance his fear of his own overwhelmingly ferocious urges.

The fragmentation of eye contact and self-regulatory behaviour

> Looking away behaviour reflects the need of each infant to maintain some control over the amount of stimulation he can take in via the visual mode.
> (Brazelton *et al.* 1974: 60)

Sean had seemed to lack an inner voice or awareness which could have monitored his physical state and helped him to modulate his level of excitement so that he could let go within himself, and rest. The ways in which he made and avoided eye contact also revealed his difficulty in regulating his experiences. In the early days of our work, there was no normal eye contact with me. As he moved around the room his large eyes were usually very wide open but empty, and I had the impression that the rims of his eyes were held taut as if he were holding something in place.

By contrast, his characteristic way of looking at me was to look from a distance of several feet and bat his eyes shut, then open again; at other times he would quickly look away and then back again repeatedly. These gaze behaviours were perhaps particularly striking at the end of sessions:

> Sean was up in his mother's arms and looking away. I said 'bye-bye'. He remained averted, as if deaf. I repeated 'bye-bye', more insistently, 'You

nt to see me go'. 'Bye-bye'. I touched his arm. Sean turned his
ine and at precisely the moment at which our eyes would have
)atted them shut. As they reopened, he was already averting his
gaze by turning his head.

I felt that he was making me disappear and reappear at will. However, in this as
in other aspects of my work with Sean, I found that to bear in mind the developmental dimension of his behaviour provided a useful counterpart to thinking
exclusively in terms of pathology. As Alvarez says,

> We should not ... confuse the building of the house with the building of
> the defensive fortifications which may eventually surround it. We build
> houses with walls to keep the weather out, but also to mark, frame and
> preserve that which may take place within.
>
> (Alvarez 1992a: 112)

From a developmental perspective, therefore, it is possible to think of Sean's
gaze aversion not simply as a means of shutting me out, but as a way of
'preserving' the tolerability of knowing me by looking. This, then, could be
thought of as an area in which Sean had found a way of regulating his experience of taking me in with his eyes (see Alvarez, this volume: Chapter 4).

However, it is equally important to acknowledge that whatever its function
for Sean, the effect of this self-regulation on the person he was with was qualita-
tively different from that created by the gaze and gaze aversion of a normal
infant. The rapidity and frequency of this eye-batting contributed to this difference; the period of attention was effectively chopped into small fragments by
these frequently occurring withdrawals of gaze. But it is also to do with how
they are placed in time in the context of what is happening between the two
people. There are moments in an interaction at which gaze aversion 'feels right',
feels part of an interactive curve with natural ups and downs. In contrast, Sean's
gaze aversion had the feeling of a switch being abruptly thrown, not in the
context of what was happening between the couple, but in accordance with
some private sense he had of what should happen next.

Despite this qualitative difference, however, I found it helpful to tilt the
experience he presented to me: to view it not, I hope, through rose-coloured
glasses, but through 'developmentally informed' ones. This tilting process has
helped me to keep doors open within my own vision of him, rather than finding
myself repeatedly hammering on closed ones.

The beginnings of reciprocity: more normal forms of regulation

> The infant first has to learn to be with someone and to create and share the
> experiences that a relationship is built on.
>
> (Stern 1977a: 81)

Given the way Sean evoked my preoccupation with his bodily state, it is perhaps not surprising that when he and I began to make lively, pleasurable and personal contact with each other, it was his body and his physical activities which were the vehicle for doing so.

Noticing the importance of his feet to him in jumping and climbing, and occasionally catching him gazing at them while he brought them together and apart, I allowed them to become a focus of my attention. The 'baby toes' (his bare feet) became our first object of mutual attention and affection. Sean seemed more able to tolerate this than when I looked him directly in the face, or when I touched or looked at his hands and fingers. Play with the baby toes involved my warm greeting to them as they emerged from within Sean's socks and shoes, followed by games such as this-little-piggy-went-to-market. Sometimes he found this hard to tolerate in spite of, or perhaps because of, its sequential nature and the small waits between each toe being attended to. Then he would jump up as I was in mid-sentence, and dash away. More acceptable to Sean was his feet being held over my eyes so that a sort of peekaboo game evolved. I became used to talking to his toes, and he began to gaze and smile at them affectionately when I did so. At the end of the session, he would watch them solemnly as I bid them goodbye and again they were concealed within his socks and shoes.

The session in which I found myself once again talking to his toes but realising that we had outgrown this, was especially important. Sean was now 'in' his eyes and ears, 'in' his face. I then began to be able to address him directly. I had gone on taking the toes as my interlocutor without noticing that now I could speak to Sean himself about them.

Jumping was also significant. Like his climbing and rocking, it served to isolate him and to immunise him against my attempts to engage him. However, encouraged in supervision to 'get in on it', I began to praise his jumping with warmth and enthusiasm in my voice: 'What a big jump! What a big strong boy you are!'. This caught his attention. He would turn to look at me, a small smile betraying his pleasure. I offered him my hands to support his jumping, and sang in time with it. He seemed surprised at first by this offer, but soon began to enjoy my 'supporting role' in it. This element of surprise at finding he was not after all alone interested me. It seemed to indicate that rather than simply turning away from contact, he forgot that there was someone there who wanted to be in touch with him.

Another of Sean's solo activities was to climb up on to the tabletop and walk backwards and forwards along it. When I took his hands he would use the support I offered to take the opportunity to jump down off the end of the table. This became 'the circuit game'. It entailed Sean taking my hand and leading me to the armchair, from which he climbed up onto the tabletop. He walked along it, still holding my hand, and then paused at the end before preparing to jump back down to the floor. Before the jump, I counted, 'one … two … three … ', attenuating the 'three' in such a way as to hold it with my voice until the moment at which he jumped. As he landed I would say 'down!' to match exactly the moment of his arrival on the ground, and bend my knees so that our faces were level and our eyes met at the moment of landing. Periods of prolonged and intense eye contact developed, particularly during the moments of the attenuated 'three', which rose dramatically in pitch, often until my voice could go no higher. First he began to make his own 'eeeeee' sound to match my 'three'. Then he began to vocalise on 'one' and 'two', placing his sounds in time to coincide with mine, although the sounds themselves resembled a deaf child's attempts to speak. He began to catch my eye to initiate the game, and to gaze at me throughout the 'circuit', only turning away after the landing. Then he would lead me back again to the armchair, exuding a sense of happy and purposeful anticipation. This game had the natural form of mother-infant interactions as described by Brazelton *et al.* involving the stages of initiation acceleration, peak of excitement (at the 'threeeee') and finally, deceleration (Brazelton *et al.* 1974: 56).

Providing as it did a form within which there was the opportunity for variation within repetition, it offered Sean an experience of regulating my part in the interaction. For example, much scope for variation lay in the timing of the 'threeeee'. Sometimes he would begin to jump, and I would have to cut it short; at other times he would wait and wait until I ran out of pitch and breath before releasing me by jumping. We never timed the jump exactly the same way twice. It allowed Sean the experience of pushing me forward or holding me up – of regulating my flow. I am not sure that this game could really be described as an exercise in mutual regulation, since the adaptations were made only by me rather than by the two of us. Nevertheless, its value lay in the experience it afforded him of exercising mastery over the timing of my responses to him, and of course, inseparable from the form the game took, in the fun, the pleasure we shared in it. The moment of landing came to feel increasingly important. He would turn to me and look into my face searchingly. It felt to me essential that I too survived the leap and was there to meet him safely on the other side of it.

'All gone' and 'more'

The circuit game just described was one of the gateways through which we discovered a new area of play.

From the beginning there had been moments when Sean would drop a toy (usually accidentally) and get down to retrieve it. The possible link between a disappearance and a return had always seemed to me to be a hopeful sign, although there were many other occasions on which he would not even register that something had been dropped, far less look for or retrieve it. Now emerged a nexus of games dealing with this area of experience, but in which Sean more deliberately exercised mastery of the process. Their themes were 'all gone' and 'more'.

> Sean gently pushed the hoop toy and set it rocking. He looked away. It gradually slowed down but before it could stop Sean set it rocking again. As I began to accompany this process with my voice, catching the dying

mood in the melody, he allowed the toy to stop before re-starting it. The rocking of the toy had a natural contour. There were no sharp edges. ... Sean pulled me around and I understood he wanted to do ring-a-ring-a-roses. As we repeated the game Sean gazed affectionately up into my face. When we came to 'all fall down' he would not fall down although I did. Sensing his anxiety I introduced a sung phrase, 'and then we get up'. He relaxed. Now there was a link between the down-ness of down and the going-around-ness of ring-a-ring-a-roses.

I thought of these games in terms of Sean exploring an experience of security, wholeness, completeness, and its opposite – loss, danger and collapse. In the moments of all-gone-ness and down-ness I was vividly aware of just how down and all-gone it seemed to him and of how hard it was to retain a sense of fullness, to imagine finding more. In his reluctance to 'all fall down' he conveyed how dangerous it was to be the 'down' one, something which had also been conveyed in his constant climbing up high. Nevertheless he had the opportunity of watching me 'all fall down' many many times and my ability to get up and restart the process.

Another game exploring this experience involved Sean climbing into the cupboard under the sink and pulling the door shut. As he began to shut the door from inside, our eyes would meet. I said 'Goodbye, see you in a minute'. When this had become established he would sometimes try to shut the door whilst averting his gaze. I would resist this, attenuating the moment of departure rather than allowing it to be passed over as quickly as possible without acknowledgement. Once he was inside with the door shut there would be a period, variable in length, of silence. Then I would knock or speak: 'Where's Sean? Where is he? Where's that boy?' Slowly or quickly, gradually or suddenly, quietly or loudly, the door would open and Sean would be revealed to me, usually already on his way out.

It was during this game that warm and lively feelings began to be part of our work together, and it was only with their arrival that I registered how absent they had previously been. At the moment of re-finding each other I felt a great, unexpected rush of feeling and easily betrayed my delight in re-encountering him through my words, my voice and doubtless through my facial expression and body language. He noticed my pleasure, and at first seemed shyly pleased, with perhaps also a hint of the surprise mentioned earlier. Soon he began to seem as pleased to be found as I was to find him.

I felt that an important aspect of this game was of Sean exploring his own mastery of the gone-ness and there-ness of his important figures. We repeated it many times and I felt that he now was building up a muscle, not in his legs, but rather the infant's sense of rediscovering time and time again the survival of these figures.

With the development of the mutual, regulating rhythmical games, Sean began to greet me affectionately in the waiting room, coming forward with a smile, sometimes with hands outstretched. He would turn towards me at the sound of my voice. These developments were mirrored at home, where his parents reported that he was becoming more demonstrative and affectionate. Initially when I had collected him there was no word, look or gesture of farewell to the person we were leaving, and this was always a painful moment to witness. Then came a time when Sean and I would be setting off. I would pause with him at the waiting room door and say, 'Let's say goodbye to Mummy'. I noticed that Sean looked confused and disorientated and would step back towards his mother as if he wasn't after all coming with me. I realised that by introducing the idea of parting from someone else at that moment, I was disrupting Sean's tenuous sense of 'what-it-is-to-be-with-Mrs-Bartram-on-the-way-to-the-therapy-room'. Then I understood that until he had the feel of what it was to be with someone, it didn't make sense to ask him to let someone go. He was too busy struggling with the puzzle of a hello, to be able simultaneously to manage a goodbye.

The water play: movement between absence and presence

Like the other games described, the water play allowed Sean to explore the cycle of 'going', 'gone' and 'more'. The going-away-ness of the water began to find a place in his attention, as he listened carefully and unhurriedly to it going down the plughole. It felt as if a sense of contour was developing between the on-ness of more and off-ness of all gone, the linking being provided by the intermediary stage of going-away-ness. I experienced this as an almost palpable 'opening out' of a space, in which thoughts could be thought and feelings felt. Sean began to say bye-bye to me at the end of sessions, and to the person he was leaving in the waiting room at the beginning. Anticipating the water, he would say 'on, wawa on' and try to say 'all gone' ('a' go' '). It seemed to be the very nature of the liquid medium which allowed these developments to take place. In contrast to his play with solid objects such as the bricks, he was more able to allow space for the contemplation of this process in water play. This made me think about his difficulty in coping with solid foods.

However, the water play also gave me an opportunity to observe some of his difficulties with any kind of taking-in at the oral level. I have already described his 'mmm ccho' sound which he often made when playing with water. Sometimes he put a cup of water, or the teapot spout to his mouth. It was striking how impossible it was for him unequivocally to take some water into his mouth and swallow it. Sometimes he managed this with the first sip, but on the second would take water from the cup, swallow some, and in the very same action allow some to dribble back out of his mouth. With each sipful, less would be taken in and more spat or dribbled out. Similarly, when drinking, he would blow into the cup of water, or else extend his tongue that way, as if he must penetrate the water rather than have it enter him. I reflected that protruding his tongue in this way avoided the necessity for bringing the two lips together, and also for bringing the lips and the cup together. (I wondered if he was afraid that his mouth might get bitten by the cup.) He seemed really to need these methods of preventing the wholesale introjection of what he appeared to imagine was a very dangerous object. What was painful to contemplate was how much these restrictions limited his intake of what would be nourishing for both mind and body. The water play afforded us an area in which we could mutually negotiate the questions of starting and stopping, of how much and how little, and of when and when not.

There were many struggles over the setting of limits on how much water and wetting was allowed. His usual response to my limit setting was apparent total indifference.

An important development came when Sean, having moved with apparent unconcern away from the sink, sat up high on the table at the window and looked back across the room at the tap which I had refused to switch on. I said, 'You *still* want that water'. He looked away and moved off, but again, from his new vantage point, turned to look at the tap. In all, he looked back at the tap seven times. He was allowing me, and himself, to know there was something he didn't have, that he wanted: that there is a gap between the ideal and the real. An absent something or someone was not instantly consigned to oblivion. Timelessness can be created by the endless repetition of an action. Sean used to open and close the cupboard doors meticulously and incessantly. Timelessness can also be created by fragmentation so that moments are a series of dots which are not interlinked. I was often struck by how impossible it was to use any tense other than the present when speaking to him. But here was a sequence which took place in real time, the beginning of a knitting together of split seconds into a larger fabric of experience, more communicable, therefore, than his usual fleeting snatches of activity.

A world of emotions

As the therapy progressed, a world of emotionality began to be revealed, in contrast to the strange empty-feeling atmosphere of the early days in which the world of a bodily, 'sensation-dominated state' (Tustin) seemed more real than a world of feelings. The circuit game and the cupboard game both allowed me to see a Sean capable of exquisite tenderness. On one occasion when I greeted him as he re-emerged from the cupboard, I had to avert my own eyes from his gaze, not because it felt too intrusive or intense, but because it felt too human, too beautiful. On another occasion when he turned to face me before jumping, in a variation of the circuit game, I could find no words for the play of emotions I saw in his face: tenderness, love, shyness – he was infinitely shy, yet open, without reserve. This made it possible to acknowledge how chillingly dismissive of our contact he could be on other occasions.

> He would not drink any water but blew it hard in the cup, then poured it away. Twice, without warning, he threw the cup of water in a violent, speedy movement down and behind him. The third time, he simply let it drop into the sink as if it were less than nothing.

After a missed session he would not look at me. He went through the motions of the circuit game but neither looked at me nor vocalised. His demeanour was nonchalant, even superior. I felt he had taken the heart out of the game.

At this moment, he did not give the impression of someone failing to latch on because he didn't know how to, but of someone who would not, could not allow himself to latch on. At such moments, I found it hard to refer to myself by my name. I seemed to have become a 'that thing', an unspeakable object of Sean's contempt. At a similar moment, he emerged from the cupboard not shyly and tenderly, but with a kick that sent the door crashing into the plaster wall where it left a dent. He would not look at me. He repeated this unrelentingly. At other times a much 'hotter' rage was present. He kicked open the cupboard door fierily, and burst out like an explosion.

A terrible distress came into the sessions, a level of pain which I barely knew how to contain. It was difficult to understand where such immoderate feelings could be coming from in such a young child.

> Sean was on the couch and briefly quietened. A new wave of something painful broke over him. His face was stricken, he looked at me pleadingly, then lunged forward to bite me, and as I prevented him and held him, patting his chest at his heart, he quietened again. Soon there was another wave. Even in the midst of it, he seemed to be registering my response to the quality and depth of his feelings. I patted his chest as if to keep his heart beating.

There were times of despair and miserable, tearless crying.

> In the waiting room I called Sean's name. He turned to look and then turned away. He cried and moaned and had to be carried to the room. He threw himself down on the carpet, weeping tearlessly. Later I built a tower of bricks and he put one on the top, but as the tower toppled he gave a terrible cry and dashed away from it. … He went to the table of the circuit game, but pulled away from me. He took the circuit at a run, and without pausing jumped alone off the end of the table, as if from a great height (the height was not great). He let out a cry, a look of terror on his face.

It was difficult to find words for the emotions and feelings he brought. Immense tenderness, terrible rage, and as I have just described, inconsolable distress. They were very intense, as if undiluted by contact with the observable world.

Discussion

I would like to highlight two characteristics of the work with Sean which seemed particularly important in my endeavours to understand him.

The first is captured evocatively by Tennyson.

thus a delicate spark
Of glowing and growing light
Thro' the livelong hours of the dark
Kept itself warm in the heart of my dreams,
Ready to burst in a colour'd flame;
Till at last when the morning came
In a cloud, it faded, and seems
But an ashen-gray delight.

Maud, Part 1, VI, iii

As I have described in the water play, the first sip was tolerable, even welcomed and enjoyed, but each successive sip became less and less tolerable, more and more persecutory. So too, with each repetition of this-little-piggy, he became more distant. Having been intrigued by its first 'run' he began to avert his gaze and smile less as if in accordance with the law of diminishing returns: it was death by a thousand blows. I puzzled over this phenomenon, contrasting to such an extent as it did with the normal mother-baby type interactions we shared at other times, where repetition with variation is the very stuff of the play. Here, however, each new good experience became desultory, deadened, and a wealth of developmentally vital (in both senses of the word) experiences was foreclosed to him. A painful and frustrating manifestation of this was the way that Sean began to use a word meaningfully, for example 'on' in relation to the water, but then, rather than it becoming part of a growing vocabulary, the word disappeared, or else was used both in context and out of context, as if to make a 'non-sense' of it. It may be that there was a part of Sean open to finding new good experiences: but the problem lay in having to learn how to manage the feel of them and to tolerate the excitement, pleasure and anxiety of finding them. His solution seems to have been to cut off exactly at the point where another child would seek prolongation of the experience; rendering the lively contact an 'ashen-gray' delight.

The second aspect of the work with Sean was that of his need, at times, to be above and beyond the ordinary and of a particular quality I felt I needed to bring to my work with him. It had to do with what seemed to be his need for a very alive, larger-than-life person to experience. This struck me forcibly when singing the rising cadence, 'And then we get up' after 'All fall down' in ring-a-ring-a-roses. I found myself thinking that I really must try to sing higher than the top G or so that I was managing, and fleetingly considered taking singing lessons!

I dramatised: 'Oh, I'm *so* tired! Worn out! ... *Look* at that water ... *so* big' – perhaps a version of the exaggerated gestures of what Stern calls 'infant-elicited social behaviours' (Stern 1977a: 16; see Alvarez, this volume: Chapter 5, on regulation). What struck me forcibly was, 'Here is a little boy with great expectations which actuality could never match up to. The water had to be full on, gushing noisily; the pitch range of the speaking voice wasn't wide enough; the pleasure when it came was unspeakably pleasurable. This little prima donna was never going to be happy in the *corps de ballet*'.

Correspondingly, Sean's disappointment and pain did not feel like those of a three year-old child: their depth and intensity seemed to have escaped any moderating, modulating influence within.

I came to understand my interventions as serving to lay a grid over the formlessness, timelessness and unmanageability of Sean's experience, allowing it to be taken in, in smaller 'bite-sized' pieces, while at the same time I had to be sensitive to his genuine need for the experience to be big enough, dramatic enough and loving enough to hold his attention.

Conclusion

I have tried to show in this paper how this little boy was able to allow himself to become more open to people's attempts to make relationships with him. In our relationship, this process seems to have been initiated by my observations of his physical state and my showing an interest in this, and in the ways in which he used his body. I have suggested that this could be thought of as similar to the preoccupation that is aroused in a care-giver with the physical state of a very small baby.

I found that certain factors in him pulled Sean back from the experience of emotional closeness and the learning experiences which can result from it: first, when his expectations were not met, his anger and disappointment were not easily mitigated; second, there was always a tendency for ground which had been gained to be once again lost.

Nevertheless, Sean could sometimes allow himself to be drawn into an emotional relationship within which his capacity for play, exploration and mutuality did begin to grow.

The regular meetings with his parents proved very helpful in understanding where difficulties still lay. Each new developmental stage, for example toilet training, brought into focus once more the struggle between the demands of the external world and Sean's own determined efforts to evade their orbit. These meetings also enabled us to confirm that Sean had indeed developed in his capacity for relatedness, and that he was able to make some compromises with the requirements of those around him. He was more sociable, and his ability to communicate and to take in the communications of others had also grown.

I am grateful to Sean's parents for their permission to write and publish this chapter, and to Anne Alvarez, who supervised my work with him.

10 Edward

Lost and found: from passive withdrawal to symbolic functioning

Branka Pecotic

Edward was referred to the Child Guidance Clinic when he was less than three years old, following a diagnosis of moderate to severe autism, established by several independent professionals. The parents wished for another opinion, as well as some advice and help for Edward and themselves. He was assessed by my colleague and responded well. Four times weekly psychoanalytic psychotherapy was recommended which he began when he was three and a half years old.

Early history

Edward is the second child of a successful professional couple, who lived abroad for a period of time and then settled in this country before he was born. His early development was described as ordinary and he was able, at the end of his first year, to use some words and communicate. He also started walking early and showed generally good physical ability and sensory motor coordination. However, in the first part of his second year, his younger brother was born and it was during that year of his life that both his mother, and the professionals Edward came in contact with, became increasingly concerned about his withdrawals, complete lack of speech and non-reactiveness. He also developed autistic rituals and passivity; he seemed generally unreachable. It was at that time that a diagnosis of autism was first tentatively suggested.

Beginning therapy

At the time his treatment started, Edward was deeply withdrawn, cut off, unable to use words and lacking even minimal interest in his surroundings. However, he had some faint and very indirect ways of showing me that there was a bit of an observant and responsive part of him which wasn't fully extinguished or cut off.

Looking back at all the material gathered after several years of work with Edward, I am amazed at how much interaction and meaningful and creative communication, as well as development in Edward, took place during that time. It is, however, misleading to believe that our sessions were altogether interesting, creative and leading to development. Quite the contrary: most of the ιd myself struggling with boredom, emptiness, and deadness in the well as, later on, irritation at his turning away and with his rituals, would not let me interfere with. What sustained the work and my hope in its usefulness was the fact that in each session, however unbearably long it seemed, something always happened, even if it appeared to be like a tiny drop of communication in the ocean of deadness. The periods of communication, as opposed to the deadening cutting-off, increased with time and it became much easier, as the years went on, to stay attuned to Edward. I seemed at times to be the only one in the room who had hope that there was somebody there, inside of him, who was able to hear me and respond to what I had to offer. Whenever I began to despair, Edward gave me some small hope that something still survived inside him: it was like the voice of somebody who had drowned in him, but who was not yet entirely dead. This increased my hopes, and I continued talking to him and working with him, sometimes having to adapt the psychoanalytic technique in the ways devised by the Tavistock Autism Workshop in order to reach him.

In the first year, there were unbearably long periods when he would do nothing: he would pick up and move some objects from his box of toys and, just as I would start to describe what he was doing in order to look for the meaning of it, I would realise that the movements were aimless. There was clearly no story, no relationship and no meaning. It would go on and on – forever. If interrupted, he would just continue doing the same with another object. Until I started working with Edward, I was never aware that a minute could be so unbearably long. I tried to give interpretations: about his turning away; protecting himself from reality which he felt was dangerous; destroying awareness of me; killing off my mind so that I couldn't penetrate his hard shell (Tustin 1990), etc. Nothing helped. He seemed past it – past the reasons why (Alvarez 1996) – and interpretations made no difference. So, when it became unbearable for me to remain dead for him for hours, I started saying that there was a bit of Edward that wanted me to get in touch and couldn't bear this deadness any longer. There was no response to that, either. I then picked up a little boy-doll from his box of toys and started talking to him, naming him a 'live Edward', saying I knew how difficult it was for him, as well as for me, to bear this situation and keep each other in mind. At that moment Edward jumped up from his seat, furiously alert, took the doll away from me and shut it in the box. After that, it became much easier to talk about the live part of him and what he did to it. I knew that it existed and that he hated it; he knew that I knew and he hated me for it.

Unmanageable terrors

In considering what to select for this chapter, I have decided to focus on the line of development of his dread of gaps and holes, as demonstrated vividly in the assessment. I shall start with a description of the tantrums and unmanage-able terrors that Edward experienced each time he had to stay in the waiting room before the session. He was usually brought to the sessions just before they were due to start and in that case he traversed the gap from the waiting room to our therapy room smoothly. However, on a couple of initial occasions he was brought very early and then had to wait for about 15 to 20 minutes for his sessions. On each of these occasions he started screaming and created an enormous upset in the waiting room.

These tantrums and unmanageable terrors that Edward first showed while having to wait for me, seemed to reflect some elemental terror rising out of the fear of being forgotten and abandoned by me as a person who kept him in mind. When he started acknowledging me as a person that he was waiting for and who was waiting for him, his panic and distressed behaviour, if he had to wait for more than a few minutes, became overwhelming. On one occasion, for example, when he was in the waiting room, he rushed towards another therapist who had just returned a child from treatment and, screaming, got hold of this therapist's hand. He was, in his own way, showing by this that he was falling apart while waiting and had lost hope that I would ever appear or even recognise him. So any other therapist would be better than having to stay in this state of 'nameless dread' (Bion 1977). But the urgency and the desperation of his need was terrible to behold.

That was not easy for him and he struggled for a long time, particularly during periods of stress, to maintain his indifference to me, emphasised by his withdrawals and refusal to relate. In order to do that, he had to obliterate awareness of my presence as an interested and attentive person. I was allowed to start existing for him only very slowly and gradually, and when he did start to acknowledge me, he at the same time employed various devices of control. He did not like me talking for quite some time and would either close my mouth with his hand or sometimes even put Sellotape on it. This is an excerpt from a session that took place in the second term of his treatment, which describes the way he related to me in the early stages of our work:

He climbed down from the chair and up, onto my lap, while I was describing what he was doing. He picked up the Sellotape from the table and put it over my lips, sealing them off. Then he climbed down onto the floor and picked up the small string and then again climbed onto my lap, making himself comfortable. I mumbled, trying to show him that I could not talk and that I realised that that was what he had done to me. I also felt that it was immensely funny, but he, however, was deadly serious. He examined the ends of the string and then, all of a sudden, started pushing them up my nostrils. It tickled me. I again mumbled to show how I could not speak and also gently pulled his hands off when the string went up too far. Then he gave up with my nostrils for a moment, still leaving the Sellotape over my mouth and went sideways and tried to investigate my left ear. He brought the string close to it, but then, for some reason, gave it up and returned to the nostrils in a very serious and concentrated way. After some time, and after my considerable mumbling and pulling his hands down in a gentle way, he decided to take off the Sellotape and climbed down onto the floor. I then tried to tell him that he did not want to be with a therapist who could talk and think, he wanted a silent Mrs Pecotic, who would not interrupt him in what he did and who would not think about what he did. He was sitting on the floor, turning his back to me and appearing to be cut off already: the moment I started struggling and speaking, he stopped relating and cut off the part of his mind that was aware of me: the deadness returned.

He showed me clearly that he would relate to me only if I was silent, as well as linked and connected to him. The string had not only the function of connecting me to him, but also gave him the ability to pull me and control me with it, like a puppet master. Having me behave as a puppet under his control served to protect against the awareness of separation. Only a separate person can talk and think and go away, and that was what he could not allow me to be for a long time, believing that I would forget him the moment I was gone. Thus he was also trying to avoid the end and gaps which appeared when the links and strings between people got broken.

He also showed his terror of falling into nothingness, and often communicated this in his therapy by repeatedly making objects fall off the table, or by making himself fall down into my arms. For a very long time he needed me to be able to respond with physical holding when he engaged in these falling-off rituals; it seemed that the act of holding him was as important as my talking about what he was communicating to me through his actions (Reid 1990).

The beginnings of attachment

The fear of separation had the quality of looming disaster, and he tried to avoid it by denying my existence in the early stages of the work. Later on, when this was no longer possible, and when he also could not maintain the illusion that I was his puppet on a string, he started creating another illusion: that we were stuck together. That was expressed in his decision to take a little plastic mother kangaroo and baby kangaroo (out of his bag of animals) and tape them firmly together. Baby kangaroo was put in mother's pouch and then Edward put a great deal of sticky tape over both of them. This took place after about six months of treatment, and they stayed together, almost unrecognisable through thick layers of tape, for the whole of the next year. The tape created a kind of second skin (Bick 1968) which protected this inseparable couple, both against separation, as well as against aggressive intrusion. Nothing could get through. Everybody was shut out. However, if everything was wrapped up, neither mother nor baby could move. So, in a way, it was a deadly embrace. An imprisonment both for mother, who could not leave, but also for baby, who could not move, change or grow. By taping mother and baby kangaroo, he also showed how he did not trust the strength of our mutual attachment yet, which would allow us to be away and still safely keep each other in mind. Only towards the end of the next year, when there were obvious signs of the beginning of his attachment to me (e.g. he would kiss my hand while I led him out of the therapy room, or would follow me with his gaze when I left him), did he unwrap mother and baby kangaroo and leave them free to separate.

Around the time that he taped the mother and baby kangaroo together, he also taped the little elephant's head firmly to its body (it was a plastic toy with a detachable head) using a lot of tape and making him almost invisible inside. The elephant soon started representing Edward in his play (he was now beginning to be able to play symbolically). It was again a significant moment when the elephant was untaped, around the same time as mother and baby kangaroo, and his head could then go on and off. That soon became a way of communicating to me how Edward felt with regard to his own mind. Sometimes he would detach the elephant's head, indicating that he was going into a period of mindlessness in the session, therefore allowing me to think about the events which had precipitated this. It was a powerful communication in that he now trusted that there was a listening and observing mind which would register his mindless periods and react to them, share them with him, as well as try to modulate the anxieties that led to them. But taping the elephant's head onto its body in the first place was also an important communication, indicating that he was in urgent need to regain his mind and start using it.

Feeling held

His sense of both physical and mental containment in the sessions grew, and the first concrete physical expression of it was when Edward started, quite early in his treatment, defecating in the room. At the time I did not experience it as aggressive, because he would usually warn me that this was what he was going to do, and would then wait for me to put down his nappy or something else that he could defecate into. He seemed to be telling me that he could unburden himself here from whatever discomfort and distress, physical and mental, he was carrying inside. It is also interesting that defecating always occurred on a Monday, the first session after the weekend. However much it may have contained an attack on me, punishing me for being away and separate, there was also the communication of his emerging hope that I was able to receive his weekend distress and think about it.

Discovering pleasure

About a year and a half into treatment, and at the same time as Edward freed the mother and baby kangaroo, he started enjoying my interest in him as something quite new and delightful (Reid 1990). He frequently engaged in playing with my face and hair or looking into my eyes, and would show his delight in being with me, either through singing or uttering simple words, like 'delicious'. Soon we started talking of him as 'delicious little boy', and he created a little game around this. He would say 'delicious' and I would talk about his joy in seeing in my eyes that he was my delicious little boy-patient, Edward – to which he would laugh with immense joy. It was so moving to witness his new-found pleasure in our relationship, which is a necessary part of all normal development and which his autism had denied him: that of a mother-therapist seeing him as a 'delicious' baby, so that he could then see his beautiful reflection in her eyes. Around that time, his attachment grew noticeably, although his autistic withdrawals and periods of mindlessness in the sessions remained. He started using words and also began displaying considerable artistic talent. He started learning in school and knew his letters and numbers up to twenty. He also showed an awareness of beauty in the world around him, which he expressed through play.

The lost lamb

At the end of the second year of his treatment, one of his favourite metaphors became the nursery rhyme 'Mary Had a Little Lamb'. He would pick up a tiny plastic lamb and would move it around until it got 'lost'. Then he would sing the rhyme beautifully. I was meant to be Mary and look for my little lost lamb-Edward. I talked about his fear that he would get lost and forgotten by me and that, even when I remembered him, I would not be able to get in touch with him, nor he with me. However, we then also introduced the idea of the little lamb-Edward calling out and making it known that he was lost and needed help, so that his fear of abandonment changed. He could learn to seek help actively, as well as help me to find him and meet his needs, and from then on that is indeed what he began to do. He became more and more capable of expressing his needs by increased symbolic play, and also developed the new capacity to project his feelings in order to help me understand how powerful they were and how difficult it was for him to struggle with them. Outside, in his family life, his parents reported that he was now able to say what he wanted or issue orders, even to complain. It is an important sign of relatedness to other people when a child becomes able to protest and to believe that he can make an impact on others.

At that time, the periods of his autistic mindlessness in therapy reduced. He also started telling me stories. Usually these were bits and pieces of stories that he had already heard, now repeated in his own way, or combined to produce new stories. His language development began.

Edward's contribution to his autistic withdrawals

After around two years of his therapy, I became increasingly able to differentiate various threads of stories and fantasies in Edward's internal life. Simultaneously, I also became aware of how frequently I felt unequal to the task of helping him. Somehow I just did not measure up. I was always aware of his acute sensitivity, but it took my supervisor to point out that Edward was also intolerant of anything less than perfection in others. When I became aware of how he could destroy my confidence and make me feel totally responsible for any failures in communication between us, I realised what a difficult child he must have been to parent.

I acknowledged Edward's contributions to his withdrawals and that seemed to free him to become more open in showing me, in his play, how he was accusing me of all kinds of imperfections or of not meeting his needs. He was furious with me for existing separately, for going away over the weekends, for (as he imagined) being with my own family, particularly my husband: he often shrieked on Mondays, when he came back to his session, saying: 'Mister! Mister!' and looking at the light: he seemed to feel that there was a Mr Pecotic who kept me company, kept me 'lit up', alive and happy. Edward would then usually attack me physically or insist on turning off the light.

I also had other 'imperfections' that he could not tolerate, and each time he had objections, I was made to feel that his fury with me was my responsibility and not his. He was very accomplished at making me feel inadequate or wrong. But this was already a huge advance in his communication, because he was now able to tell me how angry my imperfections made him. This implied that he had started to trust that I could stay with him and look after him, even while he hated me. In this way, he slowly became able to learn to tolerate his feelings of fury, as well as those of need and attachment to me. Earlier, in his more continuous autistic and mindless periods, he would not give any messages. He would not make his needs, his resentments or his fury known: he would simply withdraw.

Surviving the disaster

Edward's therapy had to be stopped abruptly for external reasons. After several months it became possible to resume our work on a reduced basis. This interruption seemed to have had a significant effect on Edward in different ways. It appeared to have temporarily shattered his trust in adults as people who kept him in mind and who could ensure stability in his life.

When he came back to therapy, he often referred to himself as the 'lipple lost lamb'. I believe that he felt like that when he was away from therapy, but he seemed to feel very unsafe wherever he was left. Actual separation stirred up terrible feelings of hopelessness. However much we worked on it in the sessions, I constantly had the feeling that what he got from psychotherapy thus far was not enough to counteract the effect of the very difficult time the parents told me they were having in their outside life. This situation made it difficult for them to bring him regularly. Because of this uncertainty and inconsistency, it was necessary for me to recognise with Edward that we would hope to meet, but that we could not promise to meet each time.

We also needed to work on Edward's increasing strength to make his needs known and heard, instead of abandoning himself to the extreme passivity, hopelessness and mindless denial of his needs which I had encountered in him at the beginning of our work together.

The fact that we were supported by Edward's parents in continuing to work after this long break of several months, albeit in a changed form, had contributed much to Edward's trust in our mutual capacity to survive disasters. Not only was there my conviction that our work was useful for him, but he was now also becoming increasingly able to communicate to his parents, as well as to his teachers at school, that he was determined to benefit from it as much as he could.

Paddington Bear at the station

After that interruption, holiday times were particularly distressing for him. Whenever the holidays approached, Edward became very anxious. But he now also communicated his old despair and dread that he would be forgotten. Unlike the previous times, when he cut off and the sessions became emotionally flat and dead, he could now show me how upset he was with the approaching breaks. He was increasingly able to project his feelings, with some belief that I could receive them. He started showing me this distress in a more direct and powerful way than ever before.

The following extract comes from a session in his third year, a week before the holiday, when he became very openly upset and anxious, wanting me to repeat the story of Paddington Bear. Paddington was a little bear who found himself lost at Paddington station, until he was found by a very nice family, who took him to their home and decided to call him Paddington, after the station where they found him. So, even though he was lost in the beginning, he ended up having a family and being loved and cared for by them. Edward obviously knew and understood this story very well, as he did with all the other stories he had heard:

> Edward pleaded that I repeat every word that he said of the story, in the way that he told it. He kept saying: 'Paddington Bear, Paddington Bear at the station!' and wanted me to repeat it. Then he would continue: 'and they found him and they said: "I know what! We shall call him Paddington!"' His voice was raised each time, insisting that I repeat, as if his whole existence depended on whether I agreed to go along with the story and repeat it exactly as he said it or not. However, in spite of my going along, he became increasingly more distressed and anxious, until, by the end of the session, he was crying, yelling and screaming: 'Paddington Bear at the station! I know what! We shall call him Paddington! Happy Birthday to you, dear', etc.

It was a very upsetting session and it provoked strong feelings in me. Long afterwards, his words still powerfully echoed in my mind and it was difficult to think about the meaning of his communications. After some work on it, I was able, in the next session, to talk to him about his fear that, during the holiday, he would feel lost like Paddington Bear at the station. He feared that, if I went away, I would not return, and there would be nobody to recognise him and give him a family and a belonging and a name.

Only then did I understand the full depth of his anxiety: that he would completely lose himself, his identity, his name, recognition of himself as a person; and that he would have to abandon even the hope that somebody would pick him up, recognise him and look after him. These were the gaps that he feared from the beginning and that he desperately needed to close. Initially he had to shut himself away from experiencing these anxieties, because they were too powerful. Now he was able to tell me what he was struggling with when I went on holiday and did not see him: the fear that he would be abandoned, instead of understood and held onto, and that he would be psychologically lost and annihilated.

In this way, he showed me how the clinic had become like Paddington Station for him. He had arrived feeling like a little Paddington Bear, not knowing and not wishing to know why he was there and what was happening to him. Then, gradually, after several years of therapy, he became somebody who wanted a name and who felt he had found a home, a place where both his autistic and his healthy self could be known.

Becoming rebellious

From that point on I was increasingly able to witness Edward's generosity and warmth towards me. For example, in one session he painted the sun on a small plastic saucer and filled the cup with water, saying 'tea', and served it to me; then he made 'cakes' with plasticine, looked at me and said that they were 'delicious' and then suggested that I eat them with tea. As he was increasingly able to appreciate what I gave him, he gradually became able to give something back. He now trusted that there was enough goodness in him to create a 'delicious' gift for me (Williams 1997).

He also showed a much greater capacity to express anger. He started focusing it on me more and more, and I came to understand it as a proof of his increasing trust in my capacity to survive and manage it. At the same time, his own internal figures became stronger and he could allow his anger to emerge directly, instead of using it to cut himself off and become mindless. He displayed particularly furious reactions when denied something or when exposed to boundaries. When he was angry in earlier times, he would put my hands around his head, needing me to hold his mind from falling apart with the immense fury. He would then often scream: 'Elephant! Elephant!', suggesting that he was going to lose his head like the little elephant whose head could be detached, because he was so angry. This lessened until he became able to take my hands when furious and even play with them, for example tapping his mouth with them and producing a Tarzan-like sound, instead of shouting and screaming.

At the same time, he began testing the boundaries to the extreme and became rivalrous with me when I protected them, as if he were saying: 'Who are you to set the boundaries! Why don't we play the game according to my rules?' A few months before the end of treatment, he ran away while waiting for me and was found after considerable upset and effort from several members of staff, in the staff room. When he was returned to me and I again took charge of him, he immediately struggled to return to the staff room and would not tolerate at all the fact that he could not have his session where he wanted. When I insisted on the session taking place in the therapy room, he suddenly said: 'Shut up, big mouth!'

He started challenging my authority more and more and rebelling all the time. For example, he wanted deliberately to paint on the walls and then looked at me to see how I was going to react; or he performed some other mischief in the room and then got into a frenzy of fury when I refused to allow him to do so. He became much heavier and stronger physically, so that his fights with me were now looking like real ones. He could hurt me, which in fact he rarely did, but he nevertheless managed to show me very powerfully that he sometimes wished to smash me to pieces.

Acquiring a backbone

In parallel with his capacity to be openly angry, he had less need to be cut off. When he wanted to cut off in the sessions, he took a small school bus into which he put the animals and which he then drove around the room. Towards the end of treatment, he drove the bus for some time and I talked about his turning away from me because he feared that things were changing for him. He then put the bus into my lap and took my hand and said my name clearly for the first time. He said: 'Mrs Pecotic, take me to the zoo'. The zoo had always represented a most interesting place for Edward, where one could find friendly animals as well as frightening and dangerous ones, and where all kinds of things took place.

He also often talked in the past about the jungle and made it out of plasticine, using various elements of the jungle to express the happenings in his internal world. For example, when he wanted to show me what he understood to be the dangers to his development, he would represent them with big, frightening plasticine animals which would attack the little monkey just starting to climb a liana up a jungle tree. Or he would use the plasticine to make a tree on an island, with crocodiles looming all around, telling me in this way about the reasons for his autistic isolation: if you bridge the island, what will come across? Crocodiles. You open up to the beauty of the world, but instead of beauty you get danger in the shape of the crocodile's teeth. All these fears had by now lessened considerably and he became a less frightened child.

He also showed me how sweet and seductive his turning away from me was to him. Much as he had often shown his attachment to me, as well as acknowledged my attachment to him, he now became able to recognise and communicate his still-alive and powerful wish to be all-in-all to himself and turn away from everybody. He revealed this to me in an amusing way:

He came to the session and started singing the tune 'Nobody Loves Me ...'. I then asked him: 'Edward, is that how you feel today, that nobody loves you?' To which he added immediately ' ... Like I Do', and started laughing. A session later, he sang: 'I love you, I love you'.

I think that both of these now existed: his affection for others, as well as the belief that nobody loved him as dearly as he loved himself.

Edward improved in various areas of his life. He was now able to read and write fluently and he started making beautiful drawings, which showed how much his view of his internal world had changed. In the beginning, he used to construct strange objects, taping together small wooden blocks, little pots and pans, pens, etc. from his box. After some time, he began to mould animals with plasticine and at first there were some strange combined objects, consisting of various bits and pieces belonging to different animals. Towards the end of his treatment, he became able to mould very beautifully, as well as to draw with a great deal of talent and accuracy and with a particular eye for detail. He seemed to be both visually and musically a talented child, and the school reported that he was making great progress.

He was now also able to ask for what he wanted, although he was still not so clearly able to say what it was that bothered him or what he did not want; but this was something that we continued to work on in our sessions. His attacks on boundaries in the room, his disagreements with me, his attacks on me when I did not oblige, seemed to enable him more and more to integrate the angry-crocodile part of himself and get a backbone (Alvarez 1992a), get teeth to bite and grind with, as well as to chew with.

Towards the end

Edward's speech developed and his play became more creative. I observed him playing with his younger brother in the waiting room, and that too seemed to be an important part of his development: the opportunity to engage in a lively exchange with his siblings, which did not exist before. However, he remained somewhat fragile and unable to use enough of his considerable capacity for anger in a way that would provide this backbone, rather than a hard-shell autistic protection for his vulnerable self. Although his trust started to emerge and was demonstrated in many different ways in our work, it was not yet solid enough to hold him together in times of crisis. But his capacity to engage in fights and arguments with me more and more in the last year of his treatment gave me much hope that his strength was growing and would continue to do so in the months and years to come.

Towards the end of his therapy, he started moulding the planets of the solar system with plasticine and he made a solid, big and beautiful planet Earth. He put various colours on it, indicating oceans and mountains. Then he pressed a point on it and said: 'Triangle'. I found myself wondering if this intelligent boy was referring to the Bermuda Triangle in the Atlantic Ocean, where, according to the legend, ships disappeared. I understood this as referring to his early elemental terror of a hole in his universe, which swallowed the stars and extinguished the light in his eyes, destroying every energy and communication that came from him. Now it had reduced to such an extent that it had become the Bermuda Triangle on the planet Earth.

It was evident from this material that his internal figures had by now become dense, heavy and reliable, like Mother Earth. But his world still contained a potential, though now limited space for disaster – a small triangle where the 'lipple lost lamb' could get lost again.

11 Conor

Hold on or you'll fall: the struggle to become an ordinary boy

Carol Hanson

Introduction

Conor began psychotherapy when he was a little over the age of three. I saw him three times weekly for several years. This chapter describes his emergence from the state of mindlessness in which I found him. I also hope to depict the central conflicts of his disorder, and additionally to convey some of the quality of the experience of working with him.

Early history

Conor was referred to the Child Guidance Clinic at the age of two and a half years by his parents, who had already consulted various professionals. They were primarily concerned about his inability to relate to other children. At that time, he had lost what speech he had: he had no eye contact and he frequently engaged in a wild physicality which his mother described as 'hyperactivity'. The absence of any meaningful contact with his world raised further concerns about the possibility of mental handicap or deafness. This was difficult to assess, however, as Conor was uncooperative when tested. His parents also wondered about emotional factors affecting his development, having seen a deterioration in the development of his speech during his second year, which coincided with a major change in his life.

Following a lengthy assessment Conor was assessed as a child with autism, and intensive psychotherapy was recommended, together with a specialised nursery school placement.

Technical issues

It was difficult to know how to work with Conor. It was unclear how much he understood but did not respond to, and how much he did not understand. I was dependent on regular supervision and the close scrutiny of my counter-transference (monitoring of my own feelings and thoughts when with him) in the understanding of his states of mind. Addressing symbolic meaning in the material had little relevance to him as the psychotherapy toys had no representational value. Technically, I found myself working differently with him than I had with other children. He did not have an ordinary reality-based perception of the world where he learned from experience, and I frequently had to enter into new, uncharted territory. In order to engage his disparate, suspended attention, I had actively to reach for him, making dramatic use of my voice and gestures. I quickly learned that he was extremely sensitive to lapses of my attention and that it was necessary for me to be especially vigilant and mindful lest he drop into mindlessness. I found myself attending closely to detail and talking more than usual in an attempt to provide and convey the mental equivalent of holding him. Using a simplified third-person language as one does with a small infant, I laboured to articulate in words his apparently fragmented, dismantled experience. I felt I was working with a very small baby driven by a terror of falling into unbounded space.

Clinical material

When I first met Conor, I was touched by his appealing 'velveteen' quality. He was an attractive, sturdy child with dark hair and eyes. In spite of the severity of his withdrawal, the impact he had on me was immediate, evoking great warmth, interest and compassion. Although during the course of treatment his despair was at times profound, making it difficult on these occasions to be with him, this was most often mitigated by his passionate possession of me and the therapy room and his tender appreciation of my help and understanding.

At the beginning of treatment, however, his behaviour and response to me was reminiscent of a small wild animal. His relationship to the world was strikingly primitive and sensual. He whizzed around the room, slithering and sliding over the surfaces much like a 'hyped-up' snail leaving a territorial trail behind him. He had no speech, and his glazed, unfocused eyes glided over surfaces, appearing not to see or take in. This 'sliding' approach to the world seemed to reflect an internal feeling that the ordinary link between mother and baby, where the mother's face and eyes act as a magnet, drawing the baby into contact and helping him to focus, was absent. As I watched him in the treatment room he seemed to be 'rooting' around. He reminded me of a baby who found it difficult to take up the nipple or teat and suck, with the result that at times he appeared to have nothing to focus on and hold on to. In the therapy room with him I often had to struggle to keep him firmly in mind and not allow him to slide away.

The following is an extract from an early session which I hope conveys some of these qualities.

> He wriggled along the windowsill in an uncoordinated way. He seemed to have little sense of the drop to the floor and it was difficult to know how to hold him. He wriggled down me to the floor and climbed up again. He seemed to be searching for something, much like a baby rooting at the breast. He kicked at the radiator and climbed onto the armchair,

contorting himself to reach underneath, as if he thought he could find what he wanted there. He climbed across the room, over the lockers. When he got to his box, he took out his metal car and poked his fingers inside, as if in his mind he was getting into and becoming the car. He travelled around the room making driving sounds as he went. It seemed he was now the 'driver' in charge. When he got to the armchair, he tossed the cushion aside and climbed on the springs, falling about so that I felt I had to support him. He got entangled, became frightened and I had to lift him out.

Conor seemed totally preoccupied with finding something. Yet he did not seem to know what it was or where to find it, and travelled around the room, climbing up high and looking down low in his search – never at rest, never finding it. He functioned at a very primitive level, as though he did not yet experience his world as having a focus he could hold on to. Without this focus, he was relentlessly driven and so he 'snail trailed' over the room, marking out his territory. As I watched him, it became clearer that this slithering over surfaces also served the mental function of attempting to iron out any uncomfortable hard edges which confronted him. Thus he could create an illusion of being at one with a smooth, featureless universe of surfaces. But the disadvantage was that when his world was experienced as not having a focus, he seemed to have nothing to hold himself together. There was no living link to an important person. Instead, he psychically became 'it' via the car, entering into its identity in an attempt to possess it and incorporate it as part of himself. Thus he gained control and 'brmm'd' around the room, pulling away anything that got in his way. When he got entangled and frightened, he feared never getting out.

While the world consisted of slippery surfaces, nothing could emerge with any clarity, focus or structure. Conor seemed to lack a sense of a world of mindful figures who could be interested and interesting. This is thought to be essential for the development of a human mind where thoughts can occur, experiences can be remembered, links can be made and imaginative life can develop. Without such a concept of a containing person, Conor fluctuated between a state of helpless collapse and dizzy mindlessness. As I began to refuse to be smoothed out and passed over psychologically, insisting my right to exist in his world, he began to seem interested.

Age 3 years 5 months

A quality that continuously surprised me about Conor during the early period of treatment was his intense wish for a person to make his experience safe for him. As the first term progressed, there were other hopeful developments and he began to recognise the need for a figure with structure in his life.

The following extract from his ninth session illustrates the way in which he soon became able to let me know something of the representations in his inner world.

Raising his arms above his head, he said something that sounded like 'Assam' and bowed to the locker as if he felt it was inhabited by someone who controlled his access to it and whom he had to appease. He was interested in the male play figures and looked at each one carefully. He then looked out of the window saying 'car' and picked up the telephone receiver, much like a father 'at work'.

He gestured to be put down in front of the lockers where he read out the numbers, counting up to twelve. I was astonished by this leap of development from the very primitive level of functioning so apparent in the first session. He attempted to look into a locker from underneath, clearly curious about its contents. He then crawled around the room, tongue out, making a 'snail trail', marking out his territory. Saying 'me', he took out the boy and girl play children and made the boy doll push the girl. Again I was amazed by this leap of development from concrete to symbolic representation.

He lay sheets of paper ('nappies') on the floor, making sounds that sounded like 'mummy'. I talked about Conor feeling left out by a daddy and other children, wanting a mummy to look after him and put on a nappy to absorb his cross feelings. He scrunched up some paper and stuffed it into a drawer as if messing it with a dirty nappy. I talked about him wanting to make this a horrible, smelly place so that no one would want it and he could have it to himself. He counted the lockers in my room, saying 'inside'. He then got in the cupboard, conveying clearly that he wanted to be the 'baby inside'. He substituted J cloths for the paper and repeated the ritual, first putting the daddy doll on the floor to watch and perhaps keep him safe.

In this session, he clearly showed interest in a firmer figure with which he was beginning to identify, perhaps a father-figure. Although he continued to snail trail, there was evidence of curiosity and some development of aggression towards me, as if I had developed sufficient structure to be noticeable.

The concept of skin as a boundary and then as a container: an interest in being with people with depth and structure

Term 2: age 3 years 9 months

Conor's growing awareness of the need for a focusing person to regulate and make things safe for him was accompanied by the development of a concept of a skin which served as a boundary separating inside from outside. This seemed to make it possible for him to achieve some distance from his world in order to be able to think about it. Introjection, curiosity, projection and thoughtfulness became possible.

The following extract from his thirty-first session illustrates his newly developed capacity to introject and to take in the world. There was now a sense of a boy firmly lodged inside a skin who could begin to integrate and think about dynamic, living human figures. At this point in our work, the continuity of the sessions had been disrupted because of holidays. For the most part, I have left out the comments I made to him.

He seemed more comfortably 'in his skin' as he trod solidly on the stairs. As he entered the room, he 'whooped' and turned to look at me deeply, smiling. Arms outstretched, he approached me, as if about to hug me. There was a brief, awkward moment as if he suddenly felt that what he was about to do was inappropriate. He then gathered himself and grinning, led me by the hand to my chair, now designated the 'thinking chair', and pushed me into it, putting me in my correct 'thinking' place. He took off his shoes and socks and examined his feet briefly before looking at me again. He seemed thoughtful.

He silently walked across the top of the locker, waiting for me to lift him down. As I did this, he took the cushion off my chair and climbed onto the strings. One foot slipped through the strings and he quickly took it out, looking at me. I said Conor was struggling to be with Miss Hanson, he doesn't want to fall in and get lost. He repositioned himself on the strings and looked at me for a long while. I said I thought he was letting me know he had tried to hold on to a picture of me in his mind and remember me when he hadn't been to sessions. He smiled and examined the springs, as if wanting to find out what they were made of. When finished, he sat back in the chair, looking extremely content, and surveyed the room. He looked at me and smiled, seemingly satisfied that I had passed the test and was resilient and strong enough.

Using the J cloths as 'nappies', he played a baby game where he was the mummy looking after the baby. He arranged and rearranged the 'nappies' on the floor saying 'baby, me, mummy' in a baby voice, making plaintive crying sounds, angry sounds, sometimes smiling and covering his ears with a 'nappy', folding and refolding, communicating and working very hard. I was impressed by the range of different feelings and sense of time, hard work and thought which he managed to communicate, and I said so. He shook the table as if testing its strength and put the 'nappies' on top. He did the same to my chair. I said Conor's testing to see if I'm strong enough to take his cross feelings, like a nappy taking a baby's poo. He gathered the 'nappies' and climbed around the room as if wanting to fill it with the smell of dirty nappies and leave his smell behind to keep other children out. He went to the phone, lifted the receiver and uttered very thoughtful 'mmmms', letting me know, I thought, that he wanted to talk to me when I wasn't there.

This session was characterised by a thoughtful, rather than deadening quality. This was a new state for Conor. He now seemed to understand that therapy was about communication and had noticed his own play as a communication and message for both of us to think about. He constantly made eye contact with me, conveying vividly a sense of being in touch with me as a thinking person. He had an expectation of a space inside my head where thoughts could go, and he let me know that when he was not with me, he thought about me and could keep a picture in mind. He noticed that he wanted to think, and that he could think and have feelings at the same time.

The experience in the session was of a little boy who came to therapy to explore rather than to evacuate. He was beginning to use his mind to sort things out and was very interested in the construction of my mind.

Coming into the world of human relationships; curiosity and frustration

Conor's growing awareness of someone separate from himself presented him with a dilemma which exercised him for several terms. It seemed that he had three options. First, he could adopt his particular autistic way of being and merge with someone so as to avoid experiencing his separateness; second, he could perversely deny any awareness and knowledge of his separateness even though his senses told him otherwise; third, he could acknowledge his separateness and explore various ways of being together with a thoughtful person. In sessions, I saw evidence of all three ways of functioning.

His wish to merge with another is evident in the following extract from the third term.

His eyes darted to the shut locker and he said 'No, no'. He seemed to be looking to see if he could get through the locker door into the locker, as if, in his mind, the doors were like a separating skin preventing him from merging. He searched around the chair saying 't', much like a baby looking for the breast. He rubbed his hand over the surface of the chair. I mimed this as I talked to him about perhaps wanting to rub away the separating skin and fuse with a feeding mummy. He took out two cars and arranged them, fronts facing each other. I said Conor was perhaps now thinking of a mummy and daddy together. He turned them so that they were facing the same direction and drove them off. After a while, he drove the cars apart in different directions, separating them. He lay down between them, emphasising his wish to separate them. He began to say 'Hanso' and 'sockie' and slipped his hands inside his socks, holding them together, examining them. I said I thought he was telling me that he wanted to get under the sock-skin and join with Hanson and be with her all the time. This seemed to pull him out of his more merged state, because he suddenly put on his shoes and went back to playing with the cars. He drove them around together and then became angry with them, crashing them against the wall. He rubbed the motif on his box. I said Conor had put his shoes on and I thought he felt that now he was inside his own skin and Hanson was inside hers and this made him very cross. He reacted by rubbing and pushing at his penis and then rubbing the two cars together. I suddenly felt extremely sleepy and unable to follow the sequence of events. Perhaps he had found his way inside my mind; in any case I was unable to think clearly.

A few months later, he had found a more benevolent figure, separate from him, but able to stay with him in a friendly, satisfying and comfortable way.

> He searched around the chair saying 't', touching the edges. He caught sight of the reflection of himself in the radiator and began to scrape the grating, saying 'baba', using first hands, then feet. I talked about him feeling there were 'babas' inside and wanting to see. He began to say 'see now'. He then modified this to 'see ... no!', seeming to indicate that he had accepted a boundary.
>
> He lay in the chair holding on to the thread of his blanket, playing with vowel sounds, stretching them out and blending them. He reminded me of a small baby playing with the nipple or teat, filling his mouth with it, mouthing and stretching it.

This new relationship was a tenuous one. It was not always possible to stay with this quality of relationship. In a holiday break, the person he held on to became the person that shut him out. He felt that when I wasn't with him I was with other babies. His fury about this broke the connection he felt to me so that he couldn't keep a link with me in my absence. He was frightened of 'goneness' and unable to tolerate mental pain, and resorted to a more perverse attempt to bypass his awareness of me as someone separate from himself. At times he reverted to his autistic world of bodily sensation.

The following extract is from the first week back after a holiday (holidays tended to make his autism recur).

> He darted into my chair and put his hands over his ears, conveying clearly his wish not to notice me so that he could sustain the illusion that we were joined. However, he then looked at me as if waiting for me to say something. As I began to talk he turned upside down in the chair, burrowing his head into the cushion, bottom uppermost. He grinned triumphantly, looking at me. He then sat up, said 'mine', and took off his shoes and socks. He began to chatter nonsense to himself, grinning. He held the socks up to his face and pulled them over his nose, sensually, smiling. He had turned to a sensation world, and I felt he had lost contact and I was left with a powerful feeling of having been shut out. I talked to him about this and he looked at me and pulled the sock across his mouth, saying 'Papa, baba, dada', giving the impression that something was being pulled from his mouth and being given to 'papa, baba, dada's' and he was left out. He suddenly cut off contact again and began to chatter incomprehensibly, grinning and holding the two socks to himself, avoiding thinking about his feelings.

These modes of defence gradually failed to convince him. Despite the escalation of his attempts to deny it, the recognition of himself as a separate being in his own skin, with his own sense of identity, became unavoidable.

> He lay on his back on the floor for quite a long time, thoughtfully, twirling his hair, legs crossed. He held his finger up to his face, touched it with his other hand and said 'bit'. He touched his leg and said 'me' and then clasped his toes and said loudly and slowly, 'toes'. This was a beautiful, moving moment. He seemed like a baby discovering that his hands and feet belong to himself. I said 'Yes, that's you, Conor, these are your hands, these are your toes, all these bits are Conor'. He looked at me, and touching his feet said loudly, 'feet'. I said he was telling me that he's found his feet and can stand by himself, that's Conor and this is Miss Hanson. He repeated himself in a reflective, meditative way. I commented on his thoughtfulness, saying that he was showing me that he had a space inside his head and was thinking and feeling inside his skin. All the bits are Conor.

Emergence from the autistic state

End of second year

By the end of the second year of treatment, there was a real emergence from his autistic state. He began to use songs and language to communicate about his internal state. He was more able to be in a relationship to a whole person, and I found myself beginning to talk about him and me rather than Conor and Miss Hanson. He clearly felt we were separate and wanted to know about me. He was also more aware of other real children with whom he did not wish to share.

The following extract from the sixth term when he was five years old, illustrates some of these points. Conor had missed the previous week's therapy because he was ill.

> He picked up the phone and said 'see,' into it, turning to me. I said he was letting me know that he wanted to see and talk to me last week, he's had to wait a long time. He stood in front of me and poignantly said 'scared'. He repeated this, adding 'skate'. I was touched, and said he was telling me that he felt scared when he couldn't come to see me and had to wait a long time. He couldn't hold on to a picture of me inside and felt that he was left to slide, skate, over a slippery surface just as in the past. He darted to my chair and began to take off his shoes. I added that as soon as he started to think about how he felt when he couldn't have Hanson he panicked, got scared and jumped into the Hanson chair as if he wanted to jump inside me and keep me with him all the time. He was again listening and watching me carefully. After a while however, he turned upside down, grinned at me and began to make 'zz' sounds. I commented on how he could only think about it for a bit and then became scared again and wanted to muddle

things up, fill his mouth up with tickly sensations so that he didn't feel it to be empty. He then sat up and looked at me, took off his shoes and began to take off his socks. I commented on this. He appeared very much in touch and interested in what I was saying, watching me closely. It seemed that he didn't want to be inside his object, but wanted to feel a close fit with her so that he could feel safe to explore. He seemed to be drinking in my every word and I found myself talking to him in quite a different way to usual. He took his hands out of his socks, deciding to leave them on, and said 'have Han all time'. I commented that he wanted me all the time and when he felt I understood then he felt held. He felt that he and I fitted well together and he could be a boy Conor inside his own sockie-skin and didn't need mine.

An increased capacity to tolerate mental pain and frustration and its accompanying problems

Seventh term: 5 years 6 months

By the end of the seventh term he was more able to tolerate mental pain. He brought to his therapy the problem of how to get through to a person whom he felt was not receptive and seemed not to think about him. He still had little idea of how to make an impression without being aggressive, and spent many sessions stamping his footprints in water, conveying a feeling of having to stamp on other creatures to get through to an important person and make an impact. This led to a preoccupation with damage and consequent regret.

The following extract illustrates his increased capacity to tolerate intense emotional pain. He was more able to own his aggression, and because of the presence of love as well, feel guilt. This was an important development. Evident too was his impressive desire for contact and his expectation of being understood. The session is the first after a weekend. I had just interpreted his worry about me forgetting him and his fear of losing his place in my mind.

He thoughtfully began to draw a half-moon shape with indentations which looked as if chunks had been bitten out. He ignored my enquiry as to what he was drawing and silently cut along the outline. There followed a lot of cutting and messing. I talked with him about his anger at me going away for the weekend. Perhaps he felt cut out by me and in his mind he had torn and cut me into little bits. He confirmed this, saying 'small bits' as he continued cutting. He looked briefly at me but quickly averted his eyes as if he was also worried that his cutting had really damaged me and he didn't want to look and see. As he cut, he took the Sellotape from his box and laid it on the table next to him, seeming to want to keep it nearby in case something broke and needed fixing. He looked at me carefully, as if trying to establish that I was strong enough to withstand his anger. He drew a faecal shape on one of the cut pieces in brown. Watching me carefully, he said 'do poo' (this seemed very closely directed at me). It was a relief to see an ordinary, uninhibited expression of defiance.

He then curled up in the chair. There was quite a sad feeling in the room and I commented that he had been very cross with me for going away from him, and perhaps had wanted to spoil me with his cross poo feelings so that no one would want me, but now I thought he was sorry. He looked at me for a long while. He then said sadly 'want cry'. I felt so moved I could barely speak and eventually ventured weakly that he felt sad. He lay reflectively on the pillow for a long time.

As the work progressed, it became clearer that he was unable to reach more ordinary feelings of concern for other people because he was unable fully to absorb or understand the notion of a broken person in need of repair. He didn't achieve this for several terms, taking things in in only a peripheral way, not managing to put them together. He became more challenging in sessions. The material became that of a more ordinary, neurotic child who was being ordinarily difficult. He defended against feeling like a baby and seemed more tricky and withholding of language, thus keeping himself a baby. At times, I found myself feeling increasingly irritated by his apparent determination to handicap himself. It was evident that he knew there was a rich world peopled with mothers, fathers and children in various combinations that he would not let himself be part of because of his fears that he would be replaced.

However, there was also a more thoughtful part of him that wanted to understand and make connections. There were clear signs of the development of real intellectual curiosity. He was on the brink of discovering that there were things he didn't know and could find out about. By the end of the third year of treatment, there was evidence of a real person firmly lodged inside him. He had achieved a three-dimensional view of the world and had become more playful and able to show his feelings. He had almost achieved a state of healthy ambivalence, and there was a real move in his capacity to symbolise. Later in the same session:

He lay with his feet up against the chair, sucking the corner of the cushion as if it was a nipple of a breast. I said he wants to feel that he is the baby who has a mummy's breast all to himself. He said 'watch' loudly and pushed the cushion up the wall with his feet. He began to kick and stamp on it, conveying his fury. He then held the cushion lovingly to himself, as if it was his most prized possession, and ran across the room. I talked about him, realising that the Hanson he felt cross with for going away and leaving him for a long time, was also the Hanson he loved. He looked at me gently and lay down in the chair, holding the cushion tenderly to himself.

However, a moment later, love turned to cynical triumph.

Turning his bottom towards me he stroked the cushion, chuckling manically. I said that as soon as he feels love and needs me, he wants me for
himself and is so cross that he can't have me all the time. He tries to make
his own soft mummy thing so that he can feel he doesn't need me. He
looked at me sharply, stopped laughing and slid off the chair, putting his
feet straight into the bin. At the same time, he developed an air of preoccupation as if to say 'that's enough contact with you'. I commented that he
was showing me he'd rather be in the bin, breaking off contact with me if
he could not feel I was all his.

He spotted a pen under the table (which was not his) and shouting 'my
pen', darted to get it. I commented that he knew the pen wasn't his, and
perhaps he was stopping himself from growing by not letting himself know
what he knew already – namely, about other people who used the room.

He took out his own pen, and turning his back to me began to write.
He ignored everything I said to him and was clearly angry with me for not
going along with a view of him as a handicapped child.

The struggle to be 'ordinary' and independent

Fifth and sixth year of therapy: age 8–9 years

At this point in his therapy, Conor was functioning sufficiently well in the
external world to begin to phase into mainstream school, which he initially
attended part-time. He became increasingly aware of the very painful fact that
he was not as able as other children in his new class, and that he did not know
as much as others of his age. He conveyed vividly some of his general confusion
about the world with its many codes to crack, and his experience of real muddle
about his slow development.

The healthier Conor became, the more he could see his autism and recognise
that he wouldn't always be coming for therapy. For a period, his use of autistic
methods of defence against psychic pain escalated as he endeavoured to handicap himself when he was no longer handicapped. He did not want to know
about differences and did not want to absorb the fact of his separateness. At this
stage he would not, rather than could not, differentiate between memory and
sense impression. He used words to blur the boundaries rather than make links.
His rivalry and over-preoccupation with other children and with couples of any
kind hampered his healthy development. His imaginary world became flattened
and two-dimensional again as a defence against these feelings. Technically, the
work became more challenging as I struggled to help him come up against
truth as a concept and to use his intelligence creatively.

By the end of the fifth year of treatment, there was much more of a sense of
ordinariness about him. Conor began to think of a time when he wouldn't be
coming to therapy anymore, and we began to talk of 'one day' ending. I then
became pregnant. I had expected him to respond with one of his old attacks on
my capacity to provide him with anything good. Instead, he became thoughtful

and his communication became surprisingly clear and articulate. Although the idea of terminating therapy had been in the air for some time, he struggled to disentangle this from the idea of me having a baby and his fear that I would chuck him out. He let me know of his concerns that if I had a baby, there wouldn't be a place for him and he would be 'thrown in the bin'. He felt that I could not possibly think about more than one baby at a time, and that if I had a baby in my tummy there would not be a place for him.

He brought to his session the problem of the Teenage Mutant Turtles who had fallen down the drain into the sewers when little and had grown up to be hard, tough turtles with protective shells on their backs. Significantly, he had chosen something which was very much in the culture – a shared image rather than a private one. (It is interesting how many of our recovering autistic patients became interested in the Turtles and what they represented.) He recognised his identification and debated the question of whether to remain the handicapped boy stuck in the sewer, or to become the more independent, ordinary boy in the outside world. Alongside this went the question of whether he could accept the notion of an adult couple and allow his infantile self to make way for other children in need of help.

The following extract, which I quote in detail, is from a session in the last term of his therapy. I think it depicts the enormous courage involved in giving up his autism, and the huge and agonising dilemmas he faced. In order to place it in context and provide a complete picture, I have included my interpretations.

He took out yesterday's drawing of inside a multi-storey building, arranged a chair for me next to him and invited me to join him. He indicated that it was an important picture and wanted to talk and think about it today. He drew in 'handles going down the stairs', explaining that 'you had to hold on or you'd fall'. He labelled the drawing 'Independent Conor'. I said I thought this was a picture to do with him moving from a dependent boy to an independent boy, and he was showing me he understood the need to feel he could 'hold on' to the work we'd done together, in order to be independent when therapy stopped.

He looked at the drawing for a long while, recapping over the parts he had done today, before showing me again the various floors from the second down to the basement. He pointed out the office of the headmaster on the ground floor and told me it was a picture 'inside the school'. He changed his mind, saying 'it isn't a school'. He wrote '58', the number he often gave my house. I said perhaps it was a picture of the inside of my house. He replied 'Not inside your house, you'. He pointed out the various floors again as if wanting to make sure I understood this was a picture of the inside of the therapist's body. I commented that I thought the differentiation was important for him. He looked at the picture for a while and then said quietly, 'I'm trying to remember'.

He drew a green figure coming down the stairs from the top floor and another, walking along the first floor. He told me they were 'children dudes' (Turtles?). The one going down the stairs stood for him, he was coming down from the second floor. The one on the first floor was another boy. He didn't know where he was going – maybe upstairs, maybe downstairs. Nobody was on the second floor now. I said that he was letting me know that he had an idea that there were other children about, but what was important for him at the moment was the idea of him coming down from the second floor, where he had had his therapy. He pointed out to me that he was holding onto the handrail or he would fall, reminding me that he was thinking and trying to hold on to the development he had made in therapy so that he didn't feel left to fall.

He suddenly panicked, and dashing to the large chair, turned himself upside down on the cushion. He examined the Turtle motifs on his boots and began to talk rubbish. I commented on the struggle to become independent. He could only think for a little while before becoming panicky and giving up thinking. In his mind he decided that the only way out for him was to go to the basement sewer and become a tough turtle boy with a hard back who didn't need anybody and could survive on eating junk food (the rubbish talk). He argued his view that the Turtles *had* grown up in the sewers, pointing out that when they were little, they couldn't talk, they could when they got bigger. He began to talk in tough Turtle language: he seemed to be avoiding a sense of his neediness, perhaps to protect himself from the pain of leaving. I commented on this. He told me not to talk about it, he wanted to cry. I said he was thinking about leaving but didn't want to feel his sad feelings and cry.

He suddenly said 'It's nice to talk to you, it's time to talk now'. He told me that today had been pancake day. He'd eaten a lot of nice pancakes, but he'd had enough for today. I commented that a moment ago he hadn't wanted to talk to me but I thought that when he felt I understood his sad feelings, he then liked to talk to me. I thought he was also letting me know that he understood he'd had enough therapy really. He asked 'When will your baby come out of your tummy?', 'Will you take it to other children's sessions?' I commented that when he felt he had had enough, he could let himself think about other children and babies having me and getting my help, as he had.

A few weeks after this session, he brought two soft cuddly toys to his therapy and told me that he had decided to let go of the Turtles and become an ordinary, healthy boy. He would do it after the summer, however, as he already had his new Turtle clothes.

Conclusion

For Conor, the struggle to emerge from a state of mindlessness and become an 'ordinary' boy in an 'ordinary' world was an agonisingly painful one. He showed an impressive degree of courage and determination to grow and develop, and during the course of treatment clearly made significant progress.

This was always supported by his parents and his special school. The strength of his autism reduced considerably and he was able to make a reasonably successful relationship to his world. His parents, too, reported considerable and continuing improvements in him at home and satisfactorily successful adjustments to his mainstream school. Although traces of his former autism were apparent, this did not significantly hamper his functioning within what could be seen as an overall pattern of normal development. However, he did lag behind his chronological age both emotionally and cognitively, and it was felt that he would be likely to benefit from more help at various significant stages of his life. It is not clear that Conor could ever catch up to his peers completely, given the extent of his early difficulties. There is little doubt, however, that he made huge strides during the course of his treatment. At the time of termination, he was indeed a far step away from his early undifferentiated mindlessness, and in most respects was able to function well and happily in the ordinary events of life.

I hope this chapter bears testimony to his determination and courage.

Acknowledgement

I should like to thank Sue Reid, whose invaluable supervision and support enabled me to do this work.

12 Carmen

Despot or subject: the discovery of beauty in a wilful, passionate child

Michele Pundick

Introduction

Carmen was four years old when she was referred for intensive psychotherapy after a diagnosis of autism. She was functioning at a very primitive level, with limited capacities for communication and relationships. She had a passionate nature and a profound intolerance of separateness. In this chapter I will focus on the first year of therapy in order to trace her development from a primitive form of relating to a genuine attachment to me, which brought in its wake all the conflicts that each of us have to negotiate in the course of ordinary development. Her central conflict was between being ruler of her world or joining the real world, which, in spite of herself, she found increasingly fascinating and beautiful, but one where she would be a mere subject like the rest of us. This is often a conflict for children with autism, but was particularly starkly revealed in the work with this child, whom I have called Carmen to give some indication of her fiery temperament.

Background

Carmen was the only child of a single mother. Her mother and father had separated in tragic circumstances, which left mother bereaved throughout Carmen's early years. She was born a few weeks prematurely and spent the first two weeks in a special care unit. She was initially tube-fed, but her mother was determined to breast-feed and succeeded in doing so. Her early development was apparently fine until about the age of two. She had rarely cried as a baby but around the age of two began crying. Her mother also noticed at this time that her speech was not developing, and sought professional advice. Over the next year and a half Carmen was referred for a variety of tests and assessments. Neurological and hearing tests found nothing abnormal. When she was three she began attending nursery, and staff became concerned about her bizarre behaviour. She tended to ignore the other children and would often cry and roll about on the floor for no apparent reason. She was referred to the Child and Family Clinic, where the assessment was that Carmen was a child with autism, but that she showed evidence of untapped potential. Intensive psychotherapy was recommended.

The beginning of treatment

I first met Carmen when she was four and a half years old. Her assessment, carried out by a colleague, left me expecting a withdrawn child, so I was surprised by the little girl I found waiting for me.

> In the waiting room, she was sitting well back in the chair, her legs outstretched, next to her mother. She was wearing a pretty, pale, multi-coloured summer dress and brightly coloured sandals and her hair was gathered up into two tiny bunches at the top of her head. I crouched down in front of her to say hello. To my surprise, I found myself holding out my hand to shake. Without looking at me, she shook my hand, giving a big smile to no-one in particular, and kicked her feet slightly. When I held out my hand to go, she didn't respond and needed to be prompted by her mother to stand up. She then took my hand and we set off to my room. I say 'took my hand' rather than 'held it' as she rarely 'held' my hand in any normal way. On this occasion, she stroked the palm of my hand with her middle finger as we walked. She did not look back or seem to notice when her mother called out goodbye.
>
> In the therapy room she sat in the chair I offered her, next to a small table where I had placed a playbox containing items such as a range of toy animals, drawing materials, a family of dolls and a ball. She looked straight ahead at the wall. For the first twenty minutes she made no sound. She smiled a lot, especially when I addressed how she might be feeling at being with me. She continually pressed the fingers of each hand against her thumb. I found myself mesmerised by her smiles and hand movements. From time to time she tentatively touched a cow in the playbox without looking at it, only to let it drop back into the box. After sitting motionless for quite some time, she picked up the roll of Sellotape, fingered the hole and then dropped it on the table, saying, 'mummy baby'. I was taken aback at this clear speech and my sense that there was some symbolic content to her activity: did she have some concept of absence?
>
> She began repeating the first syllable of her name. She then came over to me and, grinning, began saying 'mi', the first syllable of my name. When she next approached me, she leant towards me and slowly let herself fall onto me. She laughed when I held my hands out to catch her and this turned into a kind of game. She then withdrew into repetitive hand movements. I commented that Carmen had come close to Michele and maybe, then, had felt frightened. Later in the session she again came close and let herself fall onto me. At first this felt playful but then she started forcefully slumping into me. Her bright facial expression changed to dark determination and there was a moment when she looked directly at me and it was impossible to tell whether she was going to hug or headbutt me. She remained motionless for the remaining five minutes of the session except for one moment where she picked up a cow and dropped it on the floor.

When I spoke to her about coming again next week, I felt sure she was ignoring me, and when it was time to stop and I held out my hand to her, she didn't move. I then lost my conviction that she had understood me, so repeated that it was time to stop and asked her to return the cow to the box. She did this, teaching me that she had understood quite well.

Already in this first session, I was learning not to underestimate my small patient; I was expecting someone more withdrawn and yet there was something from the first moment of our meeting that had made me reach out to her. This initial contact with Carmen proved to be representative of what I was to discover in the future. She often took me by surprise, but this ran parallel with something else that felt unreachable in her.

The early sessions

Carmen always stirred powerful feelings in me. Her passionate nature and determined big gestures evoked affection and respect for this little girl, who was someone to be reckoned with. I admired her fight and spirit but I had to learn that her rage could be relentless and her wilfulness often intractable.

At the beginning, I mainly worked by describing her activities and the feelings evoked in me whilst observing all the subtleties of her character unfolding. She fluctuated between a delightful, friendly approach, an intrusive force of entry, and a turning away to her own body, in particular her hands. She filled the room with vigorous movement and excitement. This was intended both to excite and distract me, although bodily movement was also her way of communicating and discharging emotion. She would dance or skip or run up and down the room, lean into my body, push her head into my stomach, tread on my feet, clamber on my lap, try to masturbate against my knee, pull my hair, hug me and squeeze my arm. Her use of my body had different meanings. Sometimes she tried to push into me out of longing, wanting to find a way in. Other times it seemed more out of despair, when she felt the wrench of separation. But she could also try to get inside to control me in a hurtful way, as if she felt she could use me in whatever way she liked. I had to stay constantly alert to these different uses of me, and they could shift from moment to moment.

Early in the treatment, Carmen tended to pick up certain objects from the box without looking at them and quickly discard them. Initially I assumed her selection was random, but I began to notice over time that at the start of a session her hand found the cows and, when she was furious, she somehow found the lion, tiger or crocodile. She managed to find ways of doing something consistently and seemingly without intention which actually did betray consistency, selectivity and patterned meaning.

The sessions tended to be split: in the first half, she showed her pleasure and excitement at being back and her anger at having been dropped; in the second half, her behaviour became frantic, driven by her desperation and rage which could develop into cruel assaults on me. I was often to experience an overwhelming sense of wanting to push her away – a feeling I came to understand as a reflection of how overwhelmed she became after a period of being in contact with me. Her feelings were simply too big for her to contain, and too much feeling became bad feeling.

Signs of development

She tried to regulate her feelings in concrete ways. Turning her head from side to side, she would look out of the corners of her eyes, resembling a kind of haughty Cleopatra. She would purse her lips and let out spurts of air, which reminded me of a sealed bag that had been only temporarily pierced: basically, nothing much was to get in or out. And yet she also demonstrated rudimentary capacities to take a little something into herself, if only by imitation. On one occasion, I tried to explain that in future she would come three times a week. She watched with her head cocked as I used my fingers to show her the days she would and would not be coming. She smiled and held up her own fingers. Several weeks later she held up three fingers, indicating some understanding that they represented her three sessions.

She began showing intense interest in me:

> After I had sat down, she moved to the middle of the room and began swaying from one leg to the other, looking down at her feet and squealing with delight. I commented on her enjoying the swaying rhythm, moving her weight from one leg to the other. She approached me and touched my shoe with her forefinger. I named it, 'my foot', and she smiled and squealed. 'Carmen is interested in her feet and mine', I continued, 'things we have the same'. She came to stand at my side and, looking straight into my eyes, moved her face close to mine. Using her forefinger, she poked at my mouth and nose. I decided to take this up as exploratory behaviour, though there was an edge to it. 'Carmen wants to get close', I said, 'to study my face, my mouth and nose, what's inside Michele'. She yanked at my necklace. When I managed to release her hand, she pulled my hair. 'Carmen is now angry with me', I said, 'she sees things she wants from me but she doesn't want them to be Michele's, she wants them for herself'. Although she climbed onto my knees and nestled her head on my shoulder, this peaceful scene was soon shattered and she reverted to standing on my feet, kicking me and angrily kicking the toys on the floor when it was time to stop.

The early sessions foretell the story of the journey we took together – exploring the relation between self and other. The therapy became the thinking space, providing the equipment for the discovery of the intimate and of beauty. This mother-therapist looks at you and thinks about you, about what you do and how it makes you feel and what she does and how that makes you feel. Carmen loved to be looked at, and when she wouldn't take her eyes off me, it was to make sure that I didn't take my eyes off her. Often she would walk to the room gazing up at my face with a beaming smile and bright eyes, which meant she wasn't looking where she was going and I had to be the eyes for both of us, steering her around corners to prevent her from walking into a door or the wall. She also, sometimes, loved the sound of my voice and showed delight or surprise at things I said, opening her eyes wide, cocking her head or scratching the back of her head, as if showing me she was trying to take in a new idea that *my* words came out of *my* mouth, into *her* ears, and thinking went on somewhere in the head!

She became eloquent in her body language, and soon differentiated between the lower and upper part of my body. She hated my feet, which she really attacked. I came to understand that they were a source of provocation for her. Apart from needing to walk around my feet to become as close as she felt she needed to be, she seemed to feel they were the part of me that took me away. Sometimes she would literally try to take my foot off.

It is hard to convey the voracity of her emerging longings and the forcefulness and passion with which she took possession of me, not just wanting to fill me and my room but the whole building. Her arrival usually did not need announcing as everyone in the clinic could hear her entrance. The strength of her voice reflected the strength of her feelings. It conveyed her immense pleasure and excitement about seeing me, but the big noise also seemed to belie her fear that she was small and wouldn't be noticed.

Loss, sadness, 'bye-bye'

In the sixth week there was an unplanned missed session. My car had broken down on the way to see her so unfortunately I only had time to get a message to the clinic just before she arrived. The following day I could hear her in the waiting room vocalising loudly 'me, me, me', and I was surprised again by the clarity and meaningfulness of her words. When I went to collect her, she smiled and cocked her head and looked at me coyly. As I spoke about what a shock she must have had, arriving and leaving again without seeing me, she continued looking and smiling at me and vocalised short, shrill 'o! oh!' sounds. Her escort said, as if to warn me, 'She's very lively today'. But when I held out my hand to her, she ignored me and looked down at her hands. It was my turn to wait.

For the first half of the session I felt I had no impact on her. Then, suddenly, she stood up and slowly turned her head sideways, heavily closing her eyes as if drifting into a trance. I described Carmen turning off and away from me. She moved across the room, putting up three fingers of one hand as she passed me. 'Yes', I said, 'she's showing me the three times she comes here but yesterday Carmen came and Michele wasn't here'. She looked at me and there was a tear falling from one eye. 'She'd missed me yesterday', I exclaimed. She approached me, tentatively stood at the side of my chair, and as I talked about finding a way back to me, tears fell from her eyes. She climbed onto my lap and shuffled about trying to find a comfortable position. She found my hand and held it gently, every so often looking at it. Although the head shuffling continued as I talked about her disappointment, she held onto my finger until it was time to stop and then smiled proudly, seemingly aware of her achievement. After I had said goodbye to her in the waiting room, I heard her calling out 'Bye-bye'.

I was very moved by her new-found capacity to feel the sadness of loss. After this session I found I could tolerate her rage much more. The sight of one tear falling from one eye somehow reassured me of our connectedness and of her capacity to care about that deeply. And her acknowledgement of the 'bye-bye', which hitherto she had always ignored, was a momentous step and had she not kept repeating it I'm not sure I would have believed I had heard it.

Not surprisingly, the following week I was made to pay for what she experienced as my unreliability. She spent the entire week shouting 'me, me, me' and whimpering, throwing toys out of the box onto the floor and kicking them, dancing up and down the room trying to slap me and continually dashing out of the room. She seemed to be testing 'me, me, me' against 'you, you, you'.

She continued to test me during the following weeks – my resilience, who was the boss, had she driven me away? She would strut up and down the room like Miss Piggy from the Muppets, dramatically tossing her head and shoulders, then stand in front of me, hand on hips in a pose, and slowly lean towards me and sing in my face 'bye-bye baby', eloquently making it clear that she wanted me to be the baby who would be left out.

Making an impact

Her Miss Piggy pose and the way she threw her teasing 'bye-bye baby' into my face gave the impression that I was to find out what it was like to be carelessly discarded. Whole sessions could now be focused on the door, and endless repetition was a feature. There were brief interludes when she would surprise me by suddenly climbing onto my knees and sing 'ee-aw' (see-saw) accompanied by the actions, or bellow out 'Peter' and beam with joy when I sang 'Fly away Peter, fly away Paul … ' and then shout for 'more'. She seemed to be exploring the pull and push, the coming and goings, between us. This was also apparent in her games of peekaboo. Even running out of the room could develop into a game, when she'd wait in the corridor for me to come running after her. She developed a sense of fun about running wild and free, when she knew I would seek her out. This had a very different quality from moments when she would dash to the door, stand there with a glint in her eye and move away the moment I got out of my chair and return to the door the moment I sat down again. She knew the difference between having me on a string and having an impact on me. After many experiences like this, I came to trust that she knew what I wanted from her and she knew very well what I didn't like. She enjoyed trying to wind me up. She kept me on my toes both mentally and physically, and I often felt exhausted after only twenty minutes of a session.

There was evidence of her desire for relatedness but she had to struggle with the to and fro in any relationship. Around this time I learned that her behaviour was improving. Her mother told me that Carmen no longer refused to do what she was told, as she had done in the past, and I gained a sense of how embattled their relationship had been. She was now more cooperative and well behaved with her mother.

The first break

As we approached the first break, more evidence appeared of her wish for contact and her awareness of what was going on around her. In the third month she spent two consecutive sessions standing by my chair, wringing her hands and repeating 'car-daddy' in a wistful way. This was very uncharacteristic and puzzled me. The following day I learned she was going on holiday. It was not absolutely clear when they would return. The next time I saw her, she was looking out of the waiting room, which was a new development. She watched me walk the length of the corridor towards her. When I arrived, she bowed, with a smile, but on the way to the room put her hand limply in mine. As we neared the room she stopped and pulled back on my hand. Once in the room, as soon as I mentioned the coming holiday, she walked out. She faced the door for the entire session, either laughing manically and charging at the door, or else stretching her arms out towards it as if in some kind of mystical trance. She seemed to believe that everything she longed for was on the other side of the door from her and that she was excluded. In addition, although I had not picked up on her greeting me with a bow, which at the time seemed amusing, it was a sign, which was to become more explicit in the course of her therapy, that her growing sense of dependence on me could make me seem to her like a high and mighty queen and she responded with a cold determination to knock me off my pedestal.

The weeks preceding this first break saw very primitive behaviours. She would rub her head along my arms and legs, taking in my smell, and desperately cling onto my clothes as if terrified of falling into an abyss. Throughout this time she would repeat 'car' and 'daddy'. I wondered about this 'daddy' and where it came from, as Carmen had never known a daddy. Her mother could not shed light on this either. The daddy seemed to emerge in connection with the holiday. Perhaps any event or person she felt intruded into her space, represented the 'daddy' of the Oedipal triangle.

The last session before the holidays was extremely difficult.

> She was again looking out of the waiting room for me and seemed ready to go straight away. She gripped my hand solidly and, walking to the room, had a certain grown-up air about her. In the room she began her customary picking up and dropping the cow, but as I began to say that

today was our last time for a while, she ran out. I caught up with her near the waiting room. She wasn't laughing as she usually did when she ran out, but looked serious and readily took my hand to walk back to the room. She immediately ran out again, but when I opened the door I was surprised to see her facing it, her nose almost against the doorway. She walked back in of her own accord but then became frenzied. Using her shoulder like a propeller, she twirled herself around and hurled her body at the door. She laughed raucously when I prevented her from opening it and lifted her arm up high in an exaggerated action to hit me but then turned away, shaking her head haughtily as if I wasn't worth it, and, strutting and laughing, shouted 'mo, mo' (more). This went on for quite a while before it finally gave way to inconsolable crying and wailing, accompanied by her saying 'daddy' and, although I described how she couldn't believe she would ever be back in this room with me, nothing I said reached her. She spent the last few minutes standing with her back against the door, looking at me and crying desperately, quietening only when I said it was time to stop. Walking back to the waiting room, she ran around me and pushed into my legs to bar the way, crying and looking at me with pleading eyes, as if holding on for dear life. Finally, out of desperation, I said, she was showing me very clearly she did not want to go, but I would be waiting for her – we could then take the last few steps.

The session seemed to move from a triumphant war dance, when perhaps she felt herself to be taking 'the daddy' on, to her struggle between holding on and manically triumphing, to a third stage of complete desperation, when she appeared to be fighting for her life. Her collapse evoked in me overwhelming feelings of helplessness and inadequacy. Although I appreciated that this was again evidence of her capacity to feel, and powerfully to communicate her feelings to me, she seemed to feel that she was being mercilessly abandoned. Her desperation about separation was possibly connected to her mother's constant grieving during Carmen's early years.

Second term: the battle

To my delight she did return. She was now five years old. For the first few weeks she occupied a new place in my room: standing in a small space behind my chair. At this time she was about the same height as my chair so if I turned around I still could not see her. I understood this stance as her concrete representation of absence, and perhaps working out what it means not to see someone. Are they still there or have they gone? I believe she also needed proof that I would put myself out to reach her. But her return was accompanied by a storm of rage: slapping me, shrieking in my face, banging the door open and shut. Her rage was person-related and not at all autistic. She certainly knew I was there to know how cross she was. But her fury at my not being there all the time was so total, it cut her off from any good feelings, and in this state of mind she was untouchable. She seemed to feel that if I wasn't with her all the time, I must be against her, and she arrived pitched to do battle with me.

Sometimes the battle began from the moment I collected her from the waiting room. She would appear eager to start, running to me with her hand outstretched. Then, when I took her hand, she would twist round and the next minute be lying on the floor, looking up at me with a glint in her eye, amused by her antics and at having fooled me. Lying on the floor, pulling at my hand and pitting her weight against me, she was challenging; either she'd pull me down or I'd have to work hard to pull her up.

This was power, not passion, and it marked the first of many long sieges in the therapy. We would get stuck in endless repetition and I had to struggle against boredom when her autism was only too apparent. She did not tire of opening and closing the door or of running around the room, stopping every so often to flop over me, as if I was an inanimate object or a receptacle for her inertia, or pull roughly at my hands as if she wanted to disconnect them from the rest of my body.

In her external world she had developed a positive, affectionate relationship with her teacher, as well as maintaining closer contact with her mother. It seemed, in fact, that she was able to make a healthy split between the outside world, and its requirement for appropriate behaviour, and her therapy. One of the fascinating features of the work was her seemingly unconscious under-standing, almost from the beginning, that her therapy was the place to bring the deepest layers of her disturbance. In school, and in other social situations, she frequently presented as a 'good child' and it was only her mother who had experienced at first hand the passionate outbursts which were a feature of our work.

Her response to the next approaching holiday was to dig her heels, or more accurately her elbows, in even further. Her every jagged gesture defiantly said, *I will not fit in with you and your arrangements*. Her apparent toughness was defensive, meant to protect her against the kind of hurt and despair she'd expe-rienced before the first holiday, but it also prevented her from taking in any sustenance from me that might help prepare her for the absence over the holiday period.

Third term: collapse

The sessions after the second holiday were characterised by extreme explosions of passion followed by inconsolable wailing. She would start the sessions terribly excited and agitated. Even my voice was an intrusion, and whenever I tried to speak, she'd shriek louder, pull my hands, clothes and jewellery and slap me. Finally she would despair and howl for the rest of the session, accompanied by heaving herself at me and frantic scratching and clinging. The howling could last from twenty to forty-five minutes, and whatever I tried to do or say, she was beyond reach. By the end of the session she had often wet herself too.

Her rage and despair, exacerbated by the absence over the holidays, were more than her body could hold. Assaulted by her own feelings, she in turn assaulted me. Did she believe that people came and went only to torture her? She seemed to feel there was an impervious barrier around me, penetrated only by tearing into me, first by shrieking and finally by screaming and scratching to get under my skin.

The wailing lasted a month, both in and out of her therapy. Her mother began questioning whether therapy was helping her, and I, too, feeling stuck in hopelessness and despair, wondered whether I should be working with her at all. At these times the need for supervision was great. Should I be stopping the sessions when it felt cruel to go on, or was it important to stay with her in such grief and show her I could bear it? Whatever else it was, this raw emotion was not autistic.

Hello hand

Gradually, as the term progressed, there were fleeting and subtle signs of change, usually at the beginning of the sessions; she would take hold of my hand gently and press it against her chest. I was reminded how delightful she could be and how hungry for contact. Another part of her stayed as fiercely determined not to want me and to set herself against me, but as the weeks went by, the fleeting moments towards contact increased.

> As soon as I sat down, Carmen skipped near me, stopping every so often to touch my hand, giving me just time to say 'hello hand' before skipping off, smiling and vocalising joyfully. After doing this several times, she peered into my face, laughing in delight. She circled my chair and coming out, pointed at her box, saying 'ooh'. She ran to the door. I just had time to say 'Ooh, too much feeling, could she hold on to all these feelings, she's been so upset lately'. She skipped back to me, put one hand gently on my shoulder and then laid her head on my shoulder. 'Could she let me shoulder some of it for her', I wondered.

The sessions became rich and interesting again, but I needed to stay extremely vigilant in relation to her wildly fluctuating states of mind. A session mid-term marked a turning point.

> She took hold of my hand and for a while sat holding it. Then she lay across my lap with the upper part of her body, which felt affectionate and cosy. I commented on baby-Carmen wanting to be close. She beamed at the word baby, then got up and, standing against the door, repeated 'baby' and then wistfully, 'baby, mummy', with long pauses in between when she would look at me longingly and hold my hand gently. She then began saying, 'baby, mummy, daddy'. Returning to sit close to me, she crossed

her legs like mine, looked at my legs, then at her own and smiled proudly. Towards the end she stood beside me humming.

This was the first time she could consider a mummy, baby and daddy together as a threesome in harmony. Allowing a daddy in seemed to allow her more freedom so that she could then feel free to copy 'mummy' – a part of ordinary development.

There were now times when she demonstrated that the world was a wonderful place. She often arrived singing, and would dance around the room, expressing her joy when she felt we were in tune with one another. This was also happening at home. From mother's worker, I heard how Carmen was more approachable, as well as more manageable, and that there were now tender moments between them. However, opening up to the world of feelings heralded new fears; having discovered such wonders, she was determined that no-one else share them.

Fourth term: it hurts!

The first session back, she was looking out for me and greeted me tenderly. In the room she followed me to my chair and stayed at my side, smiling and opening her eyes wide, and then nestled her head on my shoulder. The moment I commented on her good feelings, her expression changed. She sang 'woodbye' and hit the holiday chart on the table. I spoke about her feeling close to me and then remembering the goodbye, as if a shadow came over the good feelings. 'Die', she said angrily several times (I was shocked) and then, 'i-uh' ('it hurts'). She climbed onto my knees and yanked a handful of my hair.

This marked the pattern for the term: she was initially delighted to see me and then remembered how much it hurt not to be with me. This she now put into words as well as action. Goodbye, which she was perfectly capable of saying, became 'good-*die*'. This was said either in rage, as if I deserved death for the way I treated her, or despair followed by 'i-uh': 'it hurts me wanting and missing you'.

Her repertoire extended as her range of feelings expanded, and she swiftly oscillated between sadness, longing, anger, hatred, frustration and love. At other times she seemed more coldly destructive. She would start the sessions by disengaging the telephone receiver. This was done with a quality of sadness and distance, suggesting that she couldn't hold on during the gaps and lost confidence in me as someone receptive. During the sessions she would also bang the receiver on the desk and then shriek 'ubbish' (rubbish) in my face or shout 'bye' and 'ubbish baby'. She was constantly on the alert, seeing and hearing rivals everywhere. She couldn't believe I could have her in mind as well as someone else. 'Daddy' returned in the material. Everywhere she looked she saw

HIM. Any jewellery I wore was felt to be me putting on the glitz for daddy. She yanked at my bracelet and pulled at my ring, shouting 'me'. My jewellery, the telephone, or my hands, which she'd now pushed apart, represented an attachment which was a blow to her and set off murderous jealousy. Everything I did, thought, or even felt, must be for Carmen – it was either all for 'me' or nothing for 'me'.

A cruel side to her emerged, which at times she seemed to indulge. Standing behind my chair, she could suddenly deliver a blow to my head which was calculated and remorseless and pushed me to the limits of my tolerance. She began squeezing her eyes at me with a grin and a look of satisfaction, suggesting she was defecating me out of her eyes. And on one occasion she climbed onto my knees and sat straddled across me with a glint in her eye, and before I could think what she was up to realised I was wet and that she had peed on me. The most despairing behaviour was her incessant masturbation. This first occurred towards the end of a session. I thought she may have been seeking bodily comfort to escape the crushing pain of separation, which seemed confirmed when I said this. She stopped and came over to me crying desperately. From then on, however, the quality changed. She would begin determinedly near my chair, and in this state of mind was impervious to anything I said. From time to time she would pause to glance at me, grinning, check I was watching her and then continue. (Was I to feel the excluded child watching her participating in an exciting intercourse?) Whatever other meanings there were, she knew she had got to me with her masturbatory behaviour. I told her I would not watch this and emphatically turned my head away or moved to sit somewhere else, but she would move into my line of vision, only to continue, triumphant in her new-found way of dominating me.

There were also times during this period when there was real dialogue. A session in the third month was particularly focused.

> As soon as I had sat down she sang 'good-die, i-uh', then charged towards me (walking over my feet, which hurt), repeating 'i-uh, i-uh'. 'Michele gone really hurts', I said. Shaking her fists in the air, she then started pummelling me, yelling repeatedly 'ye'. 'Oh you', I said, and spoke about how she feels I do this to her, maybe she thinks I want her to feel hurt otherwise I'd stay with her the whole time. She sat next to me and heaved a sigh. She sang 'good-die' and looked at my feet and then at her feet. The last session of the previous week suddenly came to mind, when she had been waiting outside after her session and had seen me leave the building. When I made this link, she replied 'Yup', to my amazement. She moved closer to me. She gazed at me and then moved even closer. 'Ishel', she said, wringing her hands. I talked about her trying to hold onto the Michele she feels close to, afraid she could lose me, that I could walk away and never come back. 'Yup', she said again. She leant back against the couch and said in a throaty drawn out voice, 'da-da, daddy', and gave a big smile. Then

she held up her left hand in a rigid beaked shape and turned towards it with her eyes closed, saying 'baby' wistfully and 'i-uh'.

She could not hold on to the caring me when her mind was so full of rivals. Separation equalled expulsion of the most awful kind. Her beaked hand, which frequently appeared, seemed to represent something which she could not have: possession of me (or, in the outside world, her mother), body and soul. Towards the end of sessions, she often now tried to bend my fingers back, which I understood was partly out of furious jealousy, in that she would rather break my fingers than let me hold anyone else's hand, but she also wanted me to feel what parting felt like for her; left damaged with bits torn off.

Encouraged by her growing use of words, and considering how much she liked to feel big and strong, I tried to introduce the power of mastery of language; yet whenever I spoke of the use of words and toys, as a means to growing up, she would resolutely shake her head in refusal. Somewhere she perceived that words meant being separate and she wasn't ready for that. At times it was difficult to discriminate between when she was not ready and when she was hijacking growth and reducing everything to rubbish. For example, two weeks later she began a session by calling out 'good-die' and laughing:

> She jumped on the couch, looking at me and laughing and shouting 'd, d'. I spoke about her feeling there's a real battle, if I'm with daddy she can't trust there's a space for her and then it is good-die Carmen. She charged at me and then, leaning slightly forward, said, 'shi' in my face and grinned. For the rest of the session she hit out wildly: banging the door, jumping on my chair, squeezing her eyes at me and laughing, and finally hitting me and kicking the radiator. I spoke about her spoiling any warmth, and she seemed to find this hilariously funny.

This was not desperation: she evidently was enjoying herself. She often turned away from the warmth, perhaps because it was too painful if the warmth went elsewhere. Then she would rather be queen of ice than feel her hunger for her sessions.

Conclusion

In conclusion, I would like to give an extract from a session towards the end of the fourth term which shows Carmen's movement between these different states of mind, but where she does manage to hold onto and integrate her different feelings. It also highlights her development from the first break, one year previously.

> Carmen ran to me when I arrived to collect her. Walking to the room, she gazed up at me, smiling and shrieking with delight and excitement, causing everyone who passed to look at her and smile. As we approached the room,

she let go of my hand and ran up to the door. She skipped about the room and then moved quickly to sit in my chair as I walked towards it. She smiled mischievously and watched to see my reaction. When I shared her joke, she laughed and gave back my chair. I then told her about the coming holidays. I was struck by her staying to hear about this but seeming immobilised by it. 'I don't want to know about this', I spoke for her, 'I'm listening but I don't like it'. For the next few minutes she skipped up and down the room, shrieking excitedly and waving her hand. I talked about her bye-bye hand and how she could not bear to think about goodbye feelings. She dashed about, repeating frantically, 'good-die', every so often stopping and shaking her head and saying 'i-uh'. 'It hurts', I said, 'you are shaking your head in disbelief, you have come full of smiles and then I tell you this, it's not fair'. Her eyes filled with tears. I spoke about her sadness, but she went to the door and opened and closed it hard, saying angrily 'good-die'. 'To hell with you Michele and your goodbyes', I said for her, and guided her away from the door.

She now became hard, doing mad walks, and laughing and shouting 'shi, shi, shi'. I reflected the hardness in my tone of voice: 'Don't care, won't feel sad, I'll harden my heart against you and I'll be mad and pretend that's clever, better than needing Michele who goes away and leaves me'. She continued laughing and mocking me but then opened the door and heaved her chest out. I spoke about her heart heaving with sadness. She climbed onto my lap and looked at me intently, conveying the pain of longing. Putting her arms around my neck, she rubbed her cheek against mine, then hit me and ran to the desk and disconnected the telephone. I talked about the hug and the hit, how can it be the same Michele who she loves to be with and who makes her leave. She returned to sit on my knees, then slowly started to slide off. I found myself holding onto her to stop her from falling but she removed my hands and went to stand by the lockers, letting her arms fall heavily onto them with a big sigh. 'So hard' I spoke for her, 'I only come three times a week, that's hard enough, and now you're telling me I won't come at all for two weeks'. She sat on my knees and lay her head against me. She then looked up at me and said 'baby' and smiled peacefully. 'You need me to be like a mummy-person who knows how you feel', I replied.

Summary

Carmen could be enchanting, when she became like a spirited toddler or when she was like a very young baby beginning to explore the world, and finding joy and beauty. Her vitality and her fighting spirit were her strength. But her vitality could swiftly turn to stubbornness when, if she could not have what she wanted on her terms, she would rather have nothing. At these times she cut herself off from nourishing and interesting relationships, either with hot passion or with cold fury ('good-die') and tested my resilience to its limits. Perhaps this linked to her early fight for life as a premature baby. Her connection to the world of relationships was impeded by her preoccupation with rivals, whom she experienced as determined as herself to have it all. She dared not trust. Her passionate wish to possess those she loved, to the exclusion of all others, provoked cold, murderous rage when she was faced with separation. Passionate love then changed to passionate hatred so that something deadly took hold inside her, which then revealed a cruel and aggressive side to her character. She seemed at times identified with someone she believed liked inflicting pain, whilst at other times she experienced important figures as unreachable. This in turn left her prey to feeling totally abandoned.

Discovering that the whole of life was not all for her, she could not believe that we could separate and both survive. This became the focus of the therapy. Feeling that she was ready to play, I introduced more toys, one of which was a large doll. She often focused intently on the doll. Lying on top of it, she would scrutinise the doll's face. She became terrified when she accidentally tilted the doll forwards, causing the eyes to close, and then desperately tried to breathe life into it. During one recent session, she articulated her inner struggle:

> She dropped the doll on the floor and I began to talk about her own feeling of being dropped. She stood in front of me and, looking at me with terrible sadness, said, 'no more'. 'No more?' I repeated, taken aback both by the painfulness and the clarity of this communication. Was she telling me I was asking too much from her? Pointing at the doll on the floor nearby, she said 'baby died'.

In this material Carmen seemed to convey the enormity of her task – having to resurrect her dead baby self each time we separated. We came to understand that it really was a battle between life and death for her. One question remains as the work progresses: whether her enormous capacity to make a loving attachment can become sufficiently modulated, and yet remain strong enough to melt the ice.

13 Matthew

From numbers to numeracy: from knowledge to knowing in a ten year-old boy with Asperger's Syndrome

Biddy Youell

Introduction

This chapter is an account of the way an intelligent, ten year-old autistic boy used numbers, words and definitions to sustain his autism and to mislead himself and others into believing him to be 'good at maths'. An attempt is made to describe how, in psychotherapeutic treatment, he began to allow this system to be challenged. The hypothesis is that the containing experience of a firm setting and a lively, thinking other (therapist) slowly enabled him to take the risk of allowing space in his mind in which symbolic thinking might ultimately develop.

Background

Matthew is a tall, thin, dark-haired, dark-skinned boy. When I met Matthew's parents, I was impressed by the fervour with which they had pursued every possible therapeutic avenue. They were also deeply committed to giving him every possible 'ordinary' experience within his family and community. He attended a unit for autistic children and spent part of his week in mainstream school.

History

As a baby, Matthew was a poor sleeper, a fussy eater and showed early signs of poor coordination. His teacher's description of his first appearance at the Unit, aged six, was striking. He climbed very slowly and falteringly up the steps, sat in a chair and while the adults talked, slipped further and further down, eventually saying flatly, 'I'm falling off my chair'. He made no attempt to halt his descent.

Matthew was precocious in many aspects of intellectual development and this undoubtedly served to mask some of his difficulties. His parents were worried, but were reassured by friends and relatives, who suggested that he was a 'budding genius'. At two and a half, he spent a beach holiday writing numbers in the sand. At three he knew his tables and soon began to use a calculator. His parents read to him, but did not teach him to read, and cannot really account for the fact that when he was four he could read complicated texts. He preferred his parents' books to children's stories, and it gradually became clear that stories were of no importance to him. His mother told me that she once had quite a battle with him over his choice of books to take on holiday. He wanted to take two versions of the same story, insisting that because the page numbers and illustrations were different, they were two different books, two choices.

Matthew showed all the dexterity he lacked in other, more ordinary spheres, when it came to using a calculator, and he 'played' with this 'toy' for hours. He mastered the basic operations and could memorise calculations and solutions. He could do complicated sums in his head and would bore everybody around him with explanations of mathematical terminology. Since this features so much as part of his therapy sessions, I will not describe it further here.

Matthew was not diagnosed formally until he was four and a half years old, and then he was described as being at the 'Asperger's' end of the spectrum. He was said to belong to a minority of autistic children, in that he had not withdrawn from his parents and was capable of some social interaction.

Matthew has always been capable of taking people's breath away with sudden statements showing astonishing awareness of his condition. I was given an example before I met him. His mother had been telling him the story of an opera. The issue had been about people missing something or somebody from their lives; about great loss and sadness. Matthew had taken his mother by surprise by saying that he missed 'play'. He did not know how to do it.

In the first few months of work with Matthew, I am afraid that I saw nothing to indicate that he was capable of such insight. I remember being in despair as I sat watching him and listening to him. He would move around the room, smiling as if enjoying a private joke and slipping in and out of a kind of melodious singing, almost like plainsong. I could not decipher the words. He took things out of his toy box, dropped them and appeared not to notice. He rubbed a cloth lightly between his fingers, as if combining fat with flour in pastry making. He did the same with a long piece of string and with the telephone cord. These rather insubstantial movements were punctuated by sudden explosive jumping: a sort of bunny hop. He rammed things into his mouth, under his armpit or between his legs. There was no direct speech and he made no eye contact with me.

I think I naively imagined that if I waited in a state of receptive readiness, he would eventually make a move in my direction. I very slowly realised that I could wait forever. I began to conduct the sessions in a much more robust and challenging way, telling him what I was observing, commenting on the tiniest of changes in his behaviour, and assuming a level of interest and understanding on his part. At first it felt very strange to be proceeding as if his actions had meaning, even when there appeared to be absolutely no intentionality. I have since understood this process in terms of what Alvarez (1992a) writes about as 'reclamation', both as a part of clinical technique and as a component of normal maternal functioning. In relation to work with severely deprived and autistic children, she saw active pursuit of contact as a crucial function of the therapist. If the child cannot communicate through the usual means of projective identification, he needs a therapist who will persist in her attempts to read the mood signs and to verbalise, describe, amplify and even create feeling states.

When Matthew first started to talk to me, it was about the time. His first 'nearly time to go' would come a few minutes into the session and that would give way to 'thirty minutes left', and so on. The clock seemed to act as a magnet which he was powerless to resist. It sometimes felt as if he was actually trying not to look at it, but would be drawn back again and again. When he stared into the mirror he was staring at the reflection of the clock, and every time he turned round it seemed to be waiting for him. His statements always reduced the number of minutes available to us, and I talked about his needing to control the time, to prepare himself for the end far in advance, so that there would be no shocks; nothing unexpected.

In the second month of treatment, I unwittingly added another, equally persecuting object: a calendar. It became a monstrous presence in the room, over which Matthew would stand, flapping, shaking, and repeating days, dates and numbers of sessions until I felt like tearing it up. On the other hand, it provided a focus around which it was possible to make some sense of some things. I talked about the way he was using the calendar and the similarities between it and the clock for him. I spoke about the difference between needing reasonable notice to prepare for a holiday break or the end of the session, and the sort of panicky repetition which he was going in for. I began to talk about it not being good for him to use his mind in this way; about it not really helping him to think about what was happening. It was just a way of 'filling up his mind'. I did not realise that he was also satisfying his need for his 'numbers', constantly adding sevens to extend the list of dates and calculating according to the movement of Easter and the incidence of leap years.

The obsession with the days and dates endured for some months. There was very little other talk. He would sometimes deliver an item of news or repeat something his mother had just said to him outside. He spoke in a booming voice and with eager eye contact, but would then recoil at any show of interest on my part and would rush into one of his autistic rituals. Many of my tentative interpretations would be received with a booming but utterly unconvincing 'Yes I do,' or 'Yes I am'.

I began to be more challenging in my interventions; making choices about when to interpret and when, simply, to tell him to stop. I became more confident in drawing him to me by having in mind a two-person psychology. In this way, my observation that Matthew was 'liking being quiet and still today' became a suggestion that 'Matthew is liking being quiet and still with Miss Youell today'. I offered a commentary which afforded him some agency; for example I would accompany his jumping with, 'Here I am. I'm Matthew! This is my room, my session, this is me!'. This would occasionally elicit a much more robust and convincing 'Yes!'

Numbers

In time, Matthew moved from the calendar into a full-blown display of just how central numbers had become. He had, by this time, developed a way of interacting with me which involved him saying or doing something which had become familiar to us both and waiting for my fairly predictable response.

> 'Twenty-five past ... nearly time to go'. He grinned as I said that it wasn't yet twenty-five past and that we were not yet halfway through our session. 'Not nearly time to go Matthew. You're already getting ready for the end so that it doesn't come as a shock to you'.
> 'Yes, I am. ... Nearly time to go now'. I again stressed the reality (twenty-five minutes left) and his determination to rush on to the end, filling the time with talk about minutes. He grinned at me expectantly as he said 'Fifteen minutes left', and then giggled, as I said he was on 'Matthew time' again and we still had enough time left to be interested in the session.
> 'Ten minutes left!' When I did not respond, he said more loudly and with a huge grin. 'Miss Youell, I said there are ten minutes left!'

This rather rudimentary sense of fun between us developed around his use of the clock and his use of the calendar. The sessions had become a dialogue of sorts, and although he continued to pick up and drop items from his box, the vehicle for his communication (and for his non-communication) became almost entirely verbal. He began to sit down in sessions, fixing me with his penetrating gaze as he subjected me to bombardment by numbers. He could keep up a monologue about numbers for twenty minutes at a time, stringing together definitions, calculations, questions and just straightforward counting.

> 'A million million is a trillion. What's a zillion? There are one hundred years in a century. How old is your mother? One thousand, two thousand, three thousand, four thousand, five thousand ... that's half of ten thousand. How many thousands in a million? How many millions in ten billion? A half is a fraction. What's an ordinal number? Twenty zillion billion. Trillions and trillions of thousands. Thirty-two. One, two, three, four, five, six, seven, eight, nine, ten. What's your favourite number? Three quarters is seventy-five per cent. It's a fraction. How many noughts in a billion? A half and two tenths is seven tenths. A zillion, billion squillion!'

I found myself overwhelmed by this and had to work hard not to get caught up in the content of these long speeches. Having got used to my active participation in sessions, he would become very persecuted by my silence and would repeat a question with such a sense of urgency that I would find myself searching the recesses of my mind for bits of mathematical knowledge. He became panic-stricken if he thought that I did not know something, and would then seek to soothe himself by counting or by writing out endless simple fraction sums. I began to talk to him about how I did not know everything and I did not need or want to.

The various elements in his relationship with numbers took months to emerge from the morass with which I was presented. He had become used to my verbalising ideas about his use of the clock and calendar, and now I took the same approach to his numbers talk. I concentrated on how he was using it, exclaiming if I felt he was trying to impress me with huge numbers (as a mother might be impressed by a toddler's achievements), showing boredom at his meaningless counting, commenting if I felt he was taking refuge in counting or simple calculations. I consciously built on the beginnings of humour.

At one stage, he was preoccupied with putting numbers into sentences and together we compiled a list of sentences to do with the number thirty-two: 'Thirty-second birthday; thirty-second trip to McDonalds; thirty-two children in a class; thirty-two sessions before the summer holiday; thirty-two days is more than a month'. I joined in with this and then was able to identify the point at which it ceased to be fun and became mere ritual repetition. This became an established joke and he would look at me and grin teasingly as he whispered 'Thirty-two ... ' and then would laugh delightedly as I showed mock alarm at the threat of being subjected to the whole list again.

I coined the phrase 'Just numbers!' and welcomed any input from him which was not numbers. In a session just before the first summer break, Matthew told me it was sports day and that he was going away at the weekend, and about it being his sister's birthday next week; and then he said with pride, 'That's not just numbers is it?' He very slowly edged towards monitoring his own use of numbers and introduced a phrase, 'Back to my numbers!'. He became worried that I was asking him to give up all numbers, and I had to be careful to differentiate between the maths he liked to do, and meaningless, mind-filling repetition and counting. He then became able to say, 'It's OK to do maths but not just numbers. I'm stopping my numbers'.

I also worked hard to lend meaning to the content of his numbers talk where possible. I suggested that his endless calculations about the number of minutes in two sessions, one and a half sessions, two and a quarter sessions and so on, might be about his actually wanting more time. He began to articulate such a wish. 'I want more time! I want two sessions, four sessions, a billion sessions', and then, more quietly, 'Miss Youell, I want more sessions'.

He was very worried that some numbers were so big that they could not fit on a calculator and that some time divisions are so tiny you cannot count them. He did 'approximations' at school and it was torture for him. He did not like remainders. He wanted only mathematical certainties. There was a period of preoccupation with age and how many years we might both expect to live. There was talk about pensionable age, and I interpreted this in terms of his wanting to know that I would be around for a long time to help him with this work. 'Miss Y, I don't want you to have a pension'.

Lists

Alongside the maths, we developed the beginnings of an understanding about his use of 'information'. Again, I differentiated between things he needed to know and 'just information'. I commented whenever I felt there was a spark of genuine interest, and resisted the temptation to give in and answer his hectoring questions about my mother's name, my grandparents' address, my mother's birthday and so on. Matthew was quick to equate his collecting of information with his 'counting' and began to monitor himself: 'just information', 'just a list'. He could tell me that he was just 'filling up' his mind and that it did not help him to think. He also began to recognise that there were things which he did want to know about me.

An extract from the third term of our work (age ten and three quarters) illustrates some of these developments. He had, for the first time, shown some interest in the dolls' house, but had quickly moved away from it and started to count:

> I commented that he had been a bit interested in the dolls' house furniture but now he had stopped ... not going to be interested, not going to notice, just going to carry on with his counting. There was then a lengthy sequence of insistent questions about my relations. 'Where does your mum live? I don't know her name. Have you got brothers and sisters?' I responded, as I had before, by recognising that he was interested in me but was not asking about me ... he was asking about my parents ... as if he and I are the same ... having parents and brothers and sisters. He repeated a lot of questions and I repeated my comments and then he took me by surprise by sitting quite still, staring into the dolls' house and saying, in a very normal voice, 'Do you have meetings with other children? What are their names?'. These felt like real questions and I commented on his interest and said he liked it when he came here and we talked. He wanted to interest me and make me smile and enjoy being with him. I said that he does know important things about me, such as how I think and what interests me. He jumped up and bunny-hopped across the room before coming back and asking me where my mum lived. When I commented that this was not real interest he said, 'You won't tell me your birthday because I'll just add it to my list and mess around with it'. This felt terribly sad and as if he was aware of his self-destructiveness.

Matthew had always come to therapy willingly, but by the end of the first year his enthusiasm was in full flood. He loved the work, wanted more of it and we did manage to arrange a second weekly session. It had become a very lively relationship and I was aware of many components which might be seen as echoing a mother-infant interaction. He would scan my face, try to predict my responses, try to make me laugh and love it when he succeeded. Within sessions, while we were concretely in each other's presence, we were increasingly in touch. I had the impression, however, that at the end of sessions I simply ceased to exist. He obliterated me as we went back to the waiting room and there was no parting, no space at all between being with me and being back with his mother.

In meeting with his parents and key teachers, I learned that there was nothing new about the incessant questioning, the listing of facts and the frenetic counting. (I have since wondered why it took Matthew so long to move from the silent 'flapping' sessions into this verbal mode of being, which was so much more akin to his behaviour at home and at school.) His teachers told me that they tried to steer a course between answering his questions, ignoring them, and challenging him as to what he did and did not need to know. His parents said the same. They also admitted that there were times when the bombardment would be such that their tolerance would suddenly give and they would turn on him with, 'For pity's sake, Matthew, shut up!' This seemed to me to be entirely understandable, honest and appropriate. Matthew needed to know that he was with real people with honest reactions. I stressed over and over again that my job was the easy one. I was with him for only fifty minutes at a time, and with no other demands on my attention. It was not the same as having Matthew in a school setting all day. Still less was it anything like being his parent and trying to meet all the demands of family life, with Matthew clinging to one's side, talking incessantly and demanding endless verbal responses, hour after hour, day after day.

The second year of therapy (age eleven)

By the fourth term, I felt his dilemma was on the table. Could he risk changing? If he gave up his 'numbers', what would he be left with? I think we were both aware that something had been opened up and it was probably too late to do anything but try to move forward. I remember a session in which I felt acutely for him as he tried to get lost in some calculations and found he could not do them. In another session he withdrew, saying 'I'm allowed to do my maths. I'm going to draw 600 noughts'. He filled half a page with manic speed and then stopped abruptly and looked at me with desperate appeal in his eyes. 'Miss Youell, I've stopped my noughts'.

I was encouraged to hear from Matthew's teachers that they were noticing changes. He was better able to make simple choices. When they told him he could do skating or swimming, he was able to say he wanted to go skating, even though swimming was written on his timetable. They had been concentrating on his physical coordination and he was thrilled when he learned to ride a bike. Most pleasing of all was that they said his sense of humour was developing. His attempts at 'jokes' often misfired, but he was showing much greater pleasure in all sorts of ways.

Pretend play and stories

Matthew began to talk about babies, about 'pretend play' and about stories. He seemed to have become acutely aware of areas of deficit and urged me to help him understand a great rush of new preoccupations. He struggled with ideas about the difference between things which happen in stories and those in real life. He spoke sadly of his own inability to play and fought the urge to slip away into numbers, lists and definitions. He talked about what babies can and can't do and what he could not do when he was at nursery (play). In one session, there was a moving and extremely painful moment as Matthew spoke of his need to play and to give up his numbers so as to grow up. I almost missed what he said as he mumbled 'I'm becoming like a baby'.

In subsequent sessions Matthew tried to engage in play, and in doing so showed me another aspect of the tyranny of numbers. He tried to play with the toys, but was drawn again and again into counting them. When he looked at the scissors, he saw a number eight in the handles; a swan was a number two. When I protested that he had said something lots of times already, he would ask, 'How many times? A hundred?'

In a few sessions he took things out of the box and tried to make them act out a story. These were so fast-moving and so bizarre that I was unable to record them with any accuracy. The following is an approximation, and does not succeed in conveying the chaotic feel of these attempts at 'pretend play'.

> The cup goes to school. It has a birthday and the pencil sharpener gives it a present. It gets a ruler for a present, and another cup and a pig and they play football. It's a maths lesson, and topic, and the doll is also a present and the scissors are a number eight … no, they're scissors. There are five fouls. The rubber has a penalty, and the ball has free kicks and gets knocked over and has five penalties and the crocodile is going to church and he kicks the ball and has a birthday too. A fowl is a duck.

Matthew seemed terrified by what was going on. If I questioned anything, he would look at me and protest, with agitation, 'Anything can happen in a story'. I came to understand that, when he said this, he meant that for him stories had no meaning. Events were random; there was no cause and effect. At first I felt alarmed that the material was psychotic in content, but as time went on and the stories failed to develop and he became peculiarly detached from the telling of them, I concluded that they were, actually, meaningless.

Matthew soon abandoned these attempts and returned to a more debating mode. He closed the lid on his toy box and again became focused on the inter-action between us. He seemed to be winning what he described as a battle to keep numbers at bay. 'Go away numbers. You are not going to win!'. He was cheerful and excited about his own progress. There was also some evidence that I was not entirely wiped out in his unconscious mind between sessions. He told me about a story he had written at school. The central character, Bid, had taken some children to the beach. I asked him if he knew my first name. 'No, Miss Youell, I don't think I do. I think it's Biddy'.

He showed me a way in which he seemed better able to conduct a spontaneous and potentially imaginative kind of play or storytelling. If we sang together and went on in an improvising, turn-taking kind of way, he seemed better able to let his mind wander, without it becoming bizarre or frenetic. The rhythm of the songs seemed to fulfil a containing function and we had many enjoyable and sometimes revealing 'conversations'.

Matthew: The animals go in two by two, hoorah, hoorah.
Biddy: The elephant and the kangaroo, hoorah, hoorah.
Matthew: The animals go into their teenage years, hoorah, hoorah.
Biddy: They learn new things and they have a good time, hoorah, hoorah.
Matthew: They don't do puzzles, not all of the time. They drive a car and tell some jokes.
Biddy: And they don't do puzzles ... not all of the time.
Matthew: Matthew goes into his teenage years, he's growing up.
Biddy: He talks and he talks and he works hard to think, hoorah, hoorah. He can do things slowly, a step at a time.
Matthew: He does his maths but not just counting. He tries new things and he talks and he thinks and he talks.

The end of the second year

The next stage in our work crept up on us unawares. At the end of the summer term, he fell off his bicycle and grazed his face and legs very badly. He missed Cub camp because he was sick. He missed his last day at school: an unheard-of occurrence. The Matthew who came to his last session of that term was a pale and battle-weary boy. He looked, literally, as if the stuffing had been knocked out of him. He was, however, able to review the term with me and speak calmly of the arrangements for the family holiday, and he spoke of his determination to 'hold onto my thinking'.

In speaking to his parents, I suggested that the sickness and fall from the bicycle could be seen in a positive light. Perhaps Matthew was more in touch with his feelings and not so defended? His mother confirmed that he does not readily allow himself to be ill. She also said that it is rather nice for her when he is ill, because he is so much more 'ordinary' and allows her to look after him.

After the summer holiday, Matthew told me that he had only had one 'panic' whilst away. His parents had told him it did not matter and that he should forget it. He was obviously having difficulty forgetting it, and for the first time managed to convey to me just how horrific his panics were. He had shivered and shuddered and could not sit still, could not talk clearly, could not sleep. He did not want to talk about it, but I felt the memory was very alive and troublesome, and wondered if his strategies for switching off were functioning less efficiently than before.

This memory soon got lost in a rush of material about Matthew's desire to know everything and be 'all brain'. To be a computer would be ideal. We clarified that this would mean no panics, no feelings, no shocks, no sudden cancellations, no 'not knowing'. He added to this the idea that grown-ups should be 'perfect'. They should know everything and should be utterly reliable, never changing an arrangement, never being late or absent. He was frantically idealising an illusory world which was slipping away from him. He was also able to articulate a knowledge that such a world cannot actually be achieved and that his attempts to cling to it were restricting his growth and development.

Discussion

At this point, my description of Matthew's therapy is sounding far too coherent and purposeful, as if we moved from stage to stage in an ordered and logical way with plenty of positive feedback for both of us. It did sometimes feel like that, but by no means always so. Matthew often raised my hopes and expectations by showing great sensitivity, putting an idea into his own words with interest and enthusiasm. It was then very disappointing when these words, which once had immense power and import, became stripped of meaning as they were incorporated into his system. To give an example; we worked our way around to seeing his situation as being one in which he partly wanted to change and partly did not. He verbalised this with great affect: 'A part of me wants to change and try new things and a part of me says no change, I don't want to change!'. A few days later, I was dismayed to hear him parroting this to his mother and could see from her expression that she had heard it hundreds of times.

The technical issue I raised at the beginning of the chapter was also a constant preoccupation. He needed me to go out in pursuit of him, but it had to be very carefully modulated. He felt intruded upon by too much enthusiastic questioning on my part. As he became more attached to me and more trusting, he also became more vulnerable to my mistakes. I sometimes felt that I swamped him with my own agenda; being anxious to press on and consolidate changes. I was also aware, in myself, of a desire to see the work carry over into the rest of his life in a tangible way.

I was painfully aware of what Matthew's family and teachers continued to suffer at his hands. He was never silent, hardly ever still. He could not be ignored for any length of time, because he expected answers to his questions. It was something of a mystery as to why people were so tolerant of him; indeed so fond of him. I have come to think that the explanation for this lies in the apparent absence of malicious or manipulative intent. I rarely felt that his return to his autistic defences ('I'll go back to my numbers') was a hostile move. It felt much more like a flight from something which was too terrifyingly threatening. His anxiety was such that everyone around him wanted to do whatever they could to alleviate it for him. Unlike some autistic children, Matthew could project very effectively.

Matthew had given me a clear picture of how his autism operated ... he described the process, and an observant onlooker could see it in action. But what was the autism about? What was Matthew defending himself against? What is the terror about? I have found Winnicott's formulation about the process of 'disillusion' in the mother-infant relationship extremely helpful, in highlighting what I think may have been Matthew's experience. Winnicott (1971) describes the mother's early, almost complete adaptation to her baby's needs, and the way in which the adaptation must become less complete in time. Disillusion must take place. He says 'the object that behaves perfectly becomes no better than a hallucination'. I am not suggesting that, in reality, Matthew's mother made a 'perfect' adaptation and kept to it too long. What I am suggesting is that Matthew somehow (perhaps pre-birth) managed to create an illusion of a 'perfect adaptation' and never allowed 'disillusion' to take root.

Tustin (1994b: 106) writes about the way in which she had come to see autism as a protective reaction to trauma, and suggests that while the trauma might have been an actual one, it is most often 'illusory'. She concluded that, in the majority of cases, the autism occurred 'as the result of the shock of traumatic awareness in infancy of bodily separateness from the mothering person'. She goes on to give a perfect description of Matthew:

> These children feel that they have faced a life-threatening disaster. As a result of this, they are in a state of acute panic. Nasty things seem to crowd in on them. All their efforts are directed towards controlling them. They have no trust that they will be kept safe otherwise. ... This makes them difficult children to rear.

Matthew allowed for no separation or difference. In his 'magic' world, there was only mathematical certainty and complete predictability. For him, numbers added up. He wanted whole numbers and calculations which were correct. X always equalled X. I was very struck by something his mother told me. She described the way in which Matthew would be inconsolable if his sister asked for something and then changed her mind and rejected it: 'But Sarah does want it. She does!' X always equals X. There could be no change.

Towards the end of the second year of treatment, Matthew said sadly, 'I'd like to be really good at maths, but I'm not'. This tallied with something I had been suspecting for some time and which his teachers confirmed. His ability in mathematics at that time was limited to arithmetic skills. He could do the calculations, but could not easily apply a known method to a new problem. Each new task had to be reduced into a series of operations. He could divide any number by seventeen, but could not easily think about how you would share a cake between seventeen people. The numbers were not symbols; he was not truly numerate. He had a huge vocabulary and grasp of syntax, but did not make up stories. He could read and write but was not truly literate.

It was very difficult to fit Matthew neatly into any one particular theoretical formulation. The pursuit of the perfect 'fit' in the literature mirrors, for me, the pursuit of the 'perfect' form of words, to which I found myself drawn in the consulting room. There was a phantasy which suggested that, if only one were clever enough, one could find a magic phrase which would penetrate his mind, illuminate all shadowy areas, and deliver him from the tyranny under which he lived. The intellectualisation of his problem was very seductive. I think, however, that he finally succeeded in communicating his need for a therapist who was not seduced by his pseudo-sophistication, but who could help him look at his unresolved infantile terrors. This exploration had to take place not from a safe, intellectualised distance, but within an alive and sometimes uncomfortable relationship.

Whilst recognising the theoretical developments which have taken place more recently, Bick's papers (1968, 1986) have proved of immense interest and help to me in thinking about Matthew. Bick (1968) suggested that failure to introject a containing experience in early life may result in an infant finding some way to hold himself together physically and psychically. She termed this 'second skin formation' and described it as the way in which dependence on the mother or carer is replaced by pseudo-independence. She identified the inappropriate use of certain mental functions as one such mechanism. Matthew's intellectual armour could be seen as a very powerful, if ultimately faulty, second skin formation. Its function and purpose did seem to be to hold Matthew together in a very concrete way, in the absence of true ego function.

In the second paper (1986) Bick expanded her ideas about 'adhesive identification'. Thoughts about Matthew flood in. He often talked in terms of 'sticking', 'clinging' and 'glueing'. Phrases such as 'I've got stuck to the calendar' or 'I'm glued to my numbers' were his own. He told me that he intended, at a weekend, to 'hang onto' his thinking. He was proposing something new in one sense, but the langauge was old and indicated the way in which he understood himself in terms of gripping onto something seen as external, rather than finding something inside himself. Bick wrote: 'I began to see that an adhesive relationship was on-the-surface of the object and two-dimensional, while every separation and discontinuity (in knowledge of the object for instance) was the unknown third dimension, the fall into space'. This reference to the 'fall into space' and her observations about the way in which the newborn baby is catapulted out into a world where it is subject to the force of gravity, put me in mind of Matthew's early lack of muscularity, and his fall off the chair when first he went to school.

Matthew's relationship to words and numbers can be seen as essentially two-dimensional. He bounced them off the surface of other people rather than projecting them into a receptive space for processing. He did not really let go of them and allow them to be accepted, rejected or modified by a receptive other. Nor did he seem to be able to take new words and phrases deep into the centre of himself. They were added on to his intellectualised, surface repertoire, like an accretion of sediment.

Over seven terms of work, Matthew showed me how much he needed his words and numbers and how ineffective physical 'sticking' was for him. In common with other autistic children, he flapped, twiddled and jiggled. He also tried to achieve some comfort from pressing his body against flat surfaces, but these efforts tended to trail away to nothing. I believe that Matthew used words, numbers and phrases as 'autistic sensation shapes' (Tustin 1980). He eventually allowed me to hear the words which form his accompanying 'plain-song', and they were always familiar extracts from his monologues, or from our conversations. In this way he soothed and caressed himself with the sound of the words. He sang, 'Numbers. Good for my mind. Christmas break', in a way which made me feel he was stroking his mind and rendering it useless.

Meltzer (1986) wrote about the difficulty of treating patients whose mode of relating is adhesive. He cautioned against precipitating a collapse through premature dismantling of the dependence on external supports. Bick (1968) similarly, wrote about the catastrophic anxieties of a 'dead-end, falling through space, liquifying, life-spilling-out variety', and suggested that these will not become accessible to analytic work in the transference, until containment has been experienced by the patient as a result of a constant setting and a firm technique.

Developments

A description of the seventh term of therapy, when Matthew was nearly twelve, serves to illustrate some of these points. It was a momentous term for him. Externally, he was presented with a series of new challenges. His house was occupied by builders; his father had changed his job; his mother was pregnant again; his school timetable had changed dramatically. He talked about all of these events and stated over and over again that he could manage these sorts of changes now. What seemed to throw him in an unexpected way was a coincidence of apparently minor events. I cancelled one Friday session in October and Cubs was cancelled the following Friday. This became known as 'The Friday without a session and the Friday without Cubs', and was talked about incessantly for session upon session. Matthew was angry with me for having the temerity to cancel a session and with Cubs for cancelling 'without a good enough reason'. He failed to incorporate these two events into his usual defensive system and remained unremittingly furious about them. There was interest and suspicion as to where I might be going on that Friday and with whom. He was very unforgiving.

He became increasingly troubled as half-term approached. I reminded him of our shared experience of two years of comings and goings, holidays, postponements and sudden cancellations. I talked about how we had been able to think about each one and about how much easier it became each time. I could not have been more mistaken; for Matthew, it was becoming much more difficult. He was in touch with unfamiliar feelings about these apparently familiar events.

As I began to talk more freely about fear, anxiety and worries, he rewarded me by telling me one day that he thought he was talking about the next Cub camp (five weeks ahead) because his daddy was in China. We had, of course, often talked about how he would do one thing in order to avoid another, but this example was all his own. He knew that the real anxiety was not Cub camp but his father's absence. He later said, 'My daddy's back and he's not dead', so I was able to see the scale and concrete nature of the anxiety he was attempting to avoid.

He came to one session full of talk about the way he 'rushes on' and how this does not allow any possibility of having 'an ordinary conversation'. I felt his mother was being quoted verbatim. I was stunned when he explained that it had happened in the last session; I had asked him whether he had always lived in the same house and he had rushed on because he did not want to answer. I remembered the interaction but had made no comment at the time and had no notion that he had registered anything at all. Here was a link which had been made unaided and perhaps after the event. It felt different from his surface-to-surface way of operating. My question had been parried at the time and I thought it had bounced off the surface. It had, evidently, been allowed to penetrate his mind and take shape within.

A week later, he told me that he thought he was talking about his Christmas list because his family were away for half-term and he was staying with his grandparents. He said that he liked being with them, but eventually admitted that he was really missing his family. He came to his sessions and tacitly begged me to stop it hurting.

The following week he was triumphant about their return and I felt very clumsy as I tried to stay with the upset, when he needed to be allowed to recover. He turned on me accusingly: 'I have managed all sorts of changes this term and I did not shut out last week'. He needed me to acknowledge his achievements and work at his pace, not mine.

We did not see the full impact of all this until the next session.

Matthew was in the waiting room, collapsed over his mother's lap, huge tears pouring from his eyes. She explained that things had happened which had upset him; the car had broken down and now Sarah was ill and off school. Matthew looked as white as a sheet and devastated. I asked him if he could come with me and maybe tell me about it and he got unsteadily to his feet and allowed me to put an arm around him and steer him to the door. His mother said goodbye and told him she would be waiting for him.

He continued to sob on the way to the room, and then sat down on a comfortable chair. I sat near him and held his hand as he mopped his eyes and twisted his hanky in his fingers. I talked about it being OK to be upset and we would just stay with that for the moment; we did not need to talk. He tried to launch into talk about Sarah and about the car and it being just something you can't predict, etc. ... but he kept running out of steam and I repeated that he did not need to talk. I suggested these events just felt

too much after last week when his family had been away and he was upset
and needed to rest ... to let his mind take a rest. I said he had been
working so hard this term and had done so well. He kept trying to rally but
could not and eventually laid his head on the table. He looked at me at one
point and said, 'I think it's sorrow coming in. I think it feels like that'.

We sat in this way for about twenty minutes. He then began to recover
and I felt like weeping.

Later in the session, he tried to muster his defences and wandered about
counting the animals or going back to old talk and old jokes. In the event, he
moved closer to me, took my hand and said nothing. When I enquired as to
what he was thinking, he answered 'Nothing really', and I felt he was telling me
the truth. He was, for once, taking a rest, allowing his mind to go its own way,
rather than feeling compelled to cram it full of all the familiar 'stuff'.

I felt devastated by this session and shared his parents and his teachers'
anxiety over the following two weeks, as he spun around in a highly unsettled
state. He had panic attacks at school and spent most of his session time flapping, singing and rocking in much the same way as he had at the beginning of
our contact. He was very angry with me, however, and shouted at me to tell
him why he couldn't have three sessions. I began to talk, with more conviction
than before, about him wanting me to himself and about needing to know that
I think about him, even when we are not together. I felt very worried as he
went off to Cub camp.

However, he returned from camp cheerful, calm and full of his achievements. He talked in a rather grandiose, but somehow 'real' way about how he
was going to manage the coming Christmas holiday. There was even the very
beginnings of empathetic concern for others in his determination not to nag at
his parents all the time. He told me that his mother was very tired, and
lamented the way in which he could 'drive people mad' with his numbers. (This
also, of course, suggests an awareness of what his 'numbers' did to him.)

This phase in my work with Matthew was, for me, alarming, exciting and
acutely painful. My sense was that Matthew was on a roller coaster of new ideas,
thoughts, and experiences. Feelings were stirred up, in the therapy, by the
October cancellations. He was able to feel those feelings and then to think
about them. He felt the separation from his parents at half-term and was able to
reflect upon it. He was able, in the session quoted, to experience the relief of
leaving his mind empty, if only for a very short time. His attempt to rally his
tyrannical numbers was half-hearted and unconvincing. He then managed to
draw on internal resources when faced with the real challenge of Cub camp and
to feel some sense of potency in what he achieved.

The issue of potency, or agency, is very interesting. When Matthew tried to
play out a game of football with the toys from the box, the football moved
around knocking first one player and then another. When a player was awarded
a penalty, the ball knocked him over. He did not kick it. Within the therapy,
Matthew developed a sense of agency in relation to me, knowing that he could

interest, amuse, exasperate, entertain or bore me. He could, to some extent, manage the relationship.

There is evidence, in this material, of a growing capacity to see events as interrelated. I was immensely struck by the links he made unaided. Returning to ideas about Matthew's numbers, this link-making felt like a very different kind of system, one in which X approximates to Y; something which was said one day, reminded him of something which had happened on another day. This is much more complex thinking and is on the borders of symbolisation. Two things are not the same, they are similar. It felt as if he was taking faltering steps towards real numeracy and real knowledge.

Further developments

Over the following two years Matthew made further significant moves. He became calmer and quieter; with his family and teachers as well as with me. The 'flapping' and 'bunny hopping' disappeared from sessions, as did the numbers and 'plainsong'. He became very clear about the difference between using his mind and the mind-numbing repetition which he termed 'not thinking'. He was able to monitor himself and to detect the change in his own voice when he slipped into his 'list' way of being. For the most part, his voice had become fairly ordinary and had a pleasing range of tone.

It was often very painful to watch Matthew's efforts to be 'ordinary'. He wanted an ordinary conversation long before he really understood that such a thing depends on some sort of mutual interest. His first attempts to communicate with new schoolmates was to fire bizarre questions and show no interest in the answers. He also became aware of his own responses to questions, sometimes being able to engage his mind and answer calmly, whilst at other times jumping away as if feeling invaded in a very brutal and hostile way. He knew how much he needed people to support him as he struggled towards a more ordinary way of functioning. He told me with great appreciation that his parents had stopped him playing with a calculator when he was six because he was fed up with it. When I questioned whether he had, in fact, been fed up with it, he shouted 'A bit of me was fed up but I couldn't tell anybody then!'

Matthew became very attached and felt separations acutely. A few days before he was to go away on a school trip towards the end of our fourth year of work, he became very cross and I commented on how much stronger his protesting voice was becoming. He agreed, telling me he wanted all his sessions and no breaks, even though a bit of him knew he could manage perfectly well. He fell silent, and then out popped 'When I was small and people went out, I thought they would never come back'.

Summary

This chapter charts Matthew's progress through the first two years of therapy. In those first two years he showed me just how misleading was his facility with words and numbers. For some time we both floundered under the tyranny of his autism. As the therapy sessions became a safe and lively space, he became able to get in touch with me and my thinking, and then to find a sufficiently safe space in his mind in which to develop his own thoughts. He became increasingly able to articulate his own experience and to recognise his compulsive listing, counting and questioning as ways of trying to avoid what felt to him to be catastrophic anxiety.

14 Becky

Motive in her mindlessness: the discovery of autistic features in a learning disabled adolescent

Janet Bungener

Introduction

In this chapter I am going to describe my work with an adolescent girl called Becky, who is not typical of the cases in this book. Becky was referred initially to a learning disability specialist. No one had autism in mind when assessing Becky for psychotherapy and it took me two years of clinical work before I began to become aware of the autism that had joined forces with the disability. The presence of deliberate mindlessness is not untypical in some of those classified as having a learning disability. The problem is how to recognise the autism and how to work with it.

I shall be giving a brief account of the two years of clinical work that eventually allowed Becky and me to identify the motive in her mindlessness. Then I move onto a detailed account of Becky shifting to and fro between intelligence and mindlessness within a session, and of the ways in which we struggled to keep her intelligence going.

Referral

Becky was referred by her parents at the age of fifteen. She had recently been abused by someone outside of the family. This was a traumatic event but was sensitively dealt with by Becky's parents and the relevant services. The abuse created the impetus for the referral and reawakened some long-term concerns about Becky's vulnerability and the ways in which she seemed to be functioning well below her capacity.

Becky was considered to have a moderate learning disability. There had been some indication of minimal brain damage when tested as a child, but this was insufficient to explain the extent of her disability. It was very hard for Becky's parents to know how much to expect of her, although some members of her family suspected Becky of tremendous resistance and 'laziness'. In turn, it took me years to get beyond the appearance of handicap to the recognition of other undermining forces at work in Becky. It was only when I recognised the presence of autistic mechanisms that it became possible to move what had seemed immovable before.

Family

Becky was from a caring, complex and lively family. Becky lived with her mother, stepfather, younger brother and half-sister. Her mother was closely involved in Becky's life. But inevitably the closeness could make it hard to stand back, and her instinct was to be protective towards Becky. With a greater distance, Becky's stepfather was more questioning and prepared to challenge Becky.

Becky's history

Becky's mother had an uncomplicated pregnancy and was delighted with her first baby daughter. Becky appeared to her mother to be a normal baby and they enjoyed together a very affectionate physical relationship. (Becky herself had a long-standing fondness for babies.) When she was two Becky was hospitalised for an illness, and after this episode mother felt that Becky had regressed. Around this time, mother was pregnant again and feeling unwell herself. Becky's brother was born when Becky was twenty-one months. At thirty months Becky was described as being like an angry baby, throwing toys and paint around, biting other children and seeming not to understand what was said to her. Becky also became more anxious. In certain situations she would hold herself frozen with fear or cut off emotionally in a dazed trance.

Recommendation for psychotherapy

After the incident of abuse at the age of fifteen, Becky was assessed by a learning disability specialist. The specialist found Becky enlivened by psychotherapeutic interventions, and felt that psychotherapy would be well supported by her parents.

In my introductory meeting with Becky's mother she became upset when we were talking about arrangements for Becky's psychotherapy. At first I found this puzzling, but later understood that this new venture was like a developmental marker which brought forth again the sadness and loss at having a disabled daughter. Bicknell (1983) in her classic paper 'The Psychopathology of Handicap', has emphasised the importance of loss in disability, not only at the time of birth, but at all subsequent developmental stages or at critical periods in the family's life cycle.

Account of therapy

Becky's psychotherapy lasted six years. For five of those years she came once weekly, and in her final year, twice a week.

For the first two years of Becky's therapy, abuse and disability were the main issues. Becky needed time to share the trauma of the abuse and for its many different meanings to be explored. A preoccupation with disability was present in every session but had to be looked at in slow, careful stages. At first Becky could only consider the disability she saw in others: fellow pupils at school were often used as vehicles for the expression of her feelings about various aspects of being disabled. There was the girl who always walked slowly, attracting the annoyance of others, and the boy who exposed the group in public by his immature behaviour, and so on. Then there came a point when she felt courageous enough to locate the disability in me, pointing out with delight any sign of slowness in me. Only in the second year of treatment could she begin to refer to the disability in herself. Little by little, through hundreds of observations of my willingness to bear having my own stumblings and misunderstandings explored, she became able to identify with this capacity of mine, and then became more able to tolerate exploring such qualities within herself (Joseph 1978). There was also a need for Becky at times to say, 'I'm not the disabled one, you are. I'm the competent one', so that a sense of ability and potency rather than disability and impotence, could be experimented with and fostered. We eventually reached a point where ability and disability could move much more freely backwards and forwards between us – almost in a kind of turn-taking – and at this same point I began to notice the autism within the disability.

For some time I had been experiencing despair and frustration when Becky was mindlessly repetitive or blank. When all my efforts would fail to awaken and reach Becky, even my sense of frustration became numbed and I would fall back into a feeling of resignation. I would think 'Well, this is the handicap and there is nothing we can do about it', and began considering the termination of Becky's therapy. On the verge of giving up, I told a colleague about my persistent sense of feeling stuck in my work with Becky. My colleague reminded me of how many years of experience I had, and therefore concluded that Becky might be quite an expert at getting everything to stop so that no-one could think. I began to see some connections with certain phenomena in work with autistic patients: the powerful shutting down of one's capacities and its numbing effect upon the therapist is a common event in therapeutic work with autism. It was possible to see that just like some children with autism, Becky might be making a contribution to her mindlessness. It could be understood as a communication about some form of failure and feeling stuck which Becky herself had not overcome or had not the will to overcome. When I could tolerate and digest unbearable feelings about feeling stuck and damaged, and could recover my belief in her capacities, then Becky's emotional and intellectual functioning came alive again.

The session – Becky's discovery of her mind

I would now like to focus on one particular session in the third year of treatment where Becky moved in and out of states of mindlessness.

Obliteration of her intelligence

The session in question began as all the sessions had begun over the last three years, Becky asking me 'Aren't you speaking?' Having given her dozens of different interpretations over the years, I knew that Becky's purpose was more to set the scene where nothing new was to happen – it had to be the same old way. Keeping things the same is a common feature of autism. It was close to a holiday so I had a holiday calendar on the table. Becky was very familiar with this procedure.

> She chose to lie down, on the couch, full length on her front, holding her book, looking up into my face smiling.

This was a very passive, absorbed position. Becky was losing herself in me. It seemed much easier to fit with me and to do the same old thing.

> However Becky did notice the holiday calendar, and I told her about the holiday and that I had to cancel next week as well (this was very unusual for me). She looked stunned into silence. I said: 'You're surprised by what I said about next week. You weren't expecting it'. Becky replied: 'I'm puzzled. Puzzled about why'. 'You're wanting to know why I can't see you next week. And I don't tell you why', I responded. Becky suggested: 'You're always busy'. I acknowledged this: 'You think I'm just so busy with other things'. Becky asked more insistently: 'Why aren't you coming?' I replied briefly: 'There is something else I have to do'. Becky mildly complained: 'Always busy'. I tried to support the feeling of unfairness, saying: 'That could make you fed up'. At this point Becky agreed.

There was the unusualness of a cancellation. Becky was allowing herself to be in touch with the shock. Becky was also able to let a difficult question develop – why I'm not seeing her – and she acknowledged a negative feeling. But when I tried to allow the negative feeling some more focused expression:

> I went on to say: 'Fed up and angry with me'. Becky responded flatly with: 'I don't mind'. 'Now you say you don't mind', I enquired. 'Never mind', Becky answered, her eyes becoming deadened. I still tried to hang on to the feelings: 'But first you did feel fed up with me?' 'No I didn't, I don't mind'.

Becky seemed to be obliterating her mind; she was obliterating her intelligence in the face of a painful situation, the fear that I didn't want to see her. But that was not the way I experienced it. I felt as though my brain had gone into a state of seizure, it was thick and numb. My thought was: 'She is handicapped'. Subsequently, I could see that Becky's defensiveness was obvious, but in the room with Becky there was such a powerful impact upon me that although the thought of defensiveness and denial was in my mind, what I really felt I had encountered was damage. My anxiety was that if I stopped to think about it, I too would get pulled into a quagmire – something shapeless, thick and timeless. In its lack of human imagery it felt similar to material that Bion described in a patient who had dreams that consisted of material so minutely fragmented that they were devoid of any visual component. Bion (1959) believed that without visual images one can be deprived of the elements needed for thought. I dreaded being stuck in this undeveloped substance. Mannoni (1973) has referred to it as the abyss, and has observed that workers either decide they can go no further in the treatment or become driven to train or educate rather than analyse. My urge was to forget it, to leave it behind, just to keep moving and not be stuck and stopped like this. I struggled and managed to resist the urge to give up and escape, and then I felt I had managed not to relegate her mind to the rubbish dump and had also held onto my own mind. I moved from believing that something was dead, to having a conviction that it was worth resuscitating.

> I said: 'I think you have got rid now of that part of your mind that knew you were angry', and I demonstrated with a rubbing out movement. Looking alert, Becky replied: 'Like a rubber with a mistake'.

Her intelligence had returned. Becky was then able for a while to keep her mind and emotions moving and to express different feelings about my forthcoming absence.

Passively handing her intelligence over

Although we had begun to move, we could not sustain it; there was a further way in which Becky could lose her intelligence, as illustrated in the material that followed:

> Looking at the calendar again I wondered if Becky wanted to put some kind of mark to show which day it was that we would miss. Becky was silent and eventually told me she had no idea, and giving the impression of complete emptiness, gazed up into my eyes, quite content. I said that she was looking to me for an idea. Becky agreed. I continued with the idea that Becky thought that I had the full mind with the ideas and she had the empty mind with nothing in it. Again Becky agreed.

Becky was passively handing over all the ability to me; then she didn't have to bother – a very parasitic position to take. Becky was quite prepared just to inhabit my mind and didn't believe there was anything in hers. Again, rather like Becky, I found that I simply wanted to take the easy way out, I would have liked just to be educative and supply the answer.

Instead I said that she found it hard to believe that if she just looked in her mind she could find an idea. There was a pause and Becky said, 'A cross'.

When I could believe that she had some capacity for thought, she could have some belief in herself and her intelligence could function.

The tendency to inhabit another person is a way of being, easily succumbed to in those with a learning disability or autism and can be a major dynamic in the maintenance of an apparent 'stupidity' (Sinason 1992).

Lumping it all together: the antithesis of thoughtful discrimination

Further on in the session, Becky used the phrase 'yes Mum', which had the appearance of just sliding into the haven of an appeasing relationship with me but because this 'yes Mum', included looking away from me to her book in a more defiant manner, it actually seemed to involve a development. There was more ego present. Here there was some self-assertiveness which I pursued and which to some extent Becky acknowledged.

Not long after this Becky went on to call me 'Mum' again, accompanied by an inane smile. Becky was using the same word as before but this time it meant nothing to her. The meaning had gone. I asked why Becky called me that, and in her response she revealed the way in which she had cancelled out her own understanding. Becky had called me Mum because I didn't have a baby. It was about the absence and not the presence of creativity and growth. Becky was rendering the patient-therapist couple sterile. This 'yes Mum' was now an attack on a meaningful link with me. (This may link with Bion's concept of −K, a denuding of meaning from experience [1962]. Bion used K and −K to represent different states of mind that therapists encounter in patients. K, which stands for knowledge, is a state of mind where the person wants to understand, and −K is where the patient prefers states of misunderstanding and tries to defeat the therapist's attempts at interpretation.) Added to this I also knew that Becky called everyone 'Mum' – this was not just deficit and incomprehension, it seemed to have a determination to blur differences. What I chose to focus upon was the effect it had on her capacity to use her mind.

I had just discussed with her how many people Becky called 'Mum' as if we were all the same. Becky renamed me 'Mummy Therapist' and after I queried this Becky explained that it was because her mum was a therapist. I agreed that in that way, being a therapist, I was like her mum, but that I was also a different type of therapist from her mum [her mother was a physiotherapist] and Becky wasn't bothering to sort out how I was the same and how I was different. Becky called father's girlfriend 'Mum', then changed it to 'Step-mum'. I spoke of how, when Becky gave everything the same name she lost the capacity to have many different ideas in her mind. But, if Becky sorted out the different names for people she could have all these different ideas inside. Becky further differentiated the position of her dad's girlfriend and acknowledged that his girlfriend would only be a step-mum if they got married.

Now Becky was using her mind: she was differentiating. Instead of lumping things together, there were fine discriminations made between people. This in turn gave her a more discriminating mind.

I have described three ways in which Becky could lose her intelligence. In the first, Becky could simply obliterate it; in the second, she could inhabit other minds and project her intelligence into them; in the third, she could lump everything together. Each time I managed not to be taken in, some intelligence returned. Perhaps as a result of all the work we had just been doing on losing and retrieving intelligence, Becky finally began to produce material from within herself which became increasingly rich and elaborate.

An independent thought

> I went on to speak of how Becky felt she couldn't be angry with me. Becky was able to say that she thought that people would kick her out if she showed she was angry. Becky then sat up, was quiet for a short while then said, 'flip'. Becky went on to speak of the programmes she was missing on TV.

This word 'flip', however condensed and out of context it appeared, was an unusually spontaneous expression of a private thought of her own. Unlike her usual faint signals, it was clear and forceful. Furthermore, it contained something other than a bland, blanket acceptance of therapy. Becky was allowing an independent thought to develop; she was thinking that what she would like to be doing at the moment was not therapy, but watching television. Potentially what Becky was allowing her mind to hold were thoughts that differ, that conflict and oppose each other. What Becky wanted to do – watch television – could be different from what I wanted to do – therapy. The thought that produced the word 'flip' came from inside her, not from trying to fit and merge with me or to find thoughts in me. When I tried to pursue this independent thought Becky again became mindless, denying in a most handicapped way that she had ever said the word 'flip'. Although Becky had slid back into her usual position that our thoughts had to be alike, my sense of hopelessness at being in the presence of irreparable damage was far shorter-lived than previously.

Valuable mental equipment

Throughout the session, I had been conveying to her that her states of mind-lessness seemed to be induced rather than due to actual damage. Becky acknowledged that she had feelings and thoughts of her own and then went on to speak of having the use of her own video-recorder and her own favourite film. I felt Becky was speaking of the equipment she had available to her that was hers, i.e. mental equipment of her own, and that furthermore it was equipment of interest to someone else. Becky had experienced that I was really interested in her intelligence.

The trick

Becky then enthusiastically described her favourite part of the film. This was her longest and most coherent narrative ever. (The film was *Dirty Dancing* – a delightful story about a young adolescent girl's discovery of sexuality and her own individuation.)

> What Becky really liked in the film was when the girl was put in a box – she demonstrated the shape of a box – and was cut in half. 'It's a trick', Becky explained. Becky said something about the girl's legs being off and about her head being cut off but how it wasn't really and the girl came back together again. I spoke of how Becky did tricks, how Becky cut off her head, her thinking, to make me believe that she had no brains, no ideas, but in our work, when we realised Becky had a head to think with, it came together again. With her head slightly down, rather talking into herself, Becky said that that was her problem and she needed help with it.

This was the first time ever that she had acknowledged she had some difficulty of her own that she was responsible for. It was very personal and moving. Usually Becky said that her problem was her dad, her granddad or her grandmother, the emphasis being on what had been done to her. This time Becky was acknowledging how she could lose her head and she knew she played an active part in this process.

Active aggressor, not passive victim

As a consequence of these developments, she seemed to be freed to acknowledge some of her resentments towards others. She went on to express some quite cruel feelings. In an elaborate narrative, Becky told of an experience where she was an active aggressor rather than a passive victim.

> Becky told me that she went to see her dad last weekend. (All I had ever heard about such visits was that they were okay.) However, this time, when I asked if Becky wanted to tell me anything more about it, Becky said: 'It was good'. She told me they ate in a Chinese restaurant, then corrected herself: 'No, a Japanese' (a subtle differentiation – a lovely move from the tendency to lump together previously described). Father met her off the bus. In an exaggerated and forced way Becky said she was, 'So surprised, so surprised', that Heather (father's girlfriend) was in the restaurant. She repeated this fact of being so surprised several times. Since I felt that the

surprised/pleased was covering the suprised/disappointed, I said: 'So annoyed, so annoyed!' that Heather was there. Becky denied this feeling. I spoke of Becky having thought when only Dad picked her up that Becky was going to get Dad all to herself and damn it, there was Heather. Becky laughed at my slight cursing then said that she had some thoughts that she couldn't say out loud about Heather but that she also liked Heather, she loved her driving. In the car Heather said Dad couldn't do this and Dad couldn't do that. 'It's so funny, so funny', Becky explained. Heather and Becky together seemed to be joining forces against Dad. Becky went on to say: 'The car door shut, it wouldn't open, Dad couldn't get in', and she laughed. 'Dad had to climb over'. Together Heather and Becky said: 'He can walk, he can go in the boot, he can go on the roof, tie a rope to him and pull him behind the car', and again Becky laughed. I spoke of how Becky could make Dad feel what he had made her feel, Dad had to be shut out, no place for him, treated badly. (Becky had often felt let down by the scarcity of contact with her father.) Becky spoke in an animated way about it being such fun and was clearly reliving those feelings in the room. I agreed that it really made Becky feel alive when she could know and show her anger with people. I spoke of my not giving her a place next week (the unusualness of the cancellation) and how she might wish I would be the shut out one like Dad.

In this narrative Becky had been owning instead of projecting her own feelings of vengefulness and cruelty. Developmentally and in terms of susceptibility to abuse, this was a very important shift. The capacity to own one's aggression means that it is less likely to have to be carried or enacted by others. Becky's passivity had carried the danger of drawing out and inciting sadism in others.

Finally, at the very end of the session Becky stood up saying: 'It was quick'. I agreed that it felt quick when there was so much to say and to talk about.

Becky's mental and emotional functioning had also gained momentum, livened up and become quicker. Becky had found that her internal world had been of interest to me and of interest to her, and did not have to be as she had previously described it: 'All broken and blank, blankety, blank, ha ha!'

Conclusion

In my work with Becky I took on a learning-disabled patient, recently abused; and only discovered, in the course of the psychotherapy, autistic features. Becky's psychotherapy started slowly: first came the impact and meaning of the sexual assault, alongside the slow exploration of feelings about disability. To begin with, disability could only be explored via figures kept at a considerable distance from us both. Then I began to become the subject who carried the feared and unwanted qualities. In this way, Becky could slowly process and gain a perspective on the experience of disability without it feeling too painful and overwhelming. Not only was Becky's ego strengthened by identifying with my capacity to bear being imperfect, but additional growth within her personality was fostered by identifying with the world of ability and potency. Only when ability and disability had been looked at from many different perspectives did the most elusive aspect of it come to my attention, that is, the autistic-like features in her disability. These elements were first of all felt by me before being understood. I consistently experienced an unbearable feeling of being stuck and wanted to end the therapy. When a colleague suggested that my despairing state of mind was a result of the strength and success of undermining forces at work in Becky, I began to look at the mindless periods as autistic states. This made it possible to help Becky see that this was something over which she had some power: if she could switch off her mind, then with my help she could switch it on again.

The session I have described in detail was in the third year of treatment when Becky was aged eighteen. Becky continued in psychotherapy for several years, making progress beyond everyone's expectation.

15 Warren

From passive and sensuous compliance to a more lively independence: limited therapeutic objectives with a verbal adolescent

Trudy Klauber

Introduction

Ever since Kanner's early work (1943, 1944) professionals and parents have commented on the burden pubertal changes place on the growing adolescent with autism. Every adolescent is thrown by sexual development. In the case of the adolescent with autism, the considerable changes brought about after puberty may also be distorted by the autism itself. In this chapter I am addressing the impact of adolescence on one young man. It impacted in two ways, providing a developmental opportunity which contributed to a number of positive changes, and it also manifested itself in an overabundance of dammed-up excitement which did not have the ordinary social outlets available to adolescents in general (see Alvarez, this volume: Chapter 5). This kind of excitement, combined with passivity and some overdependence on sensual stimulation, contributed to a continuing under-development of the mind in general, and, in particular, the capacity to wait for thoughts to connect. It increased my patient's fears, as he often mistook ordinary conversational contact for some kind of intrusive battle in which he would become angry, defensive in an over-heated way and then terrified and excited by fears of retaliation.

Warren was referred to me when he was fifteen years old. His parents were concerned to help him to make more use of his educational opportunities and to help him to develop as much of his potential as possible; they also reported that he would suddenly try to envelop women visitors at home in a kind of bear-hug cuddle. He was developing physically and was by then quite tall and well built. Warren's father was beginning to become a more important figure for him at this time, whereas previously his main emotional tie had been a very close one with his mother. A sister, two years younger, was sometimes quite provocative towards her autistic brother.

Howlin (1997), who believes there is little evidence that any particular programme can dramatically improve long-term outcome, goes on to say,

> That is not to suggest that appropriate treatment has no positive effects. It can make all the difference in helping to minimise or avoid secondary

behavioural problems, and can have a significant impact on ensuring that children develop their existing skills to the full.

In accepting the referral, I wanted to see whether I could make useful contact with Warren, and whether he had any interest in my thoughts about him. I wanted to understand what might specifically be impeding his development, and about the meaning of his impulsive/compulsive cuddling. I hoped that I could also make a contribution to improving the quality of life for him and for his family.

As I got to know him, I came to see that an over-sensuous self-absorption and verbal intrusiveness with others had become deeply entrenched and, to my mind, contributed considerably in itself to his cognitive and social impairment. It is easy to believe with young people like Warren that there is much more intellectual impairment than might actually be the case. For parents and teachers who spend a lot of time with them, despair and exhaustion can lead to very low expectations, acceptance of the passivity and blankness, and the conviction that more developed communication is impossible. Sinason (1986) has written about the difficulty in distinguishing between primary and secondary handicap for some patients. Whatever the degree of the original handicap, these children and young people can conform to the expectations of those who live and work with them. Low expectations with a personality such as Warren's can lead to the perpetuation of a situation where the boundary between secondary handicap and genuine disability becomes blurred.

Warren taught me a lot. He taught me about the need to distinguish between absence of intelligence and abuse of genuine capacity. I discovered how easily and addictively he could become sensually and sometimes sexually excited. His excitement had few links with an interest in others, and was inextricably tangled up with getting worked up by ruminative activity in his mind and twitching and touching his body. This seemed to be linked with a high level of persecution when the excitement died down. Adaptations in technique seemed essential. Firm limits had to be established. After some time I began to become very direct with him and actually told him to stop certain habits in order to allow some space for something more productive to develop.

History and referral

I had relatively few details of Warren's history. When his mother told me their story, very quickly, it was hard to ask as many questions as I would have liked. She had clearly told it many times to many professionals, and it was painful. The delivery was assisted by forceps. Warren was always difficult to settle as a baby; he cried a lot and was difficult to feed. He seemed to be very anxious and, not surprisingly, his anxiety made his parents very anxious too. In his second year he had several dramatic seizures, which his parents believed to be connected with the forceps delivery. He was successfully treated with medication. There was no evidence of fits subsequently and further medication was not needed. As a toddler he was interested in spinning things, especially wheels. He loved to hear the same songs repeated, and talked in tragic tones about 'broken' music. He had some individual help as a toddler, which stopped when he started a special primary school for autistic children.

He later transferred to another school, and, when it closed, moved to a third. By the time he was referred to me, aged fifteen, he had been enrolled on a college course for young people with learning difficulties. Many of the basic literacy, numeracy and social skills lessons seemed to be the kind which Warren could sail through. He was just about literate and numerate, and could readily engage teachers as well as his parents in repetitive interrogations, taking no apparent notice of any answers. Quietly he giggled and twitched and picked at his face and head, when his hands were not inside the pockets of his tracksuit. He seemed easily to be able to switch off from the other students and the staff. He had occasional, spectacular tantrums.

Warren's parents were concerned to make the right decisions about his education and to help him to be more sociable. He did not like change and had not taken well to changes in his educational placement. I agreed to see what could be done to help him to grow up – a phrase which I heard a lot from him in the early months. He would boom it at me in a flat voice, often without meaning, echoing his version of what he had heard his parents tell him was the purpose of therapy.

Beginning treatment

When I first met Warren himself, I encountered an initially anxious looking teenager, who seemed frightened at times. He sometimes wore a puzzled expression and looked a bit like a toddler trapped in an adolescent body of some solidity and apparent strength.

He talked to me in booming but flat tones, apparently echoing other people's phrases and expressions. He would gaze at me fixedly for minutes at a time, and when he talked about wanting to be grown up or independent he was not convincing. I was, however, aware of fleeting moments of communicative contact when he would look at me with a sharper focus, sometimes curious, often anxious, before the moment got wiped out and replaced by something more blank, glazed and sensuous. The moments of interest were different from others when he seemed sharp but was also more tricky, asking me to do something, such as holding his hand, to help him to feel better or more comfortable. Such requests always left me feeling uncomfortable. When I complied, because I thought it would help him, he often became excited, with a strange and triumphant expression on his face. When I refused he mostly seemed to be out of touch with my refusal, as if he had not noticed it at all. I was struck by his ability to blank out and switch himself off by touching his face or body, stroking himself or gazing at me in a rather sensual way. These moments could become intensified, with giggles of excitement, after which he would catch his breath and look frightened, sometimes able to slow down, but often returning to giggles of greater intensity. The moments of real contact were more lively; he seemed curious and alert and asked one or two genuine questions. He had 'gone' again before I could offer him answers or think about how to sustain or extend the contact.

I quickly became familiar with the pattern of his behaviour, which could have been interpreted as defences against anxiety, separation, or fear of not being in physical contact with another. However, most of the time anxiety did not predominate. Rather, there was a tense atmosphere in the sessions and he got very excited by verbal conflict and getting me to say no to him. As the pattern of relating repeated itself in session after session I began to think there was something like an addiction to ritualised exchanges with me where I felt cornered, and that any attempt of mine to move on was prevented. When we were locked in these habitual interchanges, for example about holding his hand, or about whether he should sit close to me in the room, he got excited and afraid, and the fear seemed to arouse him further. All of these habitual and distorted ways of relating cut across fleeting moments of ordinary contact, interest and longing. But the moments when he appeared to take in bits of what I said to him led to a decision that it was worth trying to see what change might be achieved through psychotherapy. I arranged to see him twice weekly, which continued for five years, before reducing to once weekly for a longer period.

The first year of treatment

I came to feel very discouraged during parts of the first year of the work. I slowly realised that I was being taken on journeys through the kind of deadly place which Warren inhabited internally; a place where life, interest, curiosity and hope were absent, and mechanical stroking, touching and squeezing contributed to the frightened excitement. Where once these might have provided some kind of actual comfort for an easily frightened, vulnerable child trying to manage overwhelming anxiety, they had become an addictive, mind-numbing activity into which he slipped without resistance. Real anxiety, interest or fear existed for microseconds only. Certain words excited him as readily as physical movement. There was no link in his mind between excitement and the terror which followed and drove him into more excited distancing.

He appeared to lack the equipment to stop himself from sliding instantly into sensuous confusion, and then to become trapped within it. I felt caught up for some time with the idea that I was forced to watch as he unconsciously but deliberately obliterated the humanity within himself by almost constant self-stimulation. Later, I have come to think that these attempts at taking himself away from overwhelming anxiety had become too successful and too easy for him. Thus he could not make use of opportunities to feel his anxiety and be comforted by a helpful other. This was no longer an option for him.

He did say that he was actually afraid of bullies at college, and I was well aware of the real possibility that this vulnerable boy could be a natural victim.

While I could not intervene at college, I could begin to show Warren that he was not only a victim but that he also wanted to push others around verbally, as I experienced repeatedly in his sessions. Within sessions he assumed he could just tell me to do things. He seemed all innocence. He would ask time after time if I would hold his hand because it made him feel comfortable. His so-called comfort, which was so much to do with arousal, and accompanied by glazed eyes and an odd grin, left me very concerned. At first I thought it might be a concrete attempt to make contact. The consequences, however, revealed that he was more out of touch than ever. I resisted his soft, seductive requests. The result was quite startling. He snapped into life – of a kind. His expression was harder and his tone was more direct. He insisted I should do what he asked. The orders seemed to follow some moments of real contact when he seemed connected to thought and feeling for a second or two. If he didn't tell me what to do next, he would instead stroke his stomach lovingly, or allow one hand to hover over his waistband. I felt concerned about whether the odd facial expressions and grins might actually attract the attention of adolescents looking for a victim to pick on. I hoped that the therapy might assist in minimising some of that danger for Warren.

My own hopes of building more verbal communication with him were dashed as he repeatedly switched himself off so effectively. I experimented with further non-compliance. I interpreted that I thought he was pushing me around, and pushing himself around when he sometimes wanted to tell me things about himself. As in the beginning, there were seconds, even moments, of struggle; fleetingly he looked like a lost soul awakened from a long sleep. Almost immediately he would put his hand to his hair, ear, nose or mouth, and go into ecstasy as he ritually smelt the finger he had rubbed behind one of his ears. When I told him again what I thought he was doing, he would accuse me of being bossy with him and that he did not like it. It was a weird distortion of some kind of playfulness, in which I, or his own healthier self was at the mercy of the pleasure and excitement of dashing hope of anything more ordinary and less frightening. My refusal to join in often made little difference: entangling me was exciting and arousing and part of a delusory system in which he had absolute control of me.

As the weeks passed he became more frightened that I would get angry as his verbally violent orders persisted. While he was having this overheated experience, I was left with all the concern about the state of affairs, about how I would be able to switch his mind on, and about the amount of damage that had been done to his mind through all the years he had spent in this state. I was very preoccupied with whether there was any real chance of development. Just occasionally there were moments when he settled and controlled himself for a little longer, when I talked straight to him about the mess and damage he was doing to himself. I also began to ask his mother sometimes to sit outside the room when he threatened to undo his belt or flies in sessions. At first he asked, apparently disingenuously, why she had to be there, what would she do, what would I do, while he got excited by the questions and the additional drama. I learnt ways of talking in a very cool way with no increase in vocal temperature. I wanted to avoid adding ammunition when he already had plenty to use.

There seemed to be a small change; he mentioned that his mother disliked all his questions and that Daddy got cross – I thought there was an incipient link with me. Dislike and anger were located somewhere in the vicinity. I suggested he had an idea that I really did dislike what he did to me and to himself and he wondered whether I would get really cross. In my own mind I longed for some hint that he might get cross, or at least fed up with the repertoire of behaviour that successfully pushed away liveliness and possible development. He began to look very persecuted. I suggested that all he could think was that I would start to bully him – perhaps throw him out. Sadly, even that thought could turn from fear to arousal in seconds.

Slowly he began to share a little interest in 'new' things (the word came from him), and found himself looking around the therapy room, the house and at me, with real interest. Each awakening of interest was accompanied by strong pulls back into the switched-off world of sensual stimulation. Increased interest itself got very muddled with his excitement and he became more preoccupied with talking about violence. It was as if interest was experienced as evidence that I was bullying him if I seemed lively or different from the accustomed predictability. He told me that sessions were boring (which was often true), and simultaneously that there was someone, a cross stranger outside, about to barge in on us. At first I had thought of this stranger as some kind of law-enforcement figure or father, who might set limits, but who was kept outside of Warren's mind. Later I began to wonder whether his insistence on the fact that it was a stranger might link with some (to him) strange, alien experience which was kept out of his relationships. Could this have been, at last, life knocking on the door, impatient to be let in and protesting that it had been excluded for so long while so many lethal substitutes numbed his mind and claimed his attention?

Age 17–19: making sense of the muddle

Some lengthier conversational contact developed at times, especially near the beginning of sessions. He would describe films he watched and would quote, 'Another fine mess you got me into', which seemed to be precisely what he did to his own mind and thought processes. He repeated a description of one scene from a musical he watched again and again. Food in a restaurant got messed up by two young men who ran out without paying, throwing bottles to trip up their pursuers. His excitement and the thrill of the provocation and escape seemed almost to fill him up, but not quite completely. I was fascinated to see that, through the detailed memory of the film, something communicative got through. Someone, an older man, was disapproving and angry at the chaos. Most of the time, however, and especially near to the end of the fourth and subsequent terms, when he knew he would have to say goodbye to me for a while, he got into further verbal and other entanglements, filled with masochistic excitement. This abuse of therapeutic time left him even more terrified of separations, without a means to sort out the mental mess, to know where he stood or whether there were any figures of strength to give him structure. As long as I was experienced as someone like an angry father-figure from whom he could escape, he remained deep in the mess, and very scared. This further excited his urge to resort to his habitual ways.

Over time I became even more convinced of the efficacy of the cool, but firm approach, and eventually told him directly to stop touching himself in sessions. He did. Initially he was very persecuted and feared there would be a real invasion of enemies – characterised frequently as builders, whom he always described as destroyers (He had a memory, two or three years later, that, when he was young, he had been terrified of the builders in the new house they had moved into. He thought they spoilt everything and caused the family cat to run away. It seemed that, for him, change was always felt to be destructive, never constructive, so he needed to make a quick getaway.)

Then came a new film character, Finn the Cheat. Warren told me that Finn stole gold, property deeds and a ring. The hero accused him of being a thief. He replied, 'Now you don't doubt me do you? Go ahead, search, you won't find anything. I couldn't care what you think'. His insistent affirmation, as he repeated the story in many sessions, began to convince me of meaning in the content. It seemed possible that there was some kind of cheating going on which I was witnessing. Perhaps he sensed that, although he might not have treasure of enormous value in his mind, there might be a possibility of some sense of hidden resources which he denied possessing: an unused and abused intelligence. It felt like a wonderfully clear image of how he treated the incipient curiosity, genuine anxiety or longing for contact which did exist in him. I was to be the one to search and search, but I would find no mindful, desperate boy. There was clearly terrible confusion, in which it was exciting to cheat me and to fear the barging builders.

Somewhere in the confusion I felt that he had some unconscious awareness that it was he who cheated himself. I also feared that awakening mental activity would mean he would also have to face the tragedy of the consequences of the long-term misuse of his mind and its subsequent emptiness after so many years of activity which blocked out meaningful experience and relationships.

An external event broke into the cycle of (my) hope and despair in his therapy sessions. He was permanently excluded from the course he attended after some inappropriate behaviour. The experience shook everyone, including Warren. I talked to him very openly about the dangers of what he had done there, what he did with his intrusive words and questions and how muddled he got when he touched, stroked and rubbed himself. I became bolder in setting stronger limits about touching his face and hair, which he still did quite a lot.

He looked me in the eye a bit more sometimes, with a disarming peekaboo quality, like a toddler, practising letting me go and finding me there again. When I said something which seemed accurate he would sneeze, and then had to wipe his nose vigorously, attempting, I think, to wipe out the surprising interest in what I had said. He no longer succeeded so efficiently in wiping away the contents of his mind. At the same time he became painfully aware of the length of time in each session and of calendars when we prepared for holiday breaks in therapy. I felt I needed to be active in helping him to use more of the time available at this vulnerable moment. I decided to suggest that tracksuit trousers were unsuitable for him to wear for therapy or in general, got his parents' agreement, and he began to wear ordinary trousers as a matter of course. He was immediately more alert. He cooperated with all the firmer limits except for very small lapses which convinced me that he felt relieved, on the whole, at my decision. He described my decision as 'banning' certain things from sessions. He continued to inflate his chest and rib-cage stiffening his shoulders as if he could excite himself through some conscious, sensual interference with his own breathing, but, to my surprise, a simple suggestion that he could calm down brought relaxation of the physical tension, he was more able to talk, and quick reminders continued to allow him to calm down and pick up conversation from then on.

The firmer limits brought some real development. Warren had a clear but very rigid idea of what was not good. It led him to be frightened if anyone innocently pointed out pretty girls to him. Also, he could not bear the idea of disco dancing and felt very frightened when he was encouraged to join in at family celebrations. What was quite natural for others frightened Warren, who could not tell the difference between looking at girls or at dancing and feeling drawn into something exciting but forbidden. It was very painful to realise how concrete he was. Thought and action were easily confused, and his fright led him to exclude thoughts for fear that they would become or be action, without any self-control. There was no idea of ordinary friendliness, to himself, his own thoughts or to other people.

Beginnings of symbolisation

Nearly four years into the work Warren began to use paper and pencil in sessions and to try drawings. He had an obsessional interest in another film which included a character who was a bully and the enemy of the personable adolescent hero. The hero uses his quick mind to defeat the bully so that justice can be done to a nice young man who will then get the girl. Warren's drawings of the hero and his helpful teacher were square and lifeless, but they nevertheless linked in his mind and mine, with telling a meaningful story. And it took effort to do them.

He also told me about books he had as a child and still read. Particularly 'The Three Little Pigs'. Both the huffing, puffing wolf of the story, and the bully in the film, felt readily recognisable to me as they threatened decent little pigs and a nice young man who wanted a life. It was important that this malevolent force now had some symbolic form and thus there would be less danger of enactment. Warren listened to me more, while I had to be alert to the moments when his own strange huffing and puffing drew him away from the conversation. He liked the brick house which would not be blown down. His parents reported that during an assessment he had around this time, he had volunteered that brick houses were better than wood 'because they hold up more firmly'.

He told me about going out when he felt very scared that he would see skinny girls. After many, many months of Warren talking about them and getting excited by scaring himself with their description, I began to wonder whether these skinny girls were like living, concrete, skinny reminders of the emaciated state of his mind, so different from his well fed but physically unfit body. His father took him to the gym and Warren complained to me. He complained about being taken out to eat or to the cinema. He seemed to expect that I would take his side and suggest he should stay in most of the time. It occurred to me that going out and about was becoming very painful for him now that he was a little more alert. I thought he might be making some comparisons between himself and other people, and that his answer to noticing the differences – his skinny life compared with theirs, for example – was to retreat from the pain of this realisation. I told him I thought he could try to do more. I added that I thought it was good for him to exercise, and to spend time with his parents and others, talking and listening, although I knew it was difficult for him to do so.

Sadly, however, at this time, he was caught, as so many young people like him do get caught, between the end of statutory education and some kind of sheltered work experience. He was spending at least two full days a week at home alone. This very common experience for people with autism or Asperger's Syndrome at nineteen years of age, was disastrous. The pull to retreat from knowing about himself compared with other people, was coupled with being at home with no planned activity for a day or more each week. He became more distant from me. I feared he might be using old ways of making himself blank and frightened a lot of the time. I encouraged him to talk to his parents and his social worker about it. He did some things himself, and his committed parents did a lot more. Some months later his weekly programme included daily occupation with training or work projects.

Work experience and greater ego strength

Work experience brought serious conversation about many things. He told me frankly, with a little encouragement, about his fears of what he had to do. He complained about change, different activities on different days, and seemed much more awake. I heard from his parents that he was very anxious about this new way of life. Warren himself told me that there were very many things he felt he could not do, that he talked very little to people and that he got stuck in repetitive, simple tasks for whole days. With his permission and the agreement of his parents I talked to his social worker and to the people running the projects. It seemed that Warren was quietly 'bullying' them. I use the term bullying because they felt unable to make certain, fairly small demands on him for fear that he was too vulnerable, frightened and learning-disabled and that he needed to be protected. He himself refused to carry out certain instructions. In passing they said he shouted a lot and that he also went into a dreamy, lost state where he almost slowed to a halt or moved at snail's pace. We had several conversations in which I felt able to share some of my understanding, especially of the benefits of kindly firmness which could remind him of what he could manage and try out. I also mentioned the dangers of excitement and fear in his dreaminess which messed up the side of him which wanted to try to move forward. They became strengthened in challenging Warren a little more. They discovered that the approach actually lessened his tantrums, improved his productivity and increased the sense in themselves, and in Warren, that he was getting more satisfaction out of work, that he seemed to feel better, more cheerful and, indeed, seemed more alive. Warren himself responded by tackling a wider range of tasks – including talking to members of the public. He did, if possible, like to spend all day with one nice woman in the office. He talked to me more about his working life, letting me know the pulls towards inactivity as well as telling me when he had done new things. I would comment that he liked telling me, and wanted me to be as pleased as he was. He became a comparatively reliable and rewarding member of the work team and the staff noted that more of his latent ability was being used and developed. His switched off or angry behaviour became more clearly associated with times of real uncertainty and anxiety: when parts of projects were coming to an end for him, or when staff were absent through illness or moved on to new posts.

Warren turned up for a session one cold spring day in a beach vest. He was grinning oddly and posturing. I asked quietly what he was doing. He said people wore vests when it was warm (I had not mentioned his clothing). It was actually a cool day, and I simply said I thought he knew what kind of clothes to wear for therapy and work. He said spontaneously, 'These are beach clothes'. I agreed. He said 'You wear working clothes for work and beach clothes on the beach'. I said he did not really like that kind of rule. He wanted to do something else here, tell himself it was all right to wear the vest for therapy and going to work. The peculiar grin disappeared and he spoke about being scared that he was to be travel-trained to work in another centre. As the struggle continued I was quite direct about what I thought was good for him and what was not, and about the link between the focus on entangling me in an excited way and the fear of doing something new, which, if he could accept the challenge and the support offered to him in trying it, would help him to feel proud of the achievement, when he managed it.

By this time Warren and I had been through a lot together, and there were some noticeable changes in his external life. He was managing public transport, both buses and trains, by himself and with considerable pride in his achievement. He was managing to remember to keep himself clean and tidy as a daily responsibility. His parents reported that he sometimes smiled and showed an incipient sense of humour. They also felt that people felt warmly towards him and that he could be charming. Lapses like the beach-vest day had an explanation: the anxiety about travel-training, a perfectly natural worry for Warren.

From there, we could work together on other specific anxieties, usually after a large part of a session spent in giggly non-contact. For example, from the time when he was seventeen Warren had been helped to take week-long holidays with his youth club group, without his parents. On the first occasion when the social worker came to his house to talk about the plans, Warren had grimaced and squirmed and giggled. These grimaces and tics not only masked his high anxiety about separation, they also made him more frightened and out of touch with the help he could have used. He began, at this period, to allow me to help him prepare for discussions and reviews with his social worker and for meetings to discuss arrangements. He actually could let me know how frightened he was of things as varied as horse-riding, loud discos and sharing a bedroom on the trips away. There were actually quiet times in his sessions when, after giggling, wild eye movements and the like, he was able to begin a description for himself of what scared him and then to allow me to help by prompting, talking and listening, so that he could leave the session feeling better and manage the trip in a more ordinary way.

Developments in young adult life

In his twenties the arousal and self-stimulation reduced to become almost non-existent within sessions, where he was able to wait for thoughts to come, which differed from becoming glazed over and stuck, and where I could sometimes prompt him gently and he would notice that he had something to say. He could also talk about incidents in his life, and seemed interested in my comments and interpretations. Outside, he could often behave in a relatively socially appropriate way. He was polite, dressed appropriately, answered people's questions and could manage meetings and new situations without the old behaviours. His parents reported their real pleasure at Warren's ability to manage change in a more ordinary way, including two house moves in quick succession. At that time he joined in conversations with me about his fear of the moves, and he managed changes of bedroom and was able to ask with real curiosity about what would happen to his possessions. He genuinely did not know and could not imagine that he and his possessions would move house with his parents, and was able to let me know it. This replaced the earlier ritual of asking a litany of meaningless questions which drove up everyone else's anxiety and made it almost impossible to notice that there were genuine fears which could be calmed. He also gave up repeating all the details of his earliest house move with a tragic expression and a total inability to move on.

I began to be able to say, 'Come on Warren. What's next?' and to be able to encourage him away from old ritualised phrases. He could sometimes say to me, spontaneously, after a silence while I was thinking he was stuck somewhere, 'Er … well … tell you something new', and then do so. He could, of course, also get himself completely lost and tangled up when he loosened his grip, particularly if he was experiencing strong emotions. For example:

One day he described a problem at Youth Club, 'You should always look after your valuables and keep them with you', he intoned. 'There are people who steal and some people at club steal as well'. He repeated a lot more in the same self-righteous imitation of the staff. He then said he had lost his wallet. He said it was lost and he could not find it. It took ages and quite a lot of questions before I understood him. I had to ask him to start at the beginning more than once. He said, at last, that he had left the wallet in his jacket hanging up in the cloakroom, and it had been stolen. I said that I noticed he repeated the things they told him at the club but in fact did not pay any heed to actually looking after his wallet. I said I thought he wanted me to believe he did think about the things they talked about at club, and we talked about here, but perhaps he forgot all about looking after things except for saying the words again and again. I suggested that he left his valuable mind somewhere, hanging up like the wallet in the jacket, forgotten about, and that he did not take care of it.

He said he wanted to talk about Sunday. I said he wanted to talk about something else, and not to talk about taking care of what he had in his head. His eyes slid away from me and he moved on again, 'Well, the next thing is about Friday at my place of work ... '.

Roughly a year later, when Warren was about twenty-two years old:

He said that, on Thursday, Simon (another member of the project) wandered off and he could not get on with his work because he was angry (he sounded terribly upset and cross). 'And I didn't remember if we should make four or six parcels and the job couldn't get finished. And the Supervisor came and told me off'. He insisted that Simon should not wander off and the Supervisor should be cross with him. I suggested that he was telling me about the pull he felt within himself towards wandering off and not being bothered (a favourite expression around this time) to use his mind and to remember what he had to do. He felt that Simon should have done that for him and, instead, he had wandered off leaving Warren feeling cross with Simon, not cross with himself. We talked at length, and when he got muddled I asked him to remember to tell me what happened in sequence. He agreed that would help and managed to say that he could get confused. Then he added, 'When you start a job you should go on until you come to the end'. I felt astonished at a thought he had developed by himself during the conversation and wondered whether he ever took that kind of insight out of the therapy room with him.

New challenges

When Warren went on a sponsored walk, in a Third World country with his youth group, he was shocked that the group had to sleep in tents and sit on the ground to eat. He fell on to some rough grass and thought his leg would bleed because it would be so hard. He reported that in fact he was not hurt. He complained that no-one had brought him pillows and he had to use his towels instead. He looked hurt and said it was not comfy in that place. He also indicated he had tried to join in and had felt pleased when he did, but that the staff had to remind him a lot not to give up. He looked hurt when I suggested that he often wanted a comfy place if he could get it, where he could be a little boy while everyone else did the work, but that he was not as frightened as he used to be, and that sometimes he liked the idea of new places and challenges which were not comfy, but could be interesting.

I began to challenge Warren myself a little more about taking regular responsibility for things such as sharing chores at home, remembering to start conversations, doing different things at work, or offering to do the shopping. Still, the possibility of semi-independent living for him seemed unlikely. When I challenged him about what therapy was for he was afraid that I would stop immediately, but also he was alerted in some way. I talked to him about the difficulty in taking the thinking with him, out of the room; I suggested that therapy could easily become something he just did, part of his routine, something comfy. He then spent twenty minutes telling me that he liked therapy and hated my holiday interruptions. I felt caught on a treadmill of old, old talk and said so to him. He sneezed loudly and then surprised me yet again: 'I've been talking to my Mum', he said, 'about learning to use the Underground so I can get from therapy to my college at the right time. I shouldn't be late should I?' Then he proceeded to list the Underground stations between therapy and college, and where he would need to change from one line to another. I had mentioned these stations to him once only, the previous session.

My technical difficulty was twofold. First, it was difficult to know how much to press him without pushing him beyond his capabilities and becoming cruel. Second, it was difficult to know how far we could go, and how far in truth he could consistently use the understanding of himself without the regular presence of the sessions, which he sometimes genuinely valued and enjoyed and sometimes clung to. He and I both felt, I think, that we had a lot of real contact and that I could notice and contain the mostly hidden anxiety which really did frighten him and inhibit his already limited life.

Discussion

My experience of working with Warren has shown that it is possible to make some real inroads into changing the quality of his life, and that of those who work or live with him. Warren's own misuse of his mind seems to have been a powerful contributor to his autism. Psychotherapy involved setting limits very firmly, limiting interpretation and trusting my counter-transference as a guide to when it was possible to encourage the use of a mind that was available and operative, and to discourage practices which blanked it out or messed it up.

Some young people like Warren can also confound some of the training and educational experiences which they are given. Warren could repeat a lot of his training, particularly in social skills and assertiveness, by rote. He used what was on offer in an apparently compliant way. For him, for example, assertiveness training and the real meaning of assertiveness (the grip on his own mind and his own thoughts) were miles apart. He picked up and used phrases like a parrot, and sometimes convinced workers that he was really doing what was asked of him. Within himself, phrases were mainly incorporated into his comfortable system and were used to ease himself out of communication, leaching out meaning. For example, when he used the words 'afraid' or 'frightened' he was not in touch with the emotion. When he was really frightened, his voice was more urgent and he said he was 'scared'.

Warren needed, in his middle twenties, like any adolescent, to be genuinely assertive. He needed to protest, at times, when he was being infantilised by help which he was offered, and at times to recognise that he would use it in a way which allowed him to give up the effort and to give up being bothered. He would, for example, allow his mind to go rather slack over the question of the circumstances in which his father would or would not offer him a lift somewhere. He would complain that he wanted to use public transport, which did give him a sense of achievement. He failed to notice that he was only offered help when he was running late, when the weather was bad or he was not well. He also had difficulty in discussing the situation. As he described more of the 'assertiveness', it became clear that he was passive, and then, in the car, became angry and threw tantrums because he felt he was being treated like a little boy.

While there were some characteristics of adolescent difficulty in knowing which part of himself (for example, child or almost-adult) he was identified with at a given moment, it was also clear that assertiveness, and having some kind of hold on what he wanted and how he wanted to express it were lost when they were actually needed. He was truly muddled, became angry and sullen and got excited and frightened by the quarrelling which further confused and distracted his vulnerable mind. I suspect that while he was quite good at assertiveness training, and probably at a lot of other training events as well, they were not very useful to him in reality. When he came to need to assert his will and to state what *he* wanted, he got lost, caught between the chronic addiction to permanent babyhood, his real fear, his over-excitement and some personal contempt for that weaker but growing part of himself which took satisfaction from achievement and small signs of independence. The balance could so easily be tipped so that he could either take a lot of what was offered and turn it into some kind of verbal massage or exciting fuddle in his head, or become confused when he wanted to try out a thought or to practice something new.

Warren is not alone in needing help to make proper use of what is offered in training programmes. The difficulty for those who work with these young people is in recognising the destructive habits which can entangle everyone in a twisted and often exciting muddle. Compliant behaviour may look like progress but may be being used by a young person with autism to avoid the very developments which teachers and trainers are seeking to achieve. Even relatively sophisticated young people with autism or Asperger's Syndrome often cannot notice or communicate their genuine fear or confusion, and, when the adults cannot see it either, a retreat can set in very quickly. Within such a system, the use of the disability in order to avoid challenge deprives the individual of a sense of achievement and satisfaction. There can be an all-too-comfortable match between workers' wishes to be helpful and these young people's apparent wish to be helped – one which actually maintains a sterile equilibrium.

It is often argued that young people with disabilities are best left in an apparently contented state rather than stirred up into painful awareness of their predicament. It is true that an opening up of the senses and wakening of the mind may lead to the realisation of the difference between themselves and others. Warren came to understand the difference between himself and his sister and her friends, and it was painful for us both to realise the gap between his development and theirs. However, when he could manage to be more like others, I am certain that a greater sense of belonging to the human race more than made up for the pain of difference. Moreover, he seemed relieved when I talked about it, and about the difference between lumpen, complacent passivity and risky but lively humanity.

I am very grateful to Warren and to his parents for allowing me to play a part in helping him towards something more real and satisfying in his life. He helped me to be more courageous about feeling free to adapt my technique to see what worked and to try to build on it in a relevant, and, I hope, realistic way. Psychotherapy for young people like Warren *must* go hand in hand with other useful and interesting opportunities in their lives.[1] Without them there is time for destructiveness to take ever deeper root. The work which revealed some normal anxieties in Warren, allowed him, from time to time, to accept such feelings as indicators that something needed to be addressed, with another (myself). Such signals, so clearly absent in so much autistic functioning, and sometimes wiped out so efficiently by Warren, are a vital part of a normal communication system within the self and with the other. The obliteration of anxiety, which can be felt to be essential for survival in some young children with autism, can lead to bizarre and increasingly deviant and self-destructive developmental pathways; the result may be that the vestiges of any healthy mental functioning may become stunted and, even actually destroyed.

Note

1 Howlin (1997: 29) suggests that those (young people with autism) who view their autism as a challenge to be overcome make the most progress, 'Although the extent to which they can succeed is likely to depend heavily on the assistance offered by families, teachers and other support systems'.

16 Joe

Towards solid ground: an adolescent's request for a second course of psychotherapy[1]

Judith Edwards

Introduction

In this chapter I would like to trace the development of thinking and sense of self in an adolescent boy whom I will call Joe. Joe's initial dread of annihilation and falling into limitless space became gradually modified as he grew more able to anchor himself within a space-time continuum and find his feet on what he came to call his 'solid ground'.

Time, according to my encyclopaedia, is:

> a concept that measures the duration of events and the periods that sepa-
> rate them. It is a fundamental parameter of all changes, measuring the rates
> at which they occur; it provides a scale of measurement enabling events that
> have occurred to be distinguished from those that are occurring and those
> that will occur. It appears intuitively to be flowing in one direction only, for
> all observers. However according to Einstein's theory of relativity this is
> not the case. The rate at which time passes (as measured by a clock) is not
> the same for observers in different frames of reference that are moving at a
> constant velocity with respect to each other. Thus according to the time
> dilation effect if two observers are moving at a constant velocity relative to
> each other it appears to each that the other's time processes are slowed
> down. In order to pinpoint an event in the universe, its position in a four
> dimensional space-time continuum must be specified. This continuum
> consists of three space dimensions and one of time.
>
> (*Macmillan Encyclopaedia* 1988)

In a black hole, defined as 'a gravitationally collapsed object', time slows down infinitely. The boundary of the black hole is defined as the 'event horizon', and Stephen Hawking (1992) quotes Dante in his evocation of their magnitude: 'Abandon hope all ye who enter here'. Frances Tustin (1972, 1981a) explored the idea of black holes in her work with children with autism. Hawking, however, goes on to assert that black holes are not eternal, and what I hope to show in this chapter is the struggle Joe went through in order to make at least a partial recovery from what might be thought of as gravitational collapse, and to enter the space-time continuum of everyday life.

Background history

Joe, who was re-referred to the Clinic when he was almost seventeen, was born several weeks premature, one of twins. He was incubated after the birth and remained in hospital for three weeks. When he finally went home he was, as his mother described him, stiff with terror; he refused the breast and had to be bottle-fed facing outwards. Although his physical developmental milestones occurred normally, his echolalia and repetitive play became evident at an early stage: he became, as his parents described, 'obsessed' with hard objects such as keys and toy cars, and expressed fears of 'leaking down' which were perhaps related to fantasies surrounding early tube feeding. Did this process induce a feeling of helplessness and lack of engagement? Perhaps a baby's first sense of agency (Alvarez and Furgiuele 1997) develops as he has to suck in order to get sustenance. When I presented Joe at the Autism Workshop, Sue Reid talked of 'liquid states of terror' experienced by some autistic children, and perhaps it was Joe's constitutional 'primitive permeability' (Meltzer *et al.* 1975) which plunged him into such a profoundly terrified state – he lacked the capacity to filter experience and so it bombarded him.

Joe received special schooling from nursery stage (he tested as ESN with an IQ of 50) and also had two years of intensive psychotherapy starting when he was six. He was diagnosed as having autistic features. Therapy was felt to be beneficial, but after two years Joe appeared unable to make further use of it (a situation which was to be repeated in his later treatment with me) and it was not until late adolescence that he himself made a request for further treatment after he had fallen in love with a girl at school and his advances had been rejected. He called this subsequently 'my little breakdown'. At this stage he was still having great difficulties separating from his parents, and was described as obsessional and as having inappropriate social boundaries. At his assessment the psychiatrist commented on Joe's 'inability to establish a secure relationship with his primary objects', and on his 'striving for further development against omnipotent defences'.

Joe comes from what his parents describe as 'an ordinary family', and they have successfully raised three other children. It was clear that his mother's experience with mothering other children had helped her cope with Joe's turning away in infancy. Without her determination it is likely that Joe would have withdrawn even further. As a family their natural, ordinary way of living life mitigated the effects many of these children have on their families (see Chapter 2 of this volume).

Beginning

I arranged to see Joe, who was then sixteen, for twice weekly sessions, but it soon became apparent that he would like much more, and we settled on three sessions a week as being a balance between what he would like and what my timetable would allow. My first impression of him was that he was slighter than I had expected and looked younger than his almost seventeen years. He had black hair and walked in an ungainly stop-go way, as if being impelled forward and held back simultaneously, which reminded me of what one of Tustin's patients called 'the undertow' (Tustin 1986) – a stubborn knot of forward and reverse thrusts which were to be enacted and re-enacted in his therapy. His characteristic movements of rubbing his hands desperately and flapping his arms to 'rid himself of the burden of accretions of stimuli' (Bion 1967) became apparent soon after his treatment began. While at times he would fix me in an unblinking and consuming stare, at other times he was gaze-avoidant, which I came to understand as communicating his enormous need and demand for some sort of symbiotic union and his enormous fear of the claustrophobia attendant on such union. This also seemed related to ideas of adhesive identification as a desperate measure. Bick wrote:

> I began to see that an adhesive relationship was on the surface of the object and two dimensional while every separation and discontinuity was the unknown third dimension, the fall into space. The catastrophic anxiety of falling into space, the dead end, haunts every demand for change and engenders a deep conservatism and demand for sameness, stability and support from the outside world.
>
> (Bick 1968)

In Joe's first session he was able to outline for me in a most graphic way the current embodiment of his catastrophic anxieties.

> He sat down and crossed his legs, saying immediately 'I feel very anxious, that's why I've come, because I went to the doctor and he said it was all anxiety and I need help'. He then proceeded to elaborate a host of physical symptoms – pains in the head, pains all over, stiff shoulders, fear of having AIDS and a brain tumour. All this was accompanied by vivid body language as he squirmed and twisted in his chair, pointing to various parts of his body as he spoke about them. He looked at me piercingly and asked if I thought it was all anxiety.

The room seemed full of his fears and I acknowledged how hard it was for him to feel so anxious in so many different parts of his body. He seemed in that moment to be in what Tustin (1986) calls 'a sensation dominated state', but a state which, far from giving him a feeling of sensuous enjoyment, filled him with terror and the dread of imminent annihilation. It made me wonder, in

hindsight, about Joe's response to the almost unbearable shock of being disconnected from his mother and also his twin brother at birth (what Tustin calls 'the
power and energy crisis' caused by the mouth disconnected from the nipple) and
being placed in an incubator where he may have experienced all interventions
designed for his survival as persecutory. Perhaps tube feeding contributed to a
feeling of not being actively engaged in the process of going on living? He
described in this first session how his only escape from his anxieties was 'to sort of
go into distance'. At this point he looked at me very intently and I had the
feeling that he both wanted to get inside me and wanted me to be inside his
mind, but also feared it. 'Distance' might hold something fearful and dangerous.

Tustin (1986) says:

> The first aim of treatment is to help the child to turn sufficiently from the
> excesses of his body-dominated world and to live over again the failed crisis
> of becoming a developing psychological being. The therapist's task is to
> heal the psychic break between mother and child.

It seemed as if the task would be with Joe, by way of what Anne Alvarez, in
supervision, called 'minimal dose transformations', to recapitulate an area of
failed infantile experience, the pain of which had recently been further exacerbated by Joe's experience of unrequited love. The task had of necessity to
proceed with painstaking slowness. Time and time again Joe showed me by his
lack of response how he absolutely could not take in my sometimes over-
complex interpretations. I had to do quite a bit of unlearning in order to be
open to being where Joe was, like a mother with a young baby, rather than half
a mile ahead and probably up the wrong turning anyway. I also had to be
constantly alert to Joe's wish to draw me into collusion with his autistic
compulsion to repeat; to go over events in a circular way, in what Joseph (1989)
has called a 'chuntering' activity, 'a kind of mental brinkmanship in which the
seeing of the self in this dilemma, unable to be helped, is an essential aspect'. As
she says, the pull towards life and sanity is located in the analyst, while the
patient is passive: 'the analyst is the only person in the room who seems actively
to be concerned about change' (Joseph 1989: 128). The masochistic use of
anxiety was a predominant feature in Joe's early sessions, and I had to be
constantly alert for the moment when an expression of real anxiety became
drawn into a more perverse use. At this time, a term into the treatment, he was
also talking of fears about his compulsive masturbation. To be able to talk about
this was in itself an achievement.

Four weeks after therapy began and not long before the first Christmas
break, Joe reported a dream – this was the only dream he ever told me about
throughout his treatment. He described being on a train: 'Everything's going
real slow and I'm really small. I was well terrified'. He did not seem to be able
to talk further about it, but then said he often got the feeling of being very
small in relation to objects in the room – 'There are big shadows and I'm well

frightened'. He said he'd had this dream/fantasy 'for ever'. At that point he seemed to abandon thinking and was not interested in the idea of linking the dream with our relationship. When I commented on this sudden lack of interest, he then began to talk about an incident with a friendly policeman as if he was not only persecuted by my attention but was pleasurably relieved that I would notice and care about him.

Yet I felt at this point a sense of profound hopelessness, which I was able later in the session to process for Joe, with the idea that he found it hard to believe that we could make this slow train journey together and sort out the worries which threatened to overwhelm him. The slow train reminded me of the infinite slowness of time described as being endemic to the black hole. For weeks at a time I was left with a feeling of fragmentation and incoherence which seemed impossible to convey in the writing-up of his sessions; it felt as if the only way to do it might be to tear up pieces of paper on which were written his disjointed thoughts, and spread them around the room! This made me feel at times as despairing as Joe became later in his treatment, when he could bear to own some of his feelings, rather than pass them over to me.

There was as yet no narrative thread: Meltzer *et al.* (1975) describe this suspension of mental life in the autistic child where 'the child is able to let his mental organisation fall passively to pieces'. They see the task of the therapist as being one of commanding 'or commandeering' attention like a magnet in order to reassemble the dismantled self. The question with Joe was how much had ever been coherent – as he said himself, 'I was born worried' – and how much he actively participated in a continuous process of dismantling. As Joseph said, 'there is a real misery which needs to be sorted out from the masochistic use and exploitation of misery' (Joseph 1989: 128). It was a struggle for Joe and a struggle for me to 'keep in touch with meaning in different circumstances within the limits of one's own tolerance' (Meltzer *et al.* 1975).

So, in many of the early sessions Joe seemed to 'sort of go off into distance' and I was left wondering how to bring him back. As Joseph says,

> when these lively parts of the patient remain split off it means that his whole capacity for wanting and appreciating, missing, feeling disturbed at losing etc, the very stuff that makes for whole object relating is projected and the patient remains with his addiction and without the psychological means of combating this. To me therefore the understanding of this apparent passivity is technically of primary importance with these patients. Moreover it means that with such splitting off of the life and instincts and of loving, ambivalence and guilt is largely evaded. As these patients improve and become more integrated and relationships become more real, they begin to feel acute pain sometimes experienced as almost physical – undifferentiated but extremely intense.
>
> (Joseph 1989: 136)

I think Joe's experience of falling in love had propelled him from what might be called comfortable masochism into a state of acute pain, echoing his earlier agony which became somatised. As our relationship grew and Joe was able to acknowledge his attachment, he also railed against me about the almost unbearable pain of his empty weekends, when all the members of his family went out and left him with the lonely solaces of a pizza and a video. For Joe, becoming alive was an often agonisingly painful business, and he frequently let me know how doubtful he was that it was really worth it.

In *Autistic States in Children* Frances Tustin talks of a premature sense of 'two-ness' – the infant becomes aware of separation from the mother too early: 'the insecurity of this precocious sense of two-ness leads to pathological manoeuvres to reinstate a sense of one-ness' (Tustin 1981a). Joe's refusal to look at his mother while feeding may well have been an enraged protest at being ripped away from all that he had been familiar with, life inside the womb.

The early work with him was very much informed by ideas of mother-infant interaction, as my supervisor pointed me in the direction of texts on child development to indicate how normal mothers of normal children claim and reclaim the attention of their babies in order to build up an ongoing sense of relationship, safety and meaning (Alvarez 1992a: chapter 5). In a very real sense Joe had not made the contact with mother's eyes and face as well as her breast. His preconceptions had not been met with realisations, but with something which must have seemed to him like a dark incomprehensible void which he evacuated wholesale. He had retreated into narcissism and autistic defences, and it seemed as though it was my task to monitor each tiny change in his mood, to go for the bits of feeling which came and went during each session and to treat his smallest communications as if they had meaning. In short, I came to understand that babies learn from pleasure and safety as well as from difficulty and danger; a state of mind which develops from what Trevarthen (1980) calls 'primary intersubjectivity'. Both of these points had technical implications which I shall illustrate later. Autistic withdrawal has a self-regulating as well as a defensive aspect, and I had to learn to respect that; like the need a baby has to digest and recover. Because of Joe's inadequate self-development and fragile ego, he found it hard to stay in touch with his own experience, and needed me initially as an auxiliary ego to process and link his disparate thoughts.

The first holiday break

I quote from a session some time after the first break:

> He said, 'Mum says I've got a lot of work to do here and I shouldn't think about leaving, that's right isn't it?' I asked what he thought and when he didn't respond I said, after a few minutes, that it was hard for him just now to see for himself how things were. He said, 'I get confused – about the times', and I acknowledged how confused he was. He said, 'So I come here Monday, Tuesday and Wednesday, is that right?' I said I thought he was

saying, as he'd said before, he'd like a Tuesday session too but we would stick to what we had agreed, Monday, Wednesday and Thursday sessions. He looked at his watch, looked up delightedly and said, 'Doesn't time go quickly when I talk to you!' Here Joe was beginning to understand and appreciate form and structure, where previously he had felt fragmented.

I said that he'd like always to feel good about me and being here, but then the time might go too quickly and he might feel too nice, so he looked at his watch instead (not perhaps only a turning away but also a piece of self-regulation). He looked reflective and then talked about his diminished fear of getting AIDS, but the wind blew at the door and he asked, 'What is that noise?' I said he wanted to be sure we were safe in here and that this was a safe place to talk about his worries (I was interpreting the need for safety rather than only the persecutory fear). There was a long pause and then he said, 'I was worried on Monday because my face went numb on one side – did I tell you that? I try hard not to be worried but I can't help it'. I said, 'And you want me to try hard to understand your worries with you'. I asked more about the numb face, what he'd been thinking about, but he looked down and stopped talking. After another long pause I said, 'You got a bit worried there', and he said, 'Well it makes me feel bad talking about it'. I said, 'And the room gets full of your worries, it's hard to feel this is a safe place to think about them'. After more silence he said, 'I don't know why' – then broke off, then said, 'I'm *into* therapy now, I do feel better'. I said you feel better just now, not so scared. He talked about liking his previous therapist and the psychiatrist who assessed him (they and I had been 'prats' in the previous session) – he'd said hello to Dr X at school. I said, 'And you like me a bit more now – you can be angry with Dr X and me and we are still there'. At this point his feet were very close to mine, there was silence in the room and a delicate feeling, fragile as eggshell, of things being OK. His foot moved nearer mine and he said, 'I've done well today haven't I?' I said I was to know how hard he struggled, that he had some good feelings now. There were a few moments of companionable silence and he said, looking at his watch, 'I do look at my watch a lot, I must try to control it'. I said he was noticing more, now he felt there was some understanding between us.

Joe allowed me to know early on in his treatment about his fear of being lost, lost in space, being swallowed by the black hole he used to imagine in the Clinic car park, and which then became relocated under the sink in the cupboard of the room we used. He would stride up and down the room, flapping his hands and arms, hardly still for a moment, and then would open the cupboard door to take a quick peek before taking up his journey up and down the room again. As Alvarez pointed out in *Live Company* (1992a) and as Joe himself demonstrated to me many times before I was sufficiently alerted to offer an appropriate interpretation, for a deprived, borderline or psychotic child it is necessary to use a different technique in interpreting. A different perspective with the holding out of hope needs to be offered to counteract the despair. Any interpretation of mine which talked of being lost or swallowed only exacerbated Joe's terror, and in one session I watched just such an escalation for some time before I had the wit to suggest that it was hard for him to believe he would be able to find me each time he came to the Clinic, and to believe that Mum would be at home when he got there. His relief was palpable. For a child with a fragile ego the first task is to offer some necessary hope rather than to confirm despair. What Joe needed was help in scaling problems down – I had to provide a maternal sorting function.

Slowly, as I attempted to contain his distress and link together his feeling states, however disparate they might appear to be, Joe developed a sense of something stronger that was possible inside his mind. He began to test the strength of the walls in the room by hitting them, to hang on the coat hook to test its endurance, and to have ideas about enlivening the appearance of our objectively very shabby room. When I commented on his having ideas to liven me up, that he felt very lively today and I should know about his ability to be creative, his response did not show an omnipotent thrust, as the following excerpt shows. Before the first break he was testing the strength of our link.

He got up and leaned on the window, opening it and saying, 'Some bolts are missing here – do people ever break in?' I said perhaps he was wondering if he could break in here over the holiday and get some of the sessions he felt I was robbing him of. He picked up the ruler from the table and started tapping the walls reflectively; I said perhaps he was testing how strong I was, if I could bear his wanting to break in and take something he felt was his. He laughed and began to walk up and down, saying, 'My Walkman's going to be really flashy. My dad's got a BMW G-reg with a sunroof and my mum's got a G-reg Mini with a sunroof'. I said I was to see him today as a smart flashy person with flashy parents. He said, 'No, they don't really have those cars, they're not rich. We're having the garden returfed and it's going to cost a fortune, we'll be really tight for money'. An acknowledgement of his potential for potency seemed to result not in omnipotence but in a realistic down-to-the-turf appraisal.

Joe appreciated music, and his one ambition was to play the double-bass like his jazz hero Charlie Mingus (his uncle had a vast jazz collection). In a session which had begun with Joe in a desperate state about being teased, he used a rubber band first to think about the link between us and its power of endurance in difficult times.

Then he stretched the band over a splinter in the table and started to twang it. He began to play it, with high and low notes, making a sort of tune which sounded like the drone of a sitar, quite rhythmical and pleasant. He looked at me as he played, and was enjoying it. I said he was beginning to think about playing a tune here in therapy, with the high notes and the low notes, and he was enjoying it, enjoying the feeling he could entertain me. He carried on and I could sense that he was having a Charlie Mingus fantasy as he made twanging double bass sounds. There was something very moving about this and his connection with me as the person entertained, his audience of one. It also seemed like a little child experimenting for the first time with sounds. Even when the band broke he held onto his mood of achievement and sat quietly saying, 'I could make a double bass, no, I could ask my uncle to buy me one'. There was some silence and he checked we had five minutes left. I thought afterwards about his growing sense of reality and his real ambitions, which if they were to be realised necessitated making demands on others: his therapist in the therapy, and other people in the world outside.

In this session it seemed that Joe was borrowing the identity of his hero Charlie Mingus, but in an anticipatory rather than an omnipotent way. Alvarez (1992a) talks of these 'anticipatory identifications' as being an essential prerequisite of growth and development:

> We need the psychoanalytic perspective to help us see the acorn in the oak tree, the baby in the child or the lost breast in the child's soft teddy. But we may need the developmentalists' and Jung's perspective to help us see the oak tree in the acorn, the man the child will become and *is in the process of becoming* ... a child more than any adult is filled with a sense of his future – provided of course that he is not severely depressed.
>
> (Alvarez 1992a: 177)

Coming in from distance

As Joe's moments of real contact increased, he nevertheless needed frequent intervals for digestion and recovery. He would stare out of the window in a peaceful way, like a growing baby able to look out from the shelter of his mother's arms and to begin to have curiosity about the world and the people in it. 'Someone lives there', he mused as he stared out of the window at other houses. He also began to have ideas about others using the room, about me and what I did when we were not together. His frustrated curiosity fuelled further developmental progress. As he said when he discovered 'eff off' written underneath the couch, 'You wait till I get the bastard who wrote eff off in my room!'

In a session which took place about a year after the beginning of his treatment, he threw and caught the cushion, reminding me of Freud's grandson with the reel game – throwing away the object and getting it back – the idea of object constancy.

Joe began to explore the puzzle of time, breaking the session into blocks of five minutes, and ten minutes, then ten and five. I talked about time going on and us going on within it, that he was interested in how things fitted together, the links between times and people. He went over to the window and looked out reflectively. After a while, he said with the sort of liveliness and ordinary curiosity of a young child, 'Where do you think the quietest place in the world is? Where there are no planes and doors and people and cars?' I asked where he thought and he said, 'In the country, I think'. He shut the window and rested his head against the glass, saying, 'So peaceful, so peaceful in here'. He came and sat down on the cushion again, looking around with real curiosity, and again it felt like a baby secure on mother's lap.

Gradually the idea of an internal space was being built up. As Joe slowly began to introject a containing capacity, so his perverse tendencies decreased to an extent.

> In one session he talked about Dad keeping him in order, reminding him of things 'That's what dads do, isn't it?' I also linked it with our work and with me as a sort of monitor of his states and he said, 'Yes', lapsed into silence for some time, took off his watch, tapped it and shook it. I said he was trying to find out things about me and how I worked. There was a lot more silence and I found my thoughts wandering. I said how hard it was for him today to keep his thoughts in the room. Later he started to make a timetable of sessions, saying, 'It's funny I can do this really well here, but not at school where there's a lot of noise'. He talked of the 'peace and quiet', looked at his work and said, 'It's a map – no in fact it's a contents page. I'll make a book, is that OK?'

It seemed as if the idea of mapping his states of mind in the therapy had given him an internal space in which to start 'the book', a narrative which had begun in a formless and terrifying void but which could now move forward, although painfully and slowly, out of the abyss. As he announced to me rather grandly, 'I don't have keys any more, I have thought'.

Creativity emerges

In one session in the fourth term of treatment he told me about a poem he'd written about space, then could not remember it and felt hopeless. The following session, however, he shyly declaimed this poem, about a silver surfer in space, and I saluted his creativity and his memory, as well as the idea that he had things inside him, he was not alone.

It was agreed that we would have a review meeting with Joe's parents, set up at his request. Although this is unusual with a late adolescent (he was now seventeen), it felt appropriate to respond to his need and use the meeting to think about how he could develop a more ordinarily adolescent stance over time. His feelings about whether or not to attend the meeting fluctuated: finally he decided he would, and the decision gave him strength and energy.

He snatched up a pencil and said, 'I'm going to write on my therapy room walls – can I?' I said he felt good at having decided, he wanted to make his mark, to shout out about how good he felt, but we should keep the walls clean; he had his paper in his folder to write on. He drew arcs with his pencil near the wall and repeated his request, and I acknowledged he wanted to make bold marks here. 'All right, I'll use the paper', he said, and sat down. Then he looked round the room and said, 'This room's a bit of a mess, a bit bloody shitty'. We then had a sort of duet, with me saying, 'Mrs E you're pretty shitty not letting me write on the walls', and him making further disparaging remarks about the room. He was laughing and enjoying this, the acknowledgement that I knew he was angry with me. He elaborated what he could do to improve this messy old room – remove the skirting, put woodchip on the walls, remove the panels and put wallpaper up, carpet the floor. I said he was full of ideas and plans today – by this time he was walking round the room as he talked rather like someone giving a quote for work they could do. I said he felt really in command of this, that he could do a pretty good job on the room, on me and on himself. After a while he came and sat very close to me on the couch, compared times on our watches and then put his hand very close to mine to compare watch faces. They both said exactly the same and he was pleased. I said how pleased he felt that we could be here and have a conversation and agree about things. By this time his legs were very close to mine and he said, 'Can I go and get my radio?' I said we'd had a good chat but he wanted to be sure that he could be close and still feel safe. 'No', he said, 'I want to hear some music'. I said I thought it was important for us to think about what it meant, that he could entertain me and play some music because he felt good today. He was quiet for a few minutes in a satisfied way, and I said perhaps it was good to have a quiet time after being very full of ideas, so that they could settle down and become solid in his mind – the need to digest and recover.

In his journey towards what he came to call the 'solid ground' of his therapy – 'On Solid Ground' was a piece by a musician he admired – there were frequent steps back as well as forward, as his claustrophobic fears overwhelmed him in what seemed almost a direct ratio with his engagement with me – perhaps inevitably so. In the session after the one just quoted he came in with his Walkman, which I saw as being simultaneously a way of blocking me out and an umbilical cord between us.

He took the headphones off and put them round his neck, saying, 'You know, I like therapy. I'd like it to happen at home, we could sit on the sofa, and listen to music, it helps me relax and get calm'. I said he'd like me to be around at home so he could tune into me any time, like he could tune into the radio and find out about the weather. At one point he asked in a slightly anxious way, 'Can you read my mind?' I said he liked us thinking about things together but then it felt too close, as if I was inside his head and he didn't like that. ... A bit later he said, 'I really like therapy. I used to look at my watch all the time, didn't I?' (and he covertly looked at his watch). I said, 'You want to be sure we can keep a safe distance' (like a baby learning to modulate the intensity of his contact – Stern 1985). He sat reflectively listening to the music, then talked about a song he wanted me to hear. He found it on the tape, stood up and played it. He said, 'This reminds me of therapy'. The words were something like 'she smiles, he tells her she is like a flower', and the song mentioned something about their love. He stood quite close as I listened. I said it was a lovely song, he wanted me to know about his loving feelings, that therapy was important to him and I was important too. It did indeed feel moving and a bit over-whelming, and I wondered how to handle it for him so he could have the feeling without being overwhelmed. He sat on the couch and said, 'Yes, I've talked to my mum and my family about my emotional problem – I get nervous, anxious, embarrassed, claustrophobic' (an impressive list of feel-ings states). I said I thought he wanted to know it was safe to play the song and that we wouldn't get mixed up together.

Klein (1975) advised, 'One should not underrate the loving impulses' which can help to mitigate hate and envy. I would like to quote from Sue Reid's paper 'The Importance of Beauty in the Psycho-analytic Experience', where she tells the moving story of little Georgie who, after a grossly deprived beginning, finally has in therapy 'the beautiful experience of being in mother's mind a loved beautiful baby'. She goes on to say:

> I think there is a deep-rooted fear that any 'confession' of a beautiful expe-rience will be automatically met with words like idealisation and with attempts to suggest that we have missed what lies behind it. I think it is time to make love, beauty, pleasure and appreciation respectable concepts in the psychoanalytic work and literature. For without an appreciation of beauty linked to love there is no impetus to live life, to enjoy it and to seek and embrace experiences.
>
> (Reid 1990: 51)

I think that in his struggle on the long journey from formless outer space to a defined internal space, Joe was able, as an adolescent, to reconstruct a vital infantile experience which he had missed, not because it had been unavailable but because he had been too locked into a delusional 'one-ness' to be able to experience the delights as well as the pains of 'two-ness'.

Getting the distance right

In a session not long before the second summer break we were talking about what he called the 'silly' part of his mind that undermined the 'sensible' part.

He held up his fingers and said, 'The sensible part's this big' (very small). I said at the moment the silly part felt quite large – perhaps, however, just now we were talking to the sensible part who wanted to work with me to get bigger and stronger and make more of a balance in his mind. He said, 'Yes, right. When I see someone I get right up close like this' (he came close to me and stared in a 'stupid' way into my face). He was half laughing and I said, 'It feels funny, but you know there's something wrong too'. He said, 'Anna won't go out with me. I said to her, "look we could go out together, we could get married, we could have a baby". She said, "Go away" – why?' I asked him what he thought and he said, 'I got too close. I go up to girls and I say, "Will you go out with me" straight away (he came up and stared again) and they don't like it'. I said he seemed to be saying he knew he went too far and too fast, got too close too quickly, perhaps he hoped he could practise this here with me and find out about getting friendly without getting too close and putting people off.

It was a constant struggle for him to achieve an appropriate distance, and we worked hard at it – could he be with someone rather than lose himself in them? As we worked through this dilemma again and again, I had to decide when to make a direct transference interpretation which could be experienced as intrusive, and when to leave interpretations in a transitional area so that he could have an experience without being overwhelmed by it. It was perhaps a question of the level of intensity of a transference interpretation: I felt it was something I did not fully work out for myself and for Joe.

I think it is particularly difficult with adolescents who are in the process of turning away quite resolutely from their primary objects in order to take the next appropriate developmental step. With Joe in particular the rather abrupt ending of his treatment meant that neither he nor I had sufficient time to work with the problem, and I think his experience of an internal object with imprisoning intentions remained to some extent, and perhaps even to a large extent, unmodified.

Like his Walkman, which seemed to embody both a defensive and communicative function, so Joe's watch seemed to metamorphose during the course of treatment from an autistic object designed to block me out into something more transitional where he was able to work out many questions about 'going on being' in the world. As the therapy progressed, Joe became more aware of his 'chuntering' tendencies: 'I do go on, don't I?' This was sometimes said complacently and sometimes in a truly self-critical way. When I first suggested that he was 'using up life time' as Meltzer *et al.* (1975) put it, he was deeply wounded; but in a subsequent session he was able to say, 'I do these foolish things don't I?', experiencing real pain at getting in touch with this. What Meltzer called 'autistic residues' became very evident in this tendency to 'go on', and he would follow the second hand of the watch round in a perseverative way which he had to be helped beyond. Just as he would sometimes quite mindlessly colour in something like the letters of his name, he would fill time rather than use it.

As Joe was able to step apart somewhat from his 'chuntering' self, he was able to discern patterns for himself. 'Things go in circles, don't they?' he said wonderingly. He began to notice the difference between his digital watch and my sweep hand watch – two ways of doing things. Session by session Joe seemed to take his place almost perceptibly within the rhythm of the universe – the 'white noise' of everyday life that Don DeLillo (1984) refers to in his novel of the same name – the thousand-and-one noises of the world which surround us but do not ordinarily overwhelm us as Joe had previously been overwhelmed.

Object constancy became the jumping-off point for self-constancy: Joe gradually achieved a sense of his own continuity just as he was also achieving a sense of his own boundaries. To illustrate this I would like briefly to describe a session which took place eighteen months after the start of therapy.

> After an angry and disillusioned session on Monday, he arrived for his Wednesday session in a cheerful mood, with a watch someone had given him which needed mending. I took this up initially in terms of his wondering whether things could be OK today after his outburst on Monday. He sat close to me and was delighted our watches synchronised – we could get back together, there could be synchrony between us. 'How do watches tell the same time?', he wondered – as if he were really searching for a meaning, an ordering principle. He was looking at the watch happily, tapping it, whistling to himself, involved and serious, checking mine against it (the watch itself was working, it was the strap that needed to be replaced). I talked of the hands going round, like his sessions going round, and the rhythm of the week which we knew he liked (this was just after the Easter break). He pushed the buttons on the watch, reflective and slow, and finally he pushed one and a tune started to play. He was delighted and I linked it to his delight with the sessions starting up, the music starting up and his pleasure in the discovery that he had a part in this flow. He was talking about time in therapy and time in school – how they seemed to go at different rates, and I recalled his talking about wanting time to slow down a bit, he was getting older and knew he had some work to do. He seemed to be reflecting on our differences, and on ways in which we might be the same, back together in the same room.
>
> The session fluctuated – at times he seemed to be obsessive and controlling, at times genuinely interested, like a toddler exploring his world. At one point he tried to put the watch in the key hole and attempted to turn it, and I said, 'You feel as if you're unlocking some secrets and understanding more about you and me when we're together and when we're apart, how it all fits together'. Before the end of the session I told him, as usual, that it was nearly time to end for today. He immediately said 'I've got to go now. Bill (the driver of the cab) likes me to be on time'. I said I would stay till the end of the session – I thought it was important that he should have all his time. He said, 'Well OK, but I'll go anyway – OK?' (a

bit anxiously). He did actually go a few minutes early. It was the first time he had managed to do this – he had felt too guilty before. I felt this was an important achievement for Joe. It seemed that he could now leave me before I left him: a major step in learning to walk away from Mummy, like a toddler, and then as an adult. He could trust me to survive and sustain a friendly interest in him (Reid [1978], unpublished paper, 'The Development of Friendliness in Children with Autism').

Emerging narrative

As time for Joe became more comprehensible, and was able to take his place in the path of 'continuous becoming' rather than cling onto his autistic rituals as a protection against the bombardment of everyday life, so his memory improved. He became much more aware of his capacity to cut out by what he called 'being asleep', and spent one session berating himself for his failure to keep awake to reality. Finally, he was able to hear my suggestion that it was perhaps the very act of waking up which make him notice how much of his lifetime he had slept away: it was a painful realisation. All infants are in a sense born into chaos and Joe had, in his terror, split off chaos so that he did not meet up with and use the modifying elements present in normal mother-baby interaction, as the infant through containment and through enlivening is enriched and becomes himself. In his book *Awakenings* (1983), Oliver Sacks describes how patients who had been victims of the sleeping sickness *encephalitis lethargica* were awakened through the use of the drug L-Dopa and 'became startlingly, wonderfully alive'. Those who could retrieve no meaning fell back into a comatose state, while those who benefited in the long term were able to reinstate themselves in their own narrative. As Sacks says, 'I do not feel alive, psychologically alive, except insofar as a stream of feeling – perceiving, imagining, remembering, reflecting, revising, recategorising, runs through me. I am that stream, that stream is me'.

As his therapy progressed, Joe's capacity to hold onto narrative for himself, rather than through the therapist as an auxiliary ego, became more evident. He talked more about music, and became interested in classical musicians. He asked me, 'Do you like Beethoven and Mozart?' He looked really excited and did not seem to be expecting an answer but to be listening. 'You can hear the silence in between, and then it comes in, da-da-da-*da*'. Just as the silences could now be perceived as part of the pattern, so he could trust in the continuity of going on being, and that he and I still existed in the silences between the sessions.

Time past, time present, time future

The following material comes from a session just before the first anniversary of Joe's therapy.

He checked the time on several occasions: dividing up what he'd had and what was to come in the session in a swift and accurate way. I said I was to see how well he could do this now. He went round tapping the walls, and I said he was getting a strong sense of time past and time to come, where he was in his session and where he was in his life. He was quiet a little, then said, 'So I've been here a year now?' I confirmed it would be a year to the exact date tomorrow. 'Oh wow, a year! That's amazing!' He slapped his palms together and walked up and down: 'So tomorrow I go to school'. I said perhaps he was saying he'd like to come here tomorrow to celebrate the exact date, to come for his therapy birthday. One year ago tomorrow he had been born into this therapy. He was silent, reflective again, and after a few moments I said how good it felt to him to be able to have the space here to think about that, to think about the past and the present. He was sitting on the couch very close, and he said after a pause, 'I'd like to see Mr Y again (his previous therapist), not that I don't like you or anything but I would'. I said he'd seen Dr X last week, he was thinking about his therapy with Mr Y and his therapy with me, linking people up in his mind. It was important for me to know this, that he could like Mr Y and Dr X as well as me, liking them didn't push me out.

He said, 'You know I was at school round here, I'd like to go back there'. I said he was thinking about the placing of everything today, and things that had happened in his life, the story of Joe. He sat down again and was quiet then said, 'I can remember a lot about it. They had a great big rope in the garden, we used to swing on it, and go-karts'. He was quiet again, clearly seeing things in his mind. After a bit I said he really enjoyed that time and enjoyed remembering it – swinging on this strong rope was a bit like swinging up and down in his mind, linking together all the things that had happened in his life. This strong rope was a bit like his life which began in – 'July 1974', he said promptly – and he was remembering things that made up this strong life. A bit later he said, 'There was a yellow door, I can remember it really well'. I said, 'So well you could walk inside', and he shot me a smile and said, 'That's right'. I said he might also be talking about walking through the therapy door each week, and he could walk into his memories too and see what was inside his mind. He took his key out and looked at it reflectively. I said his memory was the key to putting all this together, opening the door and looking back into his memories. He went to the window and stared out again, and it felt indeed as if something was being delicately strung together in his mind. I said he was putting together the story of his life here – it was very important.

Ending

A year later Joe's therapy ended, prematurely in my view. We had been talking about ending some time during the following year, at his request, because I felt that, although there was evidently much more work to be done, it was also important to respect the independent adolescent voice in him. Since he was now much more able to get on with his life, to have friends, go to pubs and generally enjoy himself socially, this voice had been growing louder and stronger. A person like Joe would quite probably need further periods of therapy interspersed with intervals of going it alone. We had a carefully planned weaning programme, which was then completely disrupted by external events to do with transport, which threw him into a state of total confusion. It became unbearable for him, try as I did to scale down his concerns. He insisted that he'd had enough, that he wanted to go. We had an emergency meeting with his parents and agreed on something which Joe himself thought he could manage, though I had many reservations about it which I expressed to him and to his parents (in terms of timing this was very similar to his first treatment: with a concentration span of just over two years). I had many concerns about my listening to a delusional omnipotent voice in the guise of a blustering adolescent; I feared he might land with a soundless bump back into some sort of hole, and lose the solid ground we had so painstakingly built together, because this ending was being acted out rather than being analysed in the therapy. He found it very difficult to come to the last few sessions and alternated between bravado, acting out by ordering the cab away, to saying plaintively, 'I'll never find anyone like you', which made me wonder about some wholesale re-projection of what I thought he had taken in. But he struggled as he always had done, and the last session was a moving testimony to his courage. He tapped the walls, jumped up and down on his 'solid ground', and lay on the couch with his legs in the air like a baby. At one point he looked at me very seriously and said, 'You know, you've got a good mind', and I said I thought he'd discovered that he had a good mind. He was able to hear that we had different thoughts about the ending, he had thoughts about missing and acknowledged his sadness. He gave a pretend drumroll on the couch to herald the end of the session, shook my hand solemnly and said, 'Carry on with the old therapy, won't you?'

Conclusion

In this account I have attempted to outline the progress and development of Joe during two years of therapy, and to link this with ideas of his gradually taking his place in the space-time continuum of everyday life as it came to be symbolised for him through the rhythm of the therapeutic work.

As Donald Meltzer describes in the material of a patient called Timmy,

> Over a period of months it became clear that certain forms of behaviour which appeared in great abundance constituted Timmy's autistic phenomena; and by culling out of the record those items which seemed clearly outside this category and linking them together like pearls on a thread, we were able to construct sequences (sometimes covering several sessions) which could then be interpreted as if they had indeed been quite

consecutive. The result was something akin to the cinematic photography of the blossoming of flowers, taken one frame every few minutes, in which the balletic unfolding and growth describes a pattern unseen by the waking eye.

(Meltzer *et al.* 1975)

Events which had for Joe previously been placed 'outside the stream of aggregated and eventually organised recollection' became linked – as Meltzer puts it, the thread of time on which are hung the pearls of recollection – and to this I would add the pearls of present collection and the pearls of anticipation.

Acknowledgement

I would like to acknowledge the vitality of Anne Alvarez's fine supervision, which supported me on every step of the journey with Joe.

Note

1 This chapter was first published as a paper in the *Journal of Child Psychotherapists*, 1994, 20, 1.

Endpiece

Anne Alvarez and Susan Reid

Working with patients with autism is fascinating, frustrating, boring, thrilling and always difficult. Despite their apparent inaccessibility and strangeness, our patients have taught us an enormous amount about themselves, and we hope that we have conveyed something of their ordinary humanity and unique personality. They have also taught us much about the nature of autism itself. Each new patient presents a fresh challenge to our theories and clinical techniques. Our struggles to find ways of reaching these puzzling children and young people have caused us to examine every aspect of our psychoanalytic technique, and the accounts presented here represent our most recent findings and reflections. We have come to think that some of our refinements of technique may have relevance for the treatment of other, non-autistic patients. We know, however, that there is still much to learn.

Many people with autism can benefit from the type of long-term intensive psychoanalytic psychotherapy described in these pages. We are currently engaged in research studies to evaluate its outcome. Autism, however, is a mysterious condition, and no single professional tradition holds the key to its complete understanding. It is our firm belief that it is only in the synthesis of findings from research in epidemiology, biology, neurology and psychology with those from qualitative research – represented by the detailed clinical case studies described here – that we shall gain a full understanding of the autistic condition. We hope that we have succeeded in describing our own developmentally informed psychoanalytic approach to treatment, in language plain enough to contribute to this synthesis. People with autism and their families have a right to expect this.

Bibliography

Alvarez, A. (1992a) *Live Company: Psychoanalytic Psychotherapy with Autistic, Borderline, Deprived and Abused Children*, London and New York: Tavistock/Routledge.

——(1992b) 'Wildest Dreams and Lies', in Alvarez, A., *Live Company*, London and New York: Tavistock/Routledge.

——(1996) 'Addressing the Element of Deficit in Children with Autism: Psychotherapy which is both Psychoanalytically and Developmentally Informed', *Clinical Child Psychology and Psychiatry*, 1 (14).

Alvarez, A. and Furgiuele, P. (1997) 'Speculations on Components in the Infant's Sense of Agency: The Sense of Abundance and the Capacity to Think in Parentheses', in S. Reid (ed.) *Developments in Infant Observation*, London: Routledge.

Auehahn, N. C. and Prelinge, E. (1983) 'Repetition in the Concentration Camp Survivor and her Child', *International Review of Psychoanalysis*, 10, 31–45.

Bailey, A., Phillips, W. and Rutter, M. (1996) 'Autism: Towards an Integration of Clinical, Genetic, Neuropsychological and Neurobiological Perspectives', *Journal of Psychology and Psychiatry*, 37 (1) 89–126.

Barocas, H. A. and Barocas, C. B. (1973) 'Manifestations of Concentration Camp Effects on the Second Generation', *American Journal of Psychiatry*, 130, 820–1.

Baron-Cohen, S. (1988) 'Social and Pragmatic Deficits in Autism: Cognitive or Affective?', *Journal of Autism and Developmental Disorder*, 18, 3.

——(1996) 'Toddler Test Detects Autism', *MRC News*, autumn/winter.

Baron-Cohen, S., Allen, J. and Gillberg, C. (1992) 'Can Autism be Detected at 18 Months? The Needle, the Haystack, and the CHAT', *British Journal of Psychiatry*, 161, 839–43.

Baron-Cohen, S., Cox, A., Baird, G., Swettenham, J., Nightingale, N., Morgan, K., Drew, A. and Charman, T. (1996) 'Psychological Markers in the Detection of Autism in Infancy in a Large Population', *British Journal of Psychiatry*, 168, 158–63.

Baron-Cohen, S., Tager-Flusberg, H. and Cohen, D. J. (1993) *Understanding Other Minds: Perspectives from Autism*, Oxford: Oxford Medical Publications.

Bergmann, M. and Jucovy, M. (eds) (1982) *Generations of the Holocaust*, New York: Basic Books.

Bick, E. (1968) 'The Experience of the Skin in Early Object Relations', *International Journal of Psycho-Analysis*, 49, 484–6.

——(1986) 'Further Considerations of the Function of the Skin in Early Object Relations', *British Journal of Psychotherapy*, 2, 4.

Bicknell, J. (1983) 'The Psychopathology of Handicap', *British Journal of Medicine*, 56, 167–78.

Bion, W. R. (1950) 'The Imaginary Twin', in *Second Thoughts* (1967) London: Heinemann. Reprinted in paperback (1984) Maresfield Reprints, London: Karnac Books.
——(1959) 'Attacks on Linking', *International Journal of Psycho-Analysis*, 40, 308–15;
republished (1967) in W. R. Bion, *Second Thoughts*, London: Heinemann, 93–109.
——(1962) *Learning from Experience*, 1984, London: Maresfield Reprints (Karnac).
——(1967) *Second Thoughts*, London: Karnac.
——(1977) *Seven Servants: Four Works by W. R. Bion*, New York: Jason Aronson.
——(1980) *Attention and Interpretation*, London: Karnac.
Bowlby, J. (1988) *A Secure Base: Clinical Applications of Attachment Theory*, London:
Routledge.
Braten, S. (1987) 'Dialogic Mind: The Infant and the Adult in Proto-conversation', in
M. Carvallo (ed.) *Nature, Cognition and Systems*, Dordrecht and Boston MA: D.
Reidel.
Brazelton, T. B., Koslowski, B. and Main, M. (1974) 'The Origins of Reciprocity: the
Early Mother-infant Interaction', in M. Lewis and L. A. Rosenblum (eds) *The Effect of
the Infant on its Caregivers*, London: Wiley Interscience.
Brenman Pick, I. (1985) 'Working Through in the Counter-transference', *International
Journal of Psycho-Analysis*, 66, 157–66; republished (1988) in E. Bott Spillius (ed.)
Melanie Klein Today: Developments in Theory and Practice, Volume 2: Mainly Practice,
London: Routledge, 34–47.
Britton, R. (1989) 'The Missing Link: Parental Sexuality in the Oedipus Complex', in J.
Steiner (ed.) *The Oedipus Complex Today*, London: Karnac Books.
——(1995) 'Second Thoughts on the Third Position', paper read at a Clinic Scientific
Meeting, Tavistock Clinic, London.
Bruner, J. S. (1968) *Processes of Cognitive Growth: Infancy*, USA: Clark University Press.
Cannon, W. B. (1914) 'The Emergency Function of the Adrenal Medulla in Pain and the
Major Emotions', *American Journal of Physiology*, 33, 356–72.
Cecchi, V. (1990) 'The Analysis of a Little Girl with an Autistic Syndrome', *Interna-
tional Journal of Psycho-Analysis*, 71, 403–10.
Dawson, G. and Lewy, A. (1989) 'Arousal, Attention, and the Socioemotional Impair-
ments of Individuals with Autism', in G. Dawson (ed.) *Autism: Nature, Diagnosis and
Treatment*, New York: Guildford Press.
DeLillo, D. (1984) *White Noise*, London: Viking.
Di Cagno, L., Lazzarini, A., Rissone, A. and Randaccio, S. (1984) *Il Neonato e il suo
Mondo Relazionale*, Rome: Borla.
Edwards, D. (1982) *My Naughty Little Sister*, illustrated by Shirley Hughes, London:
Methuen.
Evans-Jones, L. G. and Rosenbloom, L. (1978) 'Disintegrative Psychosis in Childhood',
Developmental Medicine and Child Neurology, 20, 4, 462–70.
Fenske, E., Zalenski, S., Krantz, P. and McClannahan, L. (1985) 'Age at Intervention
and Treatment Outcome for Autistic Children in a Comprehensive Intervention
Program', *Analysis and Intervention in Developmental Disabilities*, 5.
Forrest, G. and Vostanis, P. (1996) 'Advances in the Assessment and Management of
Autism', Association for Child Psychology and Psychiatry, Occasional Paper no. 13.
Fox, N., Calkins, S. and Bell, M. A. (1994) 'Neuroplasticity and Development in the
First Two Years of Life: Evidence from Cognitive and Socio-emotional Domains of
Research', *Development and Psychopathology*, 6, 677–96.
Freud, S. (1905) *Fragment of an Analysis of a Case of Hysteria*, SE 7.

——(1917) *Mourning and Melancholia*, SE 14: 243–58.

——(1918) *From the History of an Infantile Neurosis*, SE 17: 7–122.

——(1919) *A Child is Being Beaten: A Contribution to the Study of the Origin of Sexual Perversions*, SE 17: 179–204.

Frith, U. (1989) *Autism: Explaining the Enigma*, Oxford: Blackwell.

Gaensbauer, E. (1993) 'Memories of Trauma in Infancy', paper given at Colorado Psychiatric Society Conference on Post-Traumatic Stress Disorder, January, Vail CO.

Galante, R. and Foa, D. (1986) 'An Epidemiological Study of Psychic Trauma and Treatment Effectiveness for Children after a Natural Disaster', *Journal of the American Academy of Child Psychiatry*, 25, 357–63.

Garland, C. (1991) 'External Disasters and the Internal World: An Approach to Understanding Survivors', in J. Holmes (ed.) *Handbook on Psychotherapy for Psychiatrists*, London: Routledge.

Goldstein, D. (1995) *Stress, Catecholamines and Cardiovascular Disease*, New York: Oxford University Press.

Greenspan, S. I. (1997) *Developmentally Based Psychotherapy*, Madison CT: International University Press.

Grigsby, J. and Schneiders, J. (1991) 'Neuroscience, Modularity and Personality Theory: Conceptual Foundations of a Model of Complex Human Functioning', *Psychiatry*, 54, 21–37.

Guimaraes Filho, P. D. (1996) Panel of Second Latin American Psychoanalytic Congress of Children and Adolescents, Sao Paulo, Brazil.

Haag, G. (1985) 'La Mère et le Bébé dans les Deux Moitiés du Corps', *Neuropsychiatrie de l'Enfance*, 33, 107–14.

Hamilton, V. (1982) *Narcissus and Oedipus: The Children of Psychoanalysis*, London: Routledge and Kegan Paul. Reprinted 1993, Maresfield Library, London: Karnac.

Hawking, S. (1992) *A Brief History of Time*, BBC TV.

Heimann, P. (1950) 'On Counter-transference', *International Journal of Psycho-Analysis*, 31, 81–4.

Helm, D. T. and Kozloff, M. A. (1986) 'Research on Parent Training: Shortcomings and Remedies', *Journal of Autism and Developmental Disorders*, 16, 1–22.

Hill, A. E. and Rosenbloom, L. (1986) 'Disintegrative Psychosis of Childhood: Teenage Follow-up', *Developmental Medicine and Child Neurology*, 28 (1) 34–40.

Hobson, P. (1993) *Autism and the Development of Mind*, Hove: Lawrence Erlbaum.

Howlin, P. (1997) *Autism: Preparing for Adulthood*, London: Routledge.

Janert, S. (1993) personal communication.

Joseph, B. (1975) 'The Patient who is Difficult to Reach', in M. Feldman and E. Bott Spillius (eds) (1989) *Psychic Equilibrium and Psychic Change*, London: Tavistock/Routledge.

——(1978) 'Different Types of Anxiety and their Handling in the Analytic Situation', *International Journal of Psycho-Analysis*, 59, 223–8.

——(1982) 'Addiction to Near Death', in M. Feldman and E. Bott Spillius (eds) (1989) *Psychic Equilibrium and Psychic Change*, London: Tavistock/Routledge.

——(1989a) *Psychic Equilibrium and Psychic Change*, London: Tavistock/Routledge.

——(1989b) 'Transference: the Total Situation', *International Journal of Psycho-Analysis*, 66, 447–54.

——(1989c) 'The Patient who is Difficult to Reach', in M. Feldman and E. Bott Spillius (eds) (1989) *Psychic Equilibrium and Psychic Change*, London: Tavistock/Routledge.

Kanner, L. (1943) 'Autistic Disturbances of Affective Control', *Nervous Child*, 2, 217–50.

——(1944) 'Early Infantile Autism', *Journal of Paediatrics*, 25, 211–17.

Kardiner, A. (1941) 'The Traumatic Psychosis of War', *Psychosomatic Medicine Monograph*, II–III, New York: Paul B. Hoeber.

Karpf, A. (1996) *The War After*, London: Heinemann.

Klaus, M. H. and Kennell, J. H. (1982) *Parent-Infant Bonding*, London: C. H. Mosby.

Klein, M. (1932) 'The Psychoanalysis of Children', in *The Writings of Melanie Klein, Volume 2* (1975), London: Hogarth.

——(1946) 'Notes on some Schizoid Mechanisms', in *The Writings of Melanie Klein, Volume 4: Envy and Gratitude and Other Works* (1975) London: Hogarth, 1–24.

——(1955) 'On Identification', in *The Writings of Melanie Klein, Volume 4: Envy and Gratitude and Other Works* (1975) London: Hogarth, 141–75.

——(1959) 'Our Adult World and its Roots in Infancy', in *The Writings of Melanie Klein, Volume 3* (1975) London: Hogarth.

——(1961) 'Narrative of a Child Analysis', in *The Writings of Melanie Klein, Volume 4* (1975) London: Hogarth.

——(1975) *Envy and Gratitude*, London: Virago.

Klein, S. (1980) 'Autistic Phenomena in Neurotic Patients', *International Journal of Psycho-Analysis*, 61, 395–402. Also in J. S. Grotstein (ed.) (1981) *Do I Dare Disturb the Universe?*, Beverly Hills CA: Caesura Press.

Kysar, J. E. (1968) 'The Two Camps in Child Psychiatry: A Report from a Psychiatrist-Father of an Autistic and Retarded Child', *American Journal of Psychiatry*, 125, 103–9.

——(1969) 'Reactions of Professionals to Disturbed Children and their Parents', *Archives of General Psychiatry*, 19, 526–70.

Lachman, F. M. and Beebe, B. (1996) 'Three Principles of Salience in Organization of the Patient-Analyst Interaction', *Psychoanalytic Psychology*, 13 (1) 1–22.

Le Couteur, A., Rutter, M., Lord, C., Rios, P., Robertson, S., Holdgrafer, M. and McLennan, J. D. (1989) 'Autism Diagnostic Interview: A Semi-Structured Interview for Parents and Care-Givers of Autistic Persons', *Journal of Autism and Developmental Disorders*, 19, 363–87.

Leslie, A. M. (1987) 'Pretence and Representation: The Origins of Theory of Mind', *Psychological Review*, 94.

Lord, C., Rutter, M., Goode, S., Heemsberen, J., Jordan, H. and Mawhood, L. (1989) 'Autism Diagnostic Observation Schedule: Standardised Observation of Communicative and Social Behaviour', *Journal of Autism and Developmental Disorders*, 19, 185–212.

Luria, A. R. (1987) cited by J. S. Bruner in foreword to A. R. Luria, *The Mind of a Mnemonist*, Cambridge MA: Harvard University Press.

Macfarlane, A. (1977) *The Psychology of Childbirth*, London: Fontana/Open Books.

Macmillan (1988) *Macmillan Encyclopaedia*, London: Macmillan.

McEachin, J. J., Smith, T. and Lovas, O. I. (1993) 'Long Term Outcome for Children with Autism who Received Early Intensive Behavioural Treatment', *American Journal of Mental Retardation*, 97, 4, 359–72.

McDougall, J. (1989) *Theatres of the Body*, London: Free Association Books.

Main, M. and Hesse, E. (1990) 'Parents' Unresolved Traumatic Experiences are Related to Infant Disorganised Attachment Status: Is Frightened and/or Frightening Parental

Behaviour the Linking Mechanism?', in M. Greenberg, D. Cicchetti and M. Cummings (eds) *Attachment in the Pre-school Years*, Chicago IL: University of Chicago Press.

Mannoni, M. (1973) *The Retarded Child and the Mother*, London: Tavistock.

Mason, J. W. (1971) 'A Re-Evaluation of the Concept of Non-specificity in Stress Theory', *Journal of Psychiatric Research*, 8, 323–3.

Mayer, J. D. (1993) 'The Intelligence of Emotional Intelligence', *Intelligence*, 17 (4) 433–42.

Mayer, J. D. and Geher, G. (1996) 'Emotional Intelligence and the Identification of Emotion', *Intelligence*, March-April, 22 (2) 89–114.

Mayer, J. D. and Salovey, P. (1995) 'Emotional Intelligence and the Construction and Regulation of Feelings', *Applied and Preventive Psychology*, 4 (3) 197–208.

Meltzer, D. (1973) 'The Origins of the Fetishistic Plaything of Sexual Perversions', in *Sexual States of Mind*, Strath Tay: Clunie.

——(1975a) 'Dimensionality as a Parameter of Mental Functioning: Its Relation to Narcissistic Organisation', in D. Meltzer, J. Bremner, H. Hoxter, D. Weddell and I. Wittenberg, *Explorations in Autism*, Strath Tay: Clunie, 231.

——(1975b) 'Adhesive Identification', *Contemporary Psychoanalysis*, 2 (3).

——(1986) *Studies in Extended Metapsychology*, Strath Tay: Clunie, 178.

——(1988) 'On Aesthetic Reciprocity', in *The Apprehension of Beauty*, Strath Tay: Clunie.

Meltzer, D., Bremner, J., Hoxter, H., Weddell, D. and Wittenberg, I. (1975) *Explorations in Autism*, Strath Tay: Clunie.

Milgram, N. A. (1986) 'Attributional Analysis of War Related Stressmodels of Coping and Helping', in N. A. Milgram (ed.) *Generalisations from the Israeli Experience*, New York: Brunner/Mazel.

Miller, L., Rustin, M. and Shuttleworth, J. (1989) *Closely Observed Infants*, London: Duckworth.

Morgan, S. (1985). 'The Autistic Child and Family Functioning: A Developmental Family Systems Perspective', *Journal of Autism and Developmental Disorder*, 18, 2, 263–80.

Mundy, P. and Sigman, M. (1989) 'Specifying the Nature of the Social Impairment in Autism', in G. Dawson (ed.) *Autism: Nature, Diagnosis and Treamtent*, London: Guildford Press.

Murray, L. (1988) 'Effects of Postnatal Depression on Infant Development: Direct Studies of Early Mother-infant Interactions', in R. Kumar and I. F. Brockington (eds) *Motherhood and Mental Illness, 2: Causes and Consequences*, London: Wright, 159–90.

——(1991a) 'Intersubjectivity, Object Relations Theory and Empirical Evidence from Mother-infant Interactions', *Infant Mental Health Journal*, vol. 12.

——(1991b) 'The Impact of Post-Natal Depression on Infant Development', *Journal of Child Psychology and Psychiatry*, 33, 543–61.

Murray, L. and Trevarthen, C. (1985) 'Emotional Regulation of Interactions between Two-month-olds and their Mothers', in T. M. Field and N. Fox (eds) *Social Perceptions in Infants*, Norwood NJ: Ablex.

Newson, J. (1977) 'An Intersubjective Approach to the Systematic Description of Mother-infant Interaction', in H. R. Schaffer (ed.) *Studies in Mother-Infant Interaction*, London: Academic Press.

Newson, E. (1987) 'The Education, Treatment and Handling of Autistic Children', *Children and Society*, 1, 34–50.

O'Brien, S. (1996) 'The Validity and Reliability of the Wing Subgroups Questionnaire', *Journal of Autism and Developmental Disorders*, 26 (3).

Oxford English Dictionary (1971) compact edn, vol. II, Oxford: Clarendon Press.

Papousek, H. and Papousek, M. (1975) 'Cognitive Aspects of Preverbal Social Interaction between Human Infants and Adults', in *CIBA Foundation Symposium*, New York: Association of Scientific Publishers.

Parks, S. L. (1983) 'The Assessment of Autistic Children: A Selective Review of Available Instruments', *Journal of Autism and Developmental Disorders*, 13, 3, 255–67.

Perry, B. (1993) 'Neuro-development and the Neurophysiology of Trauma (I&II): The Alarm-Fear-Terror Continuum', *The Advisor*, 6 (1&2), Chicago IL: American Professional Society on the Abuse of Children.

——(1994) 'Neurobiological Sequelae of Childhood Trauma: PTSD in Children', in M. Murberg (ed.) (1994) *Catecholamines in Post-Traumatic Stress Disorder: Emerging Concepts*, American Psychiatric Press.

Perry, B., Pollard, R. A., Blakley, T. L., Baker, W. L. and Vigilante, D. (1995) 'Childhood Trauma, the Neurobiology of Adaptation and "Use-dependent" Development of the Brain: How "States" Become "Traits"', *Infant Mental Health Journal*, 16, 271–91.

Perry, R., Cohen, I. and DeCarlo, R. (1995) 'Case Study: Deterioration, Autism and Recovery in Two Siblings', *Journal of American Child and Adolescent Psychotherapy*, 2, 232–7.

Pines, D. (1993) 'The Impact of the Holocaust on the Second Generation', in *A Woman's Unconscious Use of her Body: A Psychoanalytical Perspective*, London: Virago.

Piontelli, S. (1989) 'A Study on Twins Before and After Birth', *International Review of Psychoanalysis*, 16, 4, 13–426.

Pynoos, R. (1996) 'The Transgenerational Repercussions of Traumatic Expectations', paper presented to 6th IPA Conference on Psychoanalytic Research, University of London.

Rado, S. (1942) 'Pathodynamics and Treatment of Traumatic War Neurosis (Traumatophobia)', *Psychosomatic Medicine*, 363–8.

Reid, S. (1988a) personal communication.

——(1988b) 'Interpretation: Food for Thought', unpublished paper given to the study weekend of the Association of Child Psychotherapists.

——(1990) 'The Importance of Beauty in the Psycho-analytic Experience', *Journal of Child Psychotherapy*, 16, 1, 29–52.

——(1997a) *Developments in Infant Observation: The Tavistock Model*, London: Routledge.

——(1997b) 'The Development of Autistic Defences in an Infant: The Use of a Single Case Study for Research', *The International Journal of Infant observation*, 1 (1) 51–79.

Rey, H. (1988) 'That Which Patients Bring to Analysis', *International Journal of Psychoanalysis*, 69, 457. Also in J. Magagna (ed.) (1994) *Universals of Psychoanalysis in the Treatment of Psychotic and Borderline States*, London: Free Association Books.

Rhode, E. (1994) *Psychotic Metaphysics,*, London: Clunie/Karnac Books, chs 5, 6.

Rhode, M. (1995) 'Links between Henri Rey's Thinking and Psychoanalytic Work with Autistic Children', *Psychoanalytic Psychotherapy*, 9, 149–55.

Rustin, M. (1998) 'Dialogues with Parents', *Journal of Child Psychotherapy* 24(2) 233–52.

Rutter, M. (1983) 'Cognitive Deficits in the Pathogenesis of Autism', *Journal of Child Psychology and Psychiatry*, 24.

——(1991) 'Autism as a Genetic Disorder', in P. McGuffin and R. Murray (eds) *The New Genetics of Mental Illness*, Oxford: Butterworth Heinemann.

——(1998) 'Developmental Catch-up and Deficit, Following Adoption and after Severe Global Early Privation', *Journal of Child Psychology and Psychiatry*, 39 (4) 465–76.

Rutter, M., Pickles, A., Vorria, P., Wolkind, S. and Hobsbaum, A. (1998) 'A Comparitive Study of Greek Children in Long-term Residential Group Care and in Two-parent Families: Social, Emotional and Behavioural Differences', *Journal of Child Psychology and Psychiatry*, 39 (2) 225–36.

Sacks, O. (1973) *Awakenings*, London: Duckworth.

——(1976) *Awakenings*, revised edn, London: Pelican.

——(1983) *Awakenings*, London: Picador.

——(1995) 'To See and Not to See', in *An Anthropologist on Mars*, London: Picador.

Sandler, A-M. and Sandler, J. (1958) 'Psychoses, Borderline States and Mental Deficiency in Childhood', *Bulletin of The British Psychological Society*, 35.

Schore, A. N. (1994) *Affect Regulation and the Origin of Self: The Neurobiology of Emotional Development*, Hillsdale, NJ: Lawrence Erlbaum.

Schore, A. S. (1996) 'The Experience-dependent Maturation of a Regulatory System in the Orbital Prefrontal Cortex and the Origin of Developmental Psychopathology', *Development and Psychopathology*, 8, 59–87.

Segal, H. (1950) 'Some Aspects of the Analysis of a Schizophrenic', in *The Work of Hanna Segal* (1981) New York: Jason Aronson. Reprinted in paperback (1986) London: Free Association Books/Maresfield Library.

Selye, H. (1936) 'A Syndrome Produced by Diverse Nocuous Agents', *Nature*, 138, 32–6.

Shulman, G. (1997) 'I Want to be Myself', in D. Syder (ed.) *Counselling Case Histories in Communication Disorders*, London: Whurr Publications.

Sinason, V. E. (1986) 'Secondary Mental Handicap and its Relationship to Trauma', *Psychoanalytic Psychotherapy*, 2, 2, 131–54.

——(1992) *Mental Handicap and the Human Condition*, London: Free Association Books.

Spitz, R. A. (1946) 'Anaclictic Depression: An Inquiry into the Genesis of Psychiatric Conditions in Early Childhood', in *Psychoanalytic Study of the Child*, 2.

Steiner, R. (1987) 'Some Thoughts on "La Vive Voix" by Ivan Fonagy', *International Review of Psychoanalysis*, 14.

Stern, D. (1974) 'Mother and Infant at Play: the Dyadic Interaction Involving Facial, Vocal and Gaze Behaviours', in M. Lewis and L. A. Rosenblum (eds) *The Effect of the Infant on its Caregiver*, New York: Wiley.

——(1977a) *The First Relationship: Infant and Mother*, London: Fontana/Open Books.

——(1977b) 'Missteps in the Dance', in *The First Relationship: Infant and Mother*, Cambridge MA: Harvard University Press.

——(1985) *The Interpersonal World of the Infant*, New York: Basic Books.

Stockdale-Wolfe, E. (1993) 'Fear of Fusion: Non-verbal Behavior in Secondary Autism', *Psychoanalytic Inquiry*, 13, 9–33.

Terr, L. (1988) 'What Happens to Early Memories of Trauma? A Study of Twenty Children Under Age Five at the Time of Documented Traumatic Events', *Journal of the American Academy of Child and Adolescent Psychiatry*, 27, 96–104.

Tischler, S. (1971) 'Clinical work with the Parents of Psychotic Children', *Psychiatria, Neuralgia, Neurochirurgia*, 74, 225–49.

——(1979) 'Being with a Psychotic Child: A Psycho-analytical Approach to the Problems of Parents of Psychotic Children', *International Journal of Psycho-analysis*, 60, 29–38.

Trevarthen, C. (1976) 'Descriptive Analyses of Infant Communicative Behavior', in H. R. Schaffer (ed.) *Studies in Mother-Infant Interaction*, London: Academic Press.

——(1978) 'Modes of Perceiving and Codes of Acting', in H. J. Pick (ed.) *Psychological Modes of Perceiving and Processing Information*, Hillsdale NJ: Erlbaum.

——(1980) 'The Foundations of Intersubjectivity', in D. K. Olson (ed.) *The Social Foundation of Language and Thought*, New York: Norton.

Trevarthen, C., Aitken, K., Papoudi, D. and Robarts, J. (1996) *Children With Autism: Diagnosis and Interventions to Meet Their Needs*, London and Bristol PA: Jessica Kingsley.

Trevarthen, C. and Marwick, H. (1986) 'Signs of Motivation for Speech in Infants, and the Nature of a Mother's Support for Development of Language', in B. Lindblom and R. Zetterstrom (eds) *Precursors of Early Speech*, Basingstoke: Macmillan.

Tronick, E. Z. (1989) 'Emotions and Emotional Communication in Infants', *American Psychologist*, February, 112–19.

Tronick, E. Z. and Weinberg, M. K. (1996) 'On the Psycho-Toxic Effects of Maternal Depression on the Mutual Emotional Regulation of Mother-Infant Interaction: The Failure to Form Dyadic States of Consciousness', to appear in L. Murry and P. Cooper (eds) *Postpartum Depression and Child Development*, London: Guildford Press.

Tsiantis, J., Sandler, A-M., Anastasopoulos, D. and Martindale, B. (1996) *Countertransference in Psychoanalytic Psychotherapy with Children and Adolescents*, London: Karnac.

Tustin, F. (1972) *Autism and Childhood Psychosis*, London: Hogarth Press.

——(1980) 'Autistic Objects', *International Review of Psychoanalysis*, 7.

——(1981a) *Autistic States in Children*, revised edn, 1992, London: Routledge and Kegan Paul.

——(1981b) 'Psychological Birth and Psychological Catastrophe', in J. S. Grotstein (ed.) *Do I Dare Disturb the Universe?*, Beverly Hills CA: Caesura Press.

——(1986) *Autistic Barriers in Neurotic Patients*, London: Karnac.

——(1990) *The Protective Shell in Children and Adults*, London: Karnac.

——(1994a) 'The Perpetuation of an Error', *Journal of Child Psychotherapy*, 20, 3–23.

——(1994b) 'Autistic Children Assessed as Not Brain-damaged', *Journal of Child Psychotherapy*, 20 (1).

Urwin, C. (1987) 'Developmental Psychology and Psychoanalysis: Splitting the Difference', in M. Richards and P. Light (eds) *Children in Social Worlds*, Cambridge: Polity Press.

Van der Kolk, B. and Greenberg, M. (1987) 'The Psychobiology of the Trauma Response: Hyperarousal, Constriction and Addiction to Traumatic Exposure', in B. Van der Kolk (ed.) *Psychological Trauma*, Cambridge: Cambridge University Press.

Williams, D. (1992) *Nobody Nowhere*, London: Transworld Publishers.

Williams, G. (1997) 'Self Esteem and Object Esteem', in *Internal Landscapes and Foreign Bodies*, London: Duckworth.

Wing, L. (1996) *The Autistic Spectrum: A Guide for Parents and Professionals*, London: Constable.

Wing, L. and Attwood, A. (1987) 'Syndromes of Autism and Atypical Development', in D. Cohen and A. Donnellan (eds) *Handbook of Autism and Pervasive Developmental Disorders*, New York: Wiley.

Wing, L. and Gould, J. (1979) 'Severe Impairments of Social Interactions and Associated Abnormalities in Children: Epidemiology and Classification', *Journal of Autism and Developmental Disorder*, 9.

Winnicott, D. (1960) 'The Theory of the Parent-Infant Relationship', in *The Maturational Processes and the Facilitating Environment*, London: Hogarth.

——(1967) 'Mirror-role of Mother and Family in Child Development', in *Playing and Reality* (1971) London and New York: Tavistock/Routledge.

——(1971) *Playing and Reality*, London and New York: Tavistock/Routledge.

Wolf, L., Noh, S., Fisman, S. and Speechley, M. (1989) 'Psychological Effects of Parenting Stress on Parents of Autistic Children', *Journal of Autism and Developmental Disorders*, 19, 1.

Yehuda, R. (ed.) (1998) *Psychological Trauma*, Washington DC: American Psychiatric Press.

Yehuda, R., Schmeidler, J., Giller, E. L. Jr, Siever, L. J., Binder-Brynes, K. (1998) 'Relationship between post-traumatic stress disorder characteristics of holocaust survivors and their adult offspring', *American Journal of Psychiatry*, 155 (6) 841–3.

Index

CPSIA information can be obtained at www.ICGtesting.com
Printed in the USA
LVOW08s1817180914

404753LV00004B/60/P